Teaching in t
Classroom

MW01504954

Teaching in the Game-Based Classroom is a hands-on guide to leveraging students' embrace of video games toward successful school performance. Evidence tells us that game-based learning can help teachers design classes, develop transformative learning tools, and assess progress on multiple levels not dependent on one-size-fits-all bubble sheets. Authored by game-savvy teachers in partnership with classroom-experienced academics, the highly varied chapters of this book are concise yet filled with sound pedagogical approaches. Middle and high school educators will find engaging new ways of inspiring students' intrinsic motivation, skill refinement, positive culture-building, autonomy as learners, and more.

David Seelow is Founder of the Revolutionary Learning blog and an education service provider. He is Senior Adjunct Professor of English at the College of Saint Rose, U.S.A., and was Founding Executive Director of the Center for Game and Simulation-Based Learning.

Also Available from Routledge
Eye on Education
(www.routledge.com/k-12)

The Brain-Based Classroom:
Accessing Every Child's Potential Through Educational
Neuroscience
By Kieran O'Mahony

Thriving as an Online K-12 Educator:
Essential Practices from the Field
Edited by Jody Peerless Green

The Media-Savvy Middle School Classroom:
Strategies for Teaching Against Disinformation
By Susan Brooks-Young

Coding as a Playground:
Programming and Computational Thinking in the Early
Childhood Classroom, Second Edition
By Marina Umaschi Bers

Making Technology Work in Schools:
How PK-12 Educators Can Foster Digital-Age Learning
By Timothy D. Green, Loretta C. Donovan, Jody Peerless Green

Integrating Computer Science Across the Core:
Strategies for K-12 Districts
By Tom Liam Lynch, Gerald Ardito, Pam Amendola

Teaching in the Game-Based Classroom:
Practical Strategies for Grades 6–12
Edited by David Seelow

Teaching in the Game-Based Classroom

Practical Strategies for Grades 6–12

Edited by David Seelow

Routledge
Taylor & Francis Group

NEW YORK AND LONDON

First published 2022
by Routledge
605 Third Avenue, New York, NY 10158

and by Routledge
2 Park Square, Milton Park, Abingdon, Oxon, OX14 4RN

Routledge is an imprint of the Taylor & Francis Group, an informa business

© 2022 Taylor & Francis

The right of David Seelow to be identified as the author of the
editorial material, and of the authors for their individual chapters,
has been asserted in accordance with sections 77 and 78 of the
Copyright, Designs and Patents Act 1988.

All rights reserved. No part of this book may be reprinted
or reproduced or utilised in any form or by any electronic,
mechanical, or other means, now known or hereafter invented,
including photocopying and recording, or in any information
storage or retrieval system, without permission in writing from
the publishers.

Trademark notice: Product or corporate names may be trademarks
or registered trademarks, and are used only for identification and
explanation without intent to infringe.

Library of Congress Cataloging-in-Publication Data
A catalog record for this book has been requested

ISBN: 978-0-367-48397-5 (hbk)
ISBN: 978-0-367-48749-2 (pbk)
ISBN: 978-1-003-04269-3 (ebk)

Typeset in Palatino
by Apex CoVantage, LLC

This book is dedicated to the memory of my mother Doris Helen Faulknor Fernandez R.N. (1923–2011)

Her keen intellect, boundless compassion, and enduring kindness inspired me and offer a model for others. She always served her underappreciated, but noble profession with dedication, integrity, and a passion for helping others.

In Memoriam

Stephen Tharrett (1952–2020)

Just as I was finishing the manuscript for this book, I received the news that I had lost one of my brothers, Stephen Tharrett. Among the many things we had in common the love of games and learning was paramount. Although Stephen was a titan in the fitness industry and author of several books in that field, he genuinely loved games and even owned a small game studio, Dinosaur Games, near Austin, Texas. He was so excited about this book, so I am deeply saddened he will not see this publication. Nonetheless, Stephen's dynamic, enthusiastic spirit lives through the optimism this book projects for the future of learning through games and the joyful thinking that produces game-based teaching. RIP, dear brother.

Contents

Preface

Humans learn from experience. They use the experiences they have had to build a massive web of associations in their mind, a web represented by emerging connections among the neurons in their brain. They use these associations—which can change with new experiences—to think, plan, and imagine with.

However, humans build their web of associations based on what they have cared about in an experience. What they care about guides their attention in an experience and, thus, determines what they focus on, what they background, and what they ignore altogether. Children who have experienced trauma early in life come to care deeply about avoiding danger and pay most of their attention in new experiences to looking out for possible threats to their well-being. This limits their ability to explore and take risks and, thus too, limits their wider learning.

Where do humans learn what to care about? From the families and social groups which give them a sense of belonging and mattering. Humans have a deep need to matter and will find mattering wherever they can, in good or bad groups. It is those to whom they matter and who matter to them that show learners what to care about and how to manage their attention in experiences, thus, how to build their minds. Caring and mattering are at the very heart of learning.

Developmentally, across their life span, humans need what we can call designed experiences. Designed experiences are ones a parent, teacher, mentor, or social group designs to show learners what to care about and how to manage their attention. After all, when a human is new to a domain, they do not yet know what to care about and how to let it guide their attention, so you just can't shove them out the door and say, "Go experience things".

Here is a simple example: In the video game *Dragon Box* you learn algebra by starting with simple rules for manipulating pictures that you do not associate with math in any form. You eventually come to see that the fun of the game is not in looking at the pictures, nice as they are, but in knowing what they mean in terms of what you get to do with them to accomplish a goal. Eventually, the pictures turn into algebraic symbols, but, of course, by then you clearly see that their meaning is not in what they look like, but in how you use them. You know well how to take active control of them. You have learned not just the nature of algebra but the nature of signs of all sorts (it is the insight at the heart of Wittgenstein's *Investigations* made clear to a 5-year-old).

The experiences we have had—and most centrally the designed experiences we have had that eventually set us on a path to self-teaching in new domains—represent the limits of our thinking, planning, and imagining. Without new experiences that make us revise and transform our associations we cease to develop, and our mind can stultify.

Who are experience designers? They are artists, architects, media designers, and teachers in the broad sense of people who guide us in new experiences that they have designed or curated in ways that will change our minds in new and better ways. In the realm of experience design, video games stand out, not just as one important technology through which we can design experiences for others, but as a good guide to experience design generally, with or without games, in or out of school.

Video games are the best technology we have with which to create virtual experiences that have all the important aspects of how good learning experiences work in the "real" world. Humans learn best when they have actions to take whose outcomes they care about. They learn best when they are mentored to know how to manage their attention effectively to accomplish their goals. And, they learn best in settings where failure is not so consequential that they will not explore, take risks, and view failure as a form of learning. Video games can create experiences we cannot have, or cannot as easily guide, in the real world.

Video games are also the best technology we must use to mimic how human memory and imagination work. Human memory is not particularly good at veridical recall because we most often use our memories (and, in doing so, change them) to make sense of things and plan for future actions before we act and pay the consequences. When we use our memories this way, we simulate and role play scenarios in our imagination to test out various hypotheses. Video games are external and programmable versions of human imagination that can greatly extend our ability to think, plan, imagine, and fanaticize and even build, not just new minds, but new worlds.

So, welcome to *Teaching in the Game-Based Classroom: Practical Strategies for Grades 6–12*, a book about experience design by experience designers steeped in the principles of how learning actually works best for humans. These principles are well represented in good games of all sorts, not just video games. The authors of this book will show you how to get those principles well developed in your classroom and how to become a designer for experiences that can make minds and the world they live in better for each of us and for all of us.

James Paul Gee
Mary Lou Fulton Presidential Professor of Literacy Studies
Regents' Professor (retired)
Arizona State University

About the Author

David Seelow has taught in virtually every kind of educational setting: university, college, community college, public high school, private high school, alternative high school, residential school for incarcerated youth, and prison. He has 30 years' teaching experience, including 15 in online/distance education. Dr. Seelow obtained a doctorate in comparative literature from Stony Brook (State University of New York) and MA in English from Columbia University before returning to school to earn an Advanced Certificate in educational computing, permanent teaching licenses for grades 7–12 in both English and social studies, and a School District Administrator's License for grades K–12. Lastly, Dr. Seelow also has a certificate in game design. He founded the Center for Game and Simulation-Based Learning, an award winning Online Writing Lab, and the Revolutionary Learning blog and consulting service. Dr. Seelow's last book, *Lessons Drawn: Essays on the Pedagogy of Comics and Graphic Novels*, was published in 2018. He currently resides in the Capital Region of New York State next to a nature preserve. In addition to games and comics, Dr. Seelow loves the New York Yankees, literature, tennis, film, theater, all things Irish, and, most of all, a beloved pug named Roderick.

Introduction
The Urgency of Innovation

David Seelow

Why Now?

When I proposed this book, the world was quite different. The emergence and rapid spread of the COVID-19 virus has wreaked havoc across the globe killing well over a million people, and, in the United States, disproportionately affected people of color (Rabin, 2020). Schools were suddenly forced to move into virtual environments with no time for preparation, and the social inequities of America's public education system returned to the surface of public discussion. A post-pandemic world will require different models of education. Things cannot go on as before. The need for change was already clear before COVID-19. The need for innovative and flexible approaches to teaching now has special urgency. Transplanting classroom practices onto virtual or hybrid environments will not work. Online education is fundamentally different than traditional classroom instruction and must reflect appropriate instructional strategies. However, crises are also opportunities for creative thinking and teaching. Teachers may not be quite prepared for the virtual world, but students are. Students spend considerable time online through social media, and game play, sometimes solitary and other times with friends, and strangers, near and far. A game-based learning approach to the post-pandemic classroom can thrive if teachers and administrators receive support in the transition and commit to embrace a progressive paradigm and bring the worlds of learning and gaming into deep and enduring conversation and application. This book will help you do that. Let me give you a brief explanation of why game-based learning works followed by a brief outline of the book's architecture.

Video games have provided countless hours of entertainment for kids since the golden age of arcade games in the late 1970s. The founding of Atari and the rise of home entertainment consoles like the Atari 2600 brought video games from public spaces to private homes. In the mid-1980s Apple II and the personal computer revolution gave video games a new platform that would soon connect players to each other through the Internet. Soon thereafter we had the smart phone (foreshadowed by Nintendo's Game Boy) and tablet as mobile devices. Kids could play on the go. Now, video games have become the largest entrainment medium in the world (Richter, 2020).

Just as games—and the technology that delivered them—progressed rapidly the pedagogy of learning education remained on a hamster wheel as if students' out of school activity had nothing to do with in-school learning. Starting 35 years ago with 1983's *A Nation at Risk*, policy makers bemoaned American students' poor performance vis-à-vis their peers in other advanced countries (see for example the Programme for International Student Assessment, 2015 and DeSilver, 2017). We have had No Child Left Behind, Race to the Top, Common Core, charter schools and privatization, and yet we have limited, if any, gains.

If anything, video games, when they do enter public discourse, are blamed for contributing to youth violence or compulsive behaviors that detract students from school although not supported by research. Let us turn the tables and look at one example of how even a sometimes maligned video game can help teach us a better way of educating our kids.

Doom or Doomed?

When Id Software released Doom in 1993, the same year Congress conducted hearings on the negative effects of "violent" video games like *Mortal Kombat*, the game did much more than propel the first-person shooter into the national spotlight and the hands of millions of kids. Let me pause for a personal example. In 1993, I was working full time as a community social worker serving "troubled" teenage boys, i.e., boys who cut classes, were truant, smoked marijuana, sometimes stole or otherwise were engaged with law enforcement and family court. In the late afternoon, I taught Introduction to Literature at the Old Westbury campus of the State University of New York. This campus had a large minority population drawing much of its student body from New York City's five boroughs. Whenever I visited a particular 12 year-old boy in Long Beach, on Long Island, a small city on the Atlantic Ocean, 25 miles west of New York City, I found him sitting at the computer playing Doom. He often missed school, was considered disruptive and had an Individualized Education Program (IEP) and Attention Deficit Disorder (ADHD). The boy's mother was a teacher who exhausted approaches without success and did not know what to do to help her son. They lived in an upper middle-class neighborhood right on the bay. The paradox of a boy who apparently could not pay attention or sit still long enough to do homework but could focus for hours on a game and excel at that game hit me immediately.

I had already resolved this paradox in my college class. After all, 1993 was also a golden age of hip hop and rap. The noted group Public Enemy was formed at nearby Adelphi University. Many adults spent considerable energy complaining about this controversial music. Contrarily, I embraced rap and made it part of my poetry unit. Attendance improved, discussions exploded, and students succeeded. A simple acknowledgment that what students immersed themselves with outside of class might prove useful material inside of class struck me as self-evident, but at the time the evidence slipped by most school systems. *Doom*, like hip hop, had much to offer if educators took the time to listen to and observe kids in their everyday lives.

First, *Doom* offered an engaging world that the classroom did not. Students were active participants in the game, while in school they too often remained passive not active learners. Students, like the one I worked with, could excel at the game. Opportunities to succeed seemed rarer at school where failure or cutting class could result in catastrophe not an extra life (i.e., another opportunity to succeed). *Doom* also made possible a multiplayer option. Kids could play with each other regardless of where they lived. This created an immediate community where kids could thrive and coexist in a passionate pursuit of common interests, just what we would like school to be. In a virtual or hybrid class, multiplayer games are ideal tools for learning. Even more, consider the possibility of kids playing across district lines! On Long Island, I could go from a poor district of largely minority students performing below what the state considered acceptable to a wealthy district of largely white students performing well above the national average by simply walking or driving a block or two. Two entirely different worlds, a wide inequity, and yet in such close geographic proximity. Games help bridge that gap the same way after-school programs like MOUSE (a New York City-wide youth program encouraging technology use and design projects that are equitable, www.mouse.org) do. We need a similar bridge in schools, not just after-school programs.

Finally, *Doom* offered players the opportunity to modify the game. Players could make their own levels or even variants of the game. They could become active knowledge makers, game designers and producers, not passive consumers. *Minecraft*, a topic of two chapters in this book, provides a superb way for students to become makers and knowledge producers. A game can be a mega hit and a mega learning opportunity too.

Game-Based Learning: Signs of Change

Although games have been used by the military for a long time to train soldiers as well as leaders, the serious application of video games to a secondary school classroom can be dated most strongly to distinguished educator and linguist John Paul Gee with the publication of his *What Can Video Games Teach Us About Learning and Literacy* in 2003 (Gee, 2007). They can teach us plenty. Gee articulated a full guide of 36 learning principles that can be derived from video games.

A few years later, Jane McGonigal published *Reality Is Broken* (2011) and gave a celebrated TED Talk called "Gaming can make a better world" (2010). McGonigal explained how games were "fulfilling genuine human needs" (p. 5) that were not being met. Our current global reality leaves too many people frustrated, unhappy and disappointed in many areas of their life. On the other hand, games, McGonigal argues, "They are teaching and inspiring and engaging us in ways that reality is not." Of course, games are part of reality, and we need to harness their power for social good and improved learning. McGonigal's TED Talk stressed how the skills required of large-scale video games, especially Massively Multiplayer Online Role Playing Games like *World of Warcraft* could be harnessed to solve real world problems. Middle school teacher Peggy Sheehy has used *World of Warcraft* successfully in her teaching (see Toppo, 2015) and the Games for Change organization has teamed with Epic Games to use the mega hit Fortnite for learning (see resources later in this Introduction). Positive change is happening.

However, let us be clear, problems today are global in scope and require cooperative and collaborative approaches for any resolution to be reached. The problems demand the kind of skills complex games stress: creativity, critical thinking, problem solving, systems thinking, intercultural communication and teamwork. You cannot teach these skills through a textbook nor can you assess students' capabilities through a bubble sheet response to test items. These problems are time sensitive too, hence my stress on the urgency of innovation.

Another practical text deserves mention here: Lee Sheldon's *The Multiplayer Classroom* (2020), now in its second edition. It describes how to set up a classroom like a game and gives many case studies from teachers at different levels of the education spectrum. This book extends those mentioned earlier and others as a resource for innovative and progressive teaching that engages students at a deeper level and promotes knowledge transfer and applied skills. What this text does not promote is gamification divorced of context. Let me clarify as this is an often misunderstood point, before laying out what to expect in this volume.

Game-Based Learning v. Gamification

Gamification is the application of game elements to a nongame environment (Deterding et al., 2011). Think of your credit card's reward system as an example. Gamification works through extrinsic mechanisms like trophies, prizes and leaderboards. They are not organic to learning and can easily be exploited by students who circumvent genuine learning to win the gold star. I do not suggest they do not have a place. I teach a course on superheroes and give free comic books to students who achieve perfect attendance. Do I think a student will go out of his or her way for a $4.99 comic book? No, but I have had more students obtain perfect attendance than any other course. Yet, even here, the reward had an organic connection to the nature of the class.

Game-based learning is a way of thinking and doing that stresses intrinsic motivation. Designer Ralph Koster explains this well, "We [game designers] build systems that enable people to do things they didn't think they could do—whether it's to drive a race car, score a goal in the World Cup, or blast an alien in the face" (2018, p. 10). Wouldn't you like to see your students solve a math problem they thought impossible or write a coherent essay with a strong point of view?

Game-based learning, as the name indicates, is learning based upon games, not games added onto to learning or using games for learning, but rather learning based upon the design and play of games, video, tabletop, card, board, athletic and outdoor games all included. Intrinsic motivation drives game-based learning; the passion to excel and enjoy at the same time. Find out what students' passions are, and that will launch a journey of discovery and growth.

To differentiate extrinsic v. intrinsic motivation let me give two simple examples. One of my favorite games has always been tennis. I love to play and watch the sport. The great Spanish player Rafael Nadal won his 13th French Open during the pandemic. That is significantly more than any other professional ever achieved at the Roland Garros Stadium in Paris. Nadal earned a very sizable check (over $1.8 million), spellbinding for any of us, and won a nifty trophy too. These are both extrinsic motivators, and at the top level of a sport the rewards are indeed pretty jaw dropping. But do they drive someone like Rafael Nadal? Not anymore. He has a passion for the sport, and his drive must be to be the best that he can possibly be. For Nadal, I believe motivation to be to win one more tournament at age 34, old for a professional tennis player, and prove he can beat the best younger players in their prime and not just beat, but trounce them, when most players at that age would have retired and enjoyed a life wealth and fame can bring one. He no longer needs the trophies or the money, but he enjoys the satisfaction of doing well—being in the zone, achieving bliss. You can achieve that feeling of internal joy in learning as well. In a fan interview (Pagilaro, 2020) following the Roland Garros tournament Rafa responded to a question "Do you have any more dreams?" by simply stating "My goal is to just keep going." One might have expected Nadal to say he wanted to break his tie with Roger Federer for the most all time wins of a major tournament (they both have 20 at the time of this writing), but the goal clearly remains internal or intrinsic and not an easily measured external or tangible reward. He later clarified this point in response to a question about how he motivates himself even when not playing well. He explained how even when losing a set and falling behind he is "always looking for solutions," that he never "gives up" because "there is always a chance: to turn the match around" and he wants "to be ready for it." The key in Rafa's mind seems to be the importance of being always present, keeping one's focus and fighting each moment. The interview ends with Rafa talking about the future and explaining he will retire when "I don't feel the passion, then it will be okay to say good-bye." In other words, no specific age, no extrinsic goal, but rather, the love for the game.

Okay, not even the best professional players can beat Nadal on a clay surface (his record at the French Open is 100–2), so what does success mean for these other players? You can only have one winner, right? No, that is a simplified notion of athletics and games. To say you must win is to say you must get an A grade or a 1600 SAT score. Success means self-improvement. Maybe a player wins an extra game or even a set against Nadal. What matters is that player does not shy away from the challenge. You only improve by challenging yourself. Good games always allow for such challenges. Success will look different for every player, and so should success look different for every student. What matters in game-based learning is that the student progresses according to what the student's goals, passions and capabilities are given the constraints and contexts the student works within. Students in under-resourced communities necessarily must work against obstacles those in well-resourced communities do not have to, and direct comparisons place less-resourced students at a permanent and discouraging disadvantage. Publishing a report comparing student scores from the wealthy suburban Scarsdale public schools with students from the urban Yonkers City Schools, though in the same county, makes no sense. Teachers, administrators, funders and government policy makers need to make sure all students have a fair opportunity to succeed. In a game both players start at "Go" but the paths they take to success may vary by student and district. Most important is that the student moves forward. What you do not want is backward movement or failure unless that failure is properly viewed as progress to promote learning towards eventual success. Measuring success by a single common end of year test or a standardized national exam subverts learning. Master designer Amy Jo Kim concisely makes my point, just substitute learning for game play, "Just as character transformation is the backbone of great drama, personal transformation is the backbone of great game play" (2018, p. 14).

Although game-based learning is a pedagogy and practice, the use of games, all kind of games, in the classroom is often part of the practice, but the games must be judiciously chosen and organic to course content. Applying games to a classroom setting requires careful consideration of your objectives, targeted outcomes and the game you are asking students to play. Karen (Kat) Schrier, a contributor to this volume (Chapter 13), edited a collection of essays titled *Learning, Education & Games: 100 Games to Use in the Classroom & Beyond* on how to use specific games in the classroom which will help you with this aspect of game-based learning. The game can be designed specifically to address a subject area, like the Mission US series of historical games for middle school students, which feature role playing protagonists at critical moments of U.S. history. However, games designed for entertainment that have education-relevant themes like Sid Meir's *Civilization* (see Squire, 2011) or even board games like *Diplomacy*, *Catan* or *Underground Railroad* can also be valuable texts for a middle or high school social studies class. The *Assassin's Creed* series from Ubisoft in Montreal addresses historical themes and subjects from a fictional perspective that grabs hold of students and keeps them playing, which brings along important collateral learning. Because all kids are now digital natives, they are less likely to read print texts than previous generations. This is a diminishment of culture, but you can use story-driven games to help reverse this trend and spark reading, through games like *Life is Strange* (2015) or *What Happened to Edith Finch?* (2017). *Assassin's Creed's Odyssey* (2018) has a tremendous story as well as a series of quests rooted deep in Ancient Greek history (431–422 B.C.E.) and the Peloponnesian War. I can easily see students playing this game as a gateway to Homer's *Odyssey*.

For a final example of what I mean by collateral learning, look at *Endless Ocean (Forever Blue)* (2007) published for Nintendo's Wii platform. On the surface or under the surface in this case, the game is a scuba diving adventure.

What student would not love to scuba dive in the South Pacific looking for hidden treasure? Treasure hunts were as popular in my day as today, and well before my day as well. In playing the adventure, students discover an entire world under the ocean: a magnificent world of diversity and breathtaking beauty. At a time when species are becoming extinct and our pollution has contaminated such beautiful forms of marine life, I can think of few game experiences more worthwhile.

As an aside, if you want to experience an epic win that has nothing to do with football or basketball, watch the documentary *Brooklyn Castle* (2012), and see how underserved kids from an under-resourced middle school in Bedford Stuyvesant Brooklyn ended up becoming national chess champions! In most cases, these games I have mentioned serve students far better than standard textbooks. They are more authentic, more engaging and more fun. Once the pandemic is over, turn your classroom into a mini Gen Con and students will thrive. Gen Con refers to an annual national conference for tabletop games held over four days in Indianapolis (the Gen refers to Lake Geneva, Wisconsin, where the first conference was held). The conference was started by legendary *Dungeons & Dragons* co-creator Gary Gygax in 1968. In 2019, the conference drew around 70,000 people. At the event you can play your favorite game at one of many tables occupied by game enthusiasts from around the world. After the pandemic, consider setting up your classroom for a week or so with different tables for different educational board or card games and each day rotate students from table to table. You can have students keep game journals or report out after each day. You can find games relevant to any subject area, and this mini Gen Con will promote an engaging, fun and social experience that deepens learning.

Many Paths to Success: The Architecture of This Book

Many games have multiple endings. There is no one way to play, no one way to succeed. In this volume you will discover many paths to understanding and applying game-based learning from recognized experts in the field. You can read the text in any order that best suits your interest or needs. These strategies apply to all disciplines and all grades from middle school to senior year. Of course, I encourage you to read every chapter because the collective voice will genuinely help transform your classroom, teaching and student learning. Moreover, at the end of many chapters you will find select carefully curated resources to use in your class. Likewise, the references give you a wealth of information and further reading when you have the time to explore these topics in more depth.

Playing Forward: What to Expect

Barry Fishman and colleagues at the University of Michigan begin our volume with a foundational chapter, "Improve Student Engagement With Gameful Learning." The authors demarcate the limitations of our current educational system, and then outline gameful learning as a positive alternative that engages disaffected students too often preoccupied with formal grades, fear of failure, centralized curriculum and standardized summative assessments. Fishman, Hayward and Niemer articulate ten key principles that can immediately impact your classroom and model the class as a dynamic, fully engaged game. Additionally, the authors point out the potential benefits of GradeCraft, a Learning Management System (LMS) designed to support gameful learning. Sandra Schamroth Abrams and Hannah R. Gerber build on the inaugural chapter and give a detailed description of how video games use feedback loops to promote ongoing learning and mastery. They focus on four elements of digital games that can be applied to any class: objectives/rules, progress bars, in-game maps and leader/scoreboards. In addition to showing practical uses of these feedback tools, Abrams and Gerber stress the importance of integrating student reflection with the feedback tools as a necessary ingredient to ongoing student productivity.

Chapters 3 and 4 function as a pair in their explanation of how *Minecraft* can be used both inside and outside the classroom to spur student motivation, creativity and community building. In "*Minecraft* and Socially Situated Student Centered Student Learning," Katie Salen Tekinbaş, cofounder of the celebrated Quest to Learn school in New York City, and Krithika Jagannath show how *Minecraft*'s survival mode can be used in an online environment that privileges teamwork, creativity and problem solving. In this chapter you will learn how challenge and improvisation lead to student growth, build community and manage behavior. In the next chapter Douglas Kiang, a computer science teacher at the Menlo School in Atherton, California, uses *Minecraft* for hands on learning projects. He also places a strong emphasis on *Minecraft*'s power in the virtual and hybrid classrooms.

The next nine chapters are grouped in three groups of three according to general subject matter and domain. Chapters 5 through 7 focus on the STEM (Science Technology Engineering Math) disciplines. We begin this segment with Kate Litman's step by step guide to designing a student game to address mathematical literacy. Moreover, Kate describes the seven design principles that guide the famous Quest to Learn school (Q2L) where she teaches. The entire school (middle and upper grades) bases its curriculum and instruction on gameful or game-like learning. Learn how this unique school operates, why Kate teaches there and how she implements its principles in mathematics. From New York City we move upstate to the Capital Region of New York and the innovative Tech Valley High School whose curriculum features technology and project-based learning. The school's authors walk through their game-design science projects which are based on cognitive scientist Lindsay Portnoy's Design Thinking framework (2020).

In the final chapter of this segment, Meredith Thompson describes an exciting partnership between MIT's Education Arcade and Game Lab with progressive science teachers from the Greater Boston region. The chapter discusses an evidence-based Virtual Reality (VR) game about cells. Learn how

VR can lead to "virtual hands-on learning" not possible in earlier days. Dr. Thompson also articulates what she calls "virtual constructionism," a pedagogy that builds on the pioneering work of Seymour Papert.

The following triad moves from STEM to the humanities (language arts, history, philosophy). STEM deserves the national attention it receives, but this emphasis cannot be at the expense of the humanities. The key liberal arts subjects equip students with enduring interdisciplinary skills such as critical thinking, creative problem solving and effective communication. In the social media era where disinformation proliferates these critical literacy skills become more vital than ever and games help teach them successfully.

Montreal's Paul Darvasi, a recognized expert in the application of games to education, begins this segment by talking about the world's most controversial video game: Grand Theft Auto. Paul explains how students live in media today and how schools must take advantage of students' driving interests to reach them in constructive ways. It is much better to use a controversial video game students frequently play outside of school in the classroom where context and intelligent guided discussion can structure their play, than let them off on their own path with no context to structure their experience. Many years ago, Professor Gerard Graff (1993) argued for the centrality of teaching the controversies with Mark Twain's *Huckleberry Finn* as one prime example. To ignore or deny the controversies that tear at the country does students a disservice. Paul gives some great personal examples of how this controversial text can help senior-level students who will soon be in college or working.

Text adventures like *Colossal Cave Adventure*, *Zork* and *Mystery House* drove early computer games. They placed players into active roles as they authored their own paths through an evolving text with many branches. Hap Aziz and Joy Baker explain how easy to use new software allows students to become authors. Furthermore, they point out and give examples of how text adventures can be rooted in historical events with student's role playing and authoring history from perspectives different than those of the standard history book. Imagine what the world would be like if Hitler prevailed? (Phillip K. Dick's novel *The Man in the High Castle*, [1962] 2016, imagines this very possibility.) Thinking through alternative decisions and their potential consequences can be a powerful learning experience. For Chapter 10, game designer and trainer Randall Fujimoto walks you around the latest and most innovative narrative techniques including Augmented/Mixed Realty (AR/MR), Live Action Role Play (LARP) and Immersive Theater, all examples of Live Interactive Narrative experiences. Students learn best through stories, and there are many effective ways to tell stories as all the previously mentioned authors will show you.

The volume's final triad addresses the critical, but too often overlooked area of social emotional learning (SEL). COVID-19 has made the need for SEL and support networks primary. These three chapters show how games can help students navigate the pressing anxieties of disrupted classrooms, disrupted families, and other current and future crises. You cannot learn if you are under constant stress and coping with emergency situations unless you have learned the skills necessary for coping with such situations.

Jonathan Cassie begins the segment with a wonderful discussion of how role playing games benefit students' self-management, social awareness, responsible decision making and interpersonal skills. Students can graduate with a 100 average, but if they lack these (SEL) skills, they will be at a disadvantage in the post-graduate world where our democracy demands informed, healthy, caring, stable and mindful citizens. Claudia-Santi F. Fernandes and the stellar team at play2PREVENT Lab at the Yale Center for Health & Learning Games highlight their PlayForward Prevention Platform. Following Jon's chapter, they present four games that address critical aspects of students' day to day lives: *PlayForward: Elm City Stories, smoke SCREEN, PlayTEST!*, and *Play Smart*. The pandemic did not wipe away the already pervasive opioid epidemic or the seriousness of student vaping. This team shows how their games help students face these complex stressful realities. They also describe evidence-based design, a multi-tiered system of support and implementation strategies.

Karen (Kat) Schrier rounds off this final triad of chapters with an urgent chapter, "Using Games for Empathy, Compassion, and Care." The racial conflicts, hate speech and discrimination that are too prevalent today must be addressed, and this chapter shows you how to grapple with these problems through several valuable games. We need to reduce biases and practice tolerance if our students are to be the future leaders we hope and want them to be. Kat has worked on using games to reduce bias and promote empathy, so you will find this chapter essential reading for helping students develop sound, fair and healthy habits for being in the world.

The final contribution is, most appropriately, "What We Learned From Games to Make Assessment Playful." Innovative learning demands innovative assessment. The use of multiple-choice bubble sheets, a one size fits all standardized assessment for content knowledge taken by solitary students simply does not cut it anymore. A powerhouse team made up of MIT's Playful Journey Lab's director Yoon Jeon (YJ) Kim and Kevin Miklasz from the highly regarded Noggin take you through several practical assessment games and the principles underlying these embedded assessments. The duo ends with some excellent ideas for remote/online assessment, something that will become increasing important post-pandemic.

My conclusion offers five ways game-based learning can transform your students as well as important factors in the successful implementation of game-based learning. However, just as learning never truly ends—we should all promote lifelong learning habits—this book does not end with a conclusion. Rather, you are fortunate to have some stimulating and important final thoughts in the afterword written by Justin Reich, Director of MIT's Teaching Systems Lab. An expert on educational technology and its limitations, Justin will share what he has learned during the pandemic that should prove beneficial to your instructional practices (see Reich, 2020).

Resources

When thinking about using any of the following games mentioned in this introduction think of the classroom in an expansive sense of the word. The classroom includes virtual/online learning, clubs, after-school programs and summer camps. Games are ideal for personalized learning as well as multi-player group learning and differentiated instruction. You can visit the games' publisher's website or as the first place to start I would suggest the STEAM portal (https://store.steampowered.com/).

Finally, board games have enjoyed a kind of renaissance lately. There are many cafes dedicated to board games just as there are arcades and billiard halls. Additionally, there are many retail stores that sell games and host game nights for community members. Once physical distancing requirements are relaxed board games can play a vital role in any discipline. A good general resource would be Board Game Geek (https://boardgamegeek.com).

Video Games

Assassin's Creed Odyssey (Ubisoft, 2018) www.ubisoft.com/en-us/game/assassins-creed/odyssey

An epic game developed by Montreal's superb Ubisoft studio, this game is rooted in the Peloponnesian War between Athens and Greece. You play either as Alexios or his sister Kassandra. The game mixes fiction and mythology with major historical figures and events. Students are exposed to ancient geography, the contrasting approaches to life exemplified by two great city states, Athens and Sparta, and the opportunity to interact with extraordinary historical figures like Socrates, Pericles and Herodotus. Do your students know who Aspasia is? Probably not, so this new awareness would be a valuable lesson about women and history by itself. The game offers all the mechanics, skills, battles and quests students love with numerous possibilities for customized learning adventures and personalization depending upon student interest.

Endless Ocean (Arika, 2007) www.arika.co.jp/arika_eng/

Some game critics complain this game developed for Nintendo's Wii platform is not game like enough, but they miss the point. This is an open world experience where students learn the skill of scuba diving while encountering the rich array of marine life. Side quests include befriending and training dolphins as diving companions. In the online option students can communicate with each other by leaving underwater notes. It is a beautiful antidote to the loud explosions of shooting and war games, a meditative journey to tranquil music. Students can customize their own soundtrack to the game or listen to songs from New Zealand's native Maori people and others. It reminded me of my childhood and the thrill and excitement I had watching the TV series "The Undersea World of Jacques Cousteau" (ABC, 1968–1976). Today's students most likely do not know who this pioneering French oceanographer and conservationist was, but they should. It is perfect for supplementary lessons in biology and environmental science.

Fortnite Creative (Epic Games, 2018) www.epicgames.com/fortnite/en-us/creative

A sandbox game where students create their own island worlds. Epic games has partnered with Games for Change to offer workshops for teachers on how to use Fortnite Creative in the classroom, www.gamesforchange.org/professional-programs/.

Life Is Strange (Dontnod, 2015) https://lifeisstrange.square-enix-games.com/en-us/games/life-is-strange?

An episodic storytelling game released in installments like a Charles Dickens novel. The game is excellent for junior or senior level English/language arts classes to teach interactive storytelling and narration. As a coming of age story, the game can also be used to teach the bildungsroman genre.

Mission US, www.mission-us.org/

A Public Media Project that partners WNET with various creative teams. This is an excellent series of games based on key episodes in American history. Each game has a full range of curricular support with videos, background information, activities and lesson plans. As of this writing the following games are available: *1770: The American Revolution/For Crown or Colony*; *1848: The Antebellum Era/Flight to Freedom*; *1866: Westward Expansion/A Cheyenne Odyssey*; *1907: The Immigrant Experience/City of Immigrants*; *1929: The Great Depression/Up from the Dust* and *1945: World War II/Prisoner in My Homeland*.

Sid Meier's Civilization (MicroProse, Firaxis Games and others, 1991–2016) https://civilization.com/

First designed by the legendary Sid Meier, *Civilization* now has six full scale games with many expansion packs and add-ons. Ideal for history, social studies and global studies, the game has players build cities as civilization emerges from the beginning of time and stretches toward the future of space colonization. In general, the turn-based games use Explore, Exploit, Expand, Exterminate as overarching ways of evolving civilization. Kurt Squire has discussed the educational uses of this game at length (see references later in this chapter).

What Remains of Edith Finch (Giant Sparrow, 2017) www.giantsparrow.com/games/finch/?

An excellent narrative-driven game for English/language arts where the player as protagonist Edith explores her ancestral home and learns about her family members' mysterious deaths as she moves from room to room. The game features mini stories and a variety of storytelling styles akin to a postmodern novel or short story/novel. Perfect for teaching narration and the horror genre and ideal to pair with stories by Edgar Allan Poe, Shirley Jackson or Stephen King.

World of Warcraft (Blizzard Entertainment, 2004)
https://worldofwarcraft.com/en-us/
A Massively Multiplayer Online Role Playing Game discussed by McGonigal (see References). There is a World of Warcraft in School program worth consulting. Peggy Sheehy, an English teacher at Suffern Middle School, uses the game successfully in a variety of ways as discussed by Greg Toppo in Chapter 7, "'I'm Not Good At Math But My Avatar Is': How a Subversive Suburban Teacher Is Using World of Warcraft to Teach Humanities," of his important book on games in the classroom (references, 2015). "World of Warcraft in the Classroom" http://wowinschool.pbworks.com/w/page/5268731/FrontPage.

Board Games

Catan (Klaus Teuber, 1995) www.catan.com/#start
One of many excellent German board games, *Catan: Trade Build Settle* challenges players to settle the Island of Catan through trading, resource management, roadways and such. The basic game now has expansions and spin-offs.

Diplomacy (Allan B. Calhamer, 1959) https://boardgamegeek.com/boardgame/483/diplomacy
An old but superb strategy game that I recommend for its emphasis on the use of negotiation to teach international politics. An excellent game for government classes, there is also now an online version: www.playdiplomacy.com/.

Freedom the Underground Railroad (Academy Games, 2012)
www.academygames.com/pages/freedom
An excellent cooperative game where players work for the abolitionist movement to end slavery.

Pandemic (Z-Man Games) https://store.us.asmodee.com/catalogue/pandemic_1135/
An excellent strategy game where players manage seven specialists in a race to cure four disease outbreaks. Not only is the game timely but winning in this game requires cooperation. The more students learn the value of cooperation and collaboration the better.

Documentary Film

Brooklyn Castle (2012, Katie Dellamaggiore) http://brooklyncastle.com/
An excellent documentary that follows students from Intermediate School 318 in Brooklyn, New York, as they become the first middle school to win the

national high school championship sponsored by the United Chess Federation. Chess is a game entirely skill based, and its role in schools cannot be overestimated both in terms of strategic thinking and character education. You can also visit the Chess in Schools website for information (https://chessinschools.us/).

References

DeSilver, D. (2017, February 15). U.S. students' academic achievement still lags behind that of their peers in many countries. *Pew Research Center*. Retrieved October 21, 2020, from http://pewrsr.ch/2kLfozD.

Deterding, S., Dixon, D., Kahled, R., & Nacke, L. (2011). From game design elements to gamefulness: Defining "gamification". In *Proceedings of the 15th international academic MindTrek conference* (pp. 9–15). Association for Computing Machinery.

Dick, P. K. (2016). *The man in the high castle*. Houghton Mifflin Harcourt. Originally published in 1962.

Gee, J. P. (2007). *What video games have to teach us about learning and literacy* (Revised and updated ed.). Palgrave MacMillan. Originally published in 2003.

Graff, G. (1993). *Beyond the culture wars: How teaching the conflicts can revitalize American education*. W.W. Norton & Company.

Koster, R. (2018). Foreword to Amy Jo Kim. In *Game Thinking: Innovate smarter and drive deeper engagement with design techniques from games*. Gamethinking.io

McGonigal, J. (2010, March 17). *Gaming can make a better world*. TED Talk.

McGonigal, J. (2011). *Reality is broken: Why games make us better and how they can change the world*. Penguin Books.

Pagilaro, R. (2020, November). Nadal: Accept the challenge. *Tennis Now*. www.tennisnow.com/Blogs/NET-POSTS/November-2020/watch-Nadal-Details-Dreams.aspx. Newsletter. The video interview "Chatting with Fans: Rafael Nadal" can be found at: www.youtube.com/watch?v=lyjCxZj_0GU&feature=youtu.be, November 8, 2020.

Portnoy, L. (2020). *Designed to Learn: Using design thinking to bring purpose and passion to the classroom*. ASCD.

Programme for International Student Assessment (2015). National Center for Education Statistics. https://nces.ed.gov/surveys/pisa/

Rabin, R. C. (2020, November 15). The U.S. surpasses 11 million infections; Black and Latino Americans still shoulder an outsize share. *The New York Times*. www.nytimes.com/live/2020/11/15/world/covid-19-coronavirus#the-us-surpasses-11-million-infections-black-and-latino-americans-still-shoulder-an-outsize-share.

Reich, J. (2020). *Failure to disrupt: Why technology alone can't transform education*. Harvard University Press.

Richter, F. (2020, September 22). The most lucrative entertainment industry by far. *Statista*. www.statista.com/chart/22392/global-revenue-of-selected-entertainment-industry-sectors.

Schrier, K. (2018). *Learning, education & games volume 3: 100 games to use in the classroom & beyond*. ETC Press.

Sheldon, L. (2020). *The multiplayer classroom: Designing coursework as a game* (2nd ed.). CRC Press.

Squire, K. (2011). *Video games and learning: Teaching and participatory culture in the digital age*. Teacher's College Press, Technology, Education Connection Series.

Toppo, G. (2015). *The game believes in you: How digital play can make our kids smarter*. St. Martin's Press.

1

Improve Student Engagement with Gameful Learning

Barry Fishman, Caitlin Hayward and Rachel Niemer

As educators, we want our students to be deeply engaged. We want them to work hard and take on intellectual challenges. We want them to take risks and try new things. And when things don't go as planned, we want students to be resilient and learn from their efforts. But the way our education system is designed encourages the opposite of these behaviors. Many chapters in this volume describe the use of games in learning. In this chapter, we describe how games are a metaphor for school itself, and how following principles of good game design can make a tremendous difference in how students engage with school. We introduce gameful learning, an approach to course design intended to enhance learner engagement and support them in feeling more intrinsically motivated. When students are intrinsically motivated, they learn more, are more willing to take risks, and are more resilient.

Roots of the Current System

How did we reach the point where students care more about grades than learning? This situation should not surprise us. As Cathy Davidson put it, our students

> were well-taught and learned well the lesson implicit in our society that what matters is not the process or the learning but the end result, the grade. . . . The message we're giving our students today is all that really counts is the final score.
>
> (Davidson, 2013)

The dominant, percentage-based approach to grading was intended to make education more scientific, including a purportedly objective way to compare students to each other (Kirschenbaum et al., 1971/2021). Unfortunately, this system provides only the illusion of accuracy and reliability (Brookhart et al., 2016; Guskey, 2013). There is ample evidence that percentage-based grading and grade point averages only serve to obscure information about learning (Rose, 2016) and promulgate bias and inequity (Kendi, 2019).

School Is a Terrible Game

If the current system isn't working the way we want it to, what should we do instead? We believe that well-designed games provide an excellent frame to think about supporting student motivation. Motivation researchers have been fascinated by the mechanisms that underlie effective games for decades (e.g., Malone & Lepper, 1987). James Paul Gee (2003) arguably kicked off the current movement around games and learning by dissecting popular games and explaining their success in terms of socio-cultural and cognitive theories of learning. The next step in our path towards developing gameful learning was realizing that school *itself* is a kind of game. Consider this definition of games from eminent game designers Katie Salen Tekinbaş and Eric Zimmerman: "A game is a system in which players engage in artificial conflict, defined by rules, that results in a quantifiable outcome" (Salen & Zimmerman, 2003, p. 80). If you replace the words "game" and "players" in that definition with "school" and "learners," you get a straightforward description of how school operates. The "quantifiable outcome," of course, is the grade. Inspired by Gee's analysis, we realized that the inverse of his observation also applied: If great games (and schools) are motivating and lead to learning, bad games (and schools) discourage engagement and learning.

We call attention to two critical flaws in the way grades are typically used in schools. The first is that when you design a percentage-based grading system, you put students into a losing game. Everyone starts with 100 percent. Suppose you earn 95 percent on an assignment, an A! However, you have lost your perfect score. Games typically do the opposite: you start with zero and build up. The goal of a well-designed game isn't perfection, it's progress. Struggling doesn't remove the possibility of succeeding at the highest level. In percentage-based grading, learners are punished for struggling, even if they end up learning just as much as (or more than!) students who did not struggle. People play well-designed games *because* they are challenging, not despite that fact. We have difficulty remembering the last time a student asked us for the "hardest thing" they could work on.

The second flaw is that grades reduce information about learning. What does an "A" mean? What does 90 percent mean with respect to how much one has learned? As Alfie Kohn (2019) argues, grades are more about ranking students than about describing what they know and can do. Grades were never about supporting or even accurately reporting students' learning; they merely make it easier for students to be sorted and selected by colleges and employers. To this end, schools often ration success and expect grades in a class to be distributed along something like a bell curve (Rose, 2016). This makes no sense. If we taught learners successfully, shouldn't everyone be able to achieve high marks? Instead of celebrating teachers where everyone does well, we stigmatize them as "easy graders." We need a better game.

Ten Principles to Make Learning in School a Better Game

Drawing from a wide range of scholarship and from our own experiences in designing and teaching gameful courses, we have devised ten principles that guide our thinking about how successful games can inform successful learning experiences.

Clear Learning Goals

Nobody starts playing a game without some clear idea of what they are playing for. If you have ever been told that you are learning something "because it will be on the test," or "because it is required," that isn't good enough. Good education design starts with clear goals, and then works backward to design the elements of learning (Wiggins & McTighe, 2005). If you begin a learning process with no idea why you are there or what the point is, you're most likely playing a bad game.

Balance Intrinsic and Extrinsic Motivation

In discussions of motivation, there is a general sense that doing something out of pure interest (i.e., intrinsic motivation) is better than doing something for a reward or to avoid a penalty (i.e., extrinsic motivation). And in general, this is true, especially for maintaining sustained engagement. However, in an academic context, extrinsic motivation is nearly impossible to avoid entirely, because we are often aiming for larger goals (e.g., get into a good college, become a doctor) that are not expressed clearly in any individual course. And extrinsic motivation can also be useful, helping us stick to deadlines, to follow rules, etcetera. The key is to strike a balance between these two forms of motivation (Roy & Zaman, 2017). We may start off with the extrinsic reward in mind, but as we go, a well-designed play/learning experience will engage us with the activity and learning as its own reward.

Support Autonomy

Good games give players a sense of agency, allowing them to make choices that have consequences (Gee, 2003). This design principle is drawn from Self-Determination Theory (Deci & Ryan, 2000), a foundational theory of human motivation. In a classroom, why do we insist that everyone proceed in the same order and at the same pace? Learners are diverse, and by respecting those differences, we help them succeed (Guskey, 2010; Rose, 2016). By giving learners a say in the path they follow, we deepen their buy-in to the process.

Create a Sense of Belonging

A second key principle from Self-Determination Theory (SDT) is to create a sense of belonging or relatedness. This means having your contributions or presence recognized by others and feeling supported when you need help. In games, this takes the form of being part of a team, cooperative play, and even in competition against others. Well-designed competition provides a measure of how your skills relate to those around you (Rigby & Ryan, 2011). In school, students sometimes feel misunderstood, isolated, or in the case of large classes, invisible. Grading conventions like the "curve" ration success, and pit learners against one other in unproductive ways. Good games don't do this.

Create Early Wins and Visible Progress

Good games provide opportunities for early successes, reducing player frustration and translating effort into progress. The "junior version" of baseball—tee ball—allows young players to successfully hit the ball just like the major leaguers. As they improve, there are more "just right" challenges to keep players moving along without getting overly frustrated (Perkins, 2008). This is also a principle of SDT: providing support for competence. In this frame, supporting competency means providing tasks that students are prepared for but may also find challenging (Rigby & Ryan, 2011). The feeling we get from completing easy work isn't nearly as motivating as the sense of accomplishment we feel after doing something difficult.

Allow for Productive Failure

Ask any entrepreneur: "Productive failures," where we take away lessons to apply to future attempts, are essential to success (Kapur, 2016). Sports, which are extremely well-designed games, involve a mix of winning and losing across one's career. In school we put too much emphasis on constant success. Students who are admitted to highly selective colleges have probably never experienced a significant "failure," which also means they weren't truly pushed. And as noted earlier, percentage-based grading systems punish learners who don't succeed right away, by dragging down their average. In good games, it's how you finish that counts the most.

Encourage Exploration

If you watch a serious gamer play a well-designed game, when they complete a level, they don't just move on. Instead, they go back, and they poke around to see what elements the game designers included that they missed the first time through. What they are doing is trying to understand the system of the game (Gee, 2003). And isn't that really the point of learning a subject? We don't want students to memorize the facts of science. We want them to learn to think about the world the way a scientist would. Understanding the system is more important than getting "right" answers (Collins, 2017).

Foster Identity Play

A corollary to encouraging exploration is to encourage students to explore their identity. In the "magic circle" of game play, you get to *be* a warrior, an astronaut, a basketball player. In the moment of the game, you aren't merely experimenting with these identities, you are becoming them in a meaningful, if temporary, way (Gee, 2003). This has strong parallels to education. John Seely Brown has argued that most of school is "learning about" things, mostly in the form of facts. When school works well, it is "learning to do," in the form of project-based or hands-on learning experiences. But the ultimate goal for education should be helping students "learn to become," to form images of their future selves and play with different identities (Thomas & Brown, 2011).

Include Opportunities for Practice and Reinforcement

Practice makes perfect. One of the great things about a digital game is that it never gets tired of you trying to get better. That can be hard to achieve in a regular classroom, because neither time nor patience are infinite. But harkening back to several of the principles mentioned earlier, including visible progress and productive failure, good games and good learning experiences let you practice to improve. This concept was one of the motivating factors behind the development of mastery-based learning (Guskey, 2010).

Embed Assessment in Learning

Finally, we note that you will probably never see a championship sports team sitting down to take a test on their sport after hoisting the trophy. Nor will you see a gamer complete a level and be given a quiz on key ideas from that level, at least not in a well-designed game. That's because the assessment of what these players have learned is embedded in the experience. They could not have completed the challenge of the game without having learned what was needed. We spend a lot of time on summative assessment in education, fostering a culture of measurement, instead of designing for "in game" or formative assessment to foster a culture of learning (Shepard, 2000). Good teaching also emphasizes assessment that is authentic to the task or goals. Standardized tests are a narrow way to measure understanding. Recently, educational researchers have started to focus on this idea literally, in the form of "stealth assessment" of learning in educational games (Shute & Ventura, 2013).

It's Not Gamification . . . It's Gameful

We make a distinction between gameful and the more broadly used term, gamification. Gamification, which has become increasingly prominent in many areas of modern life, primarily leverages superficial elements of games to create extrinsic motivations to take actions. Gamification has the power to be coercive and deceptive (Bogost, 2011), but there are also many good applications of game design for learning that are called gamification (Landers et al., 2018). We do want to stress the difference between shallow vs. deep approaches to gamification (Roy & Zaman, 2017), and emphasize the importance of redesigning the system to support meaningful engagement and learning.

Be Gameful in Your Own Way

Gameful learning works in any subject area, for any teaching style, and for learners of all ages. At the University of Michigan alone, we've supported the use of gameful learning across more than 50 different academic program areas. We also note that the learning experience doesn't have to feel "like a game." The point is that well-designed learning environments have the affordances to support learner motivation. You can make a gameful approach work in *your* context, no matter what that context may be.

Gameful Principles in Practice: Examples From Real Courses

Over the past decade, we have helped hundreds of instructors design gameful learning experiences that suit their own goals and preferences. Along the way, we have observed myriad variations in how gameful ideas can be successfully implemented, and delight in discovering new approaches that address our shared goals. Instructors *support autonomy* and *encourage exploration* by providing more assignment choice, encouraging students to complete assignments in different ways, and allowing students to design their own assignments. Some instructors even allow students to assign weights to different assignment types to suit their individual strengths. *Productive failure* is supported through techniques like dropping the lowest score on a group of assignments, allowing for revision or resubmission, and enabling students to choose to complete additional assignments to demonstrate growth. Some instructors *create early wins and visible progress* by using badges to recognize progression through different levels of competency; others use unlocks to ask students to achieve a specific performance level on an assignment before opening more difficult tasks. Competitions between teams of students help *create a sense of belonging* and *balance intrinsic and extrinsic motivation*. As noted earlier, these principles align with what many consider good instruction in general, and practices such as using *embedded assessments* begin to feel more natural in gameful settings.

We have also observed the use of gameful learning beyond formal courses. Professional development programs leverage these practices to *foster identity play, encourage exploration,* and *include opportunities for practice and reinforcement* as learners develop new skills and mindsets. Just as with games, there are endless ways to combine gameful design principles, and the principles complement each other in use.

Gameful Infrastructures

One impediment to realizing our vision for gameful learning is the tremendous infrastructure built up around the current poorly designed percentage-based grading game. Grade point averages, transcripts, college admissions, job markets . . . all are built around the current system. Sociologists point out that, though we often think of infrastructure as something physical, like roads or plumbing, it is much deeper, comprising embedded standards and conventions that shape both culture and practice (Star & Ruhleder, 1996). In most schools, the gradebooks built into learning management systems (LMS) default to percentage-based grading. This creates a logistical challenge to teachers who want to implement gameful learning and sends a strong cultural message about what is "normal." While you don't need special tools to implement gameful learning, it is important to think carefully about how existing systems and structures represent grades or progress, and provide students with alternative representations of their learning to shift how they view the grading game.

Conclusion

Gameful learning is designed to make school a better game, one where learners feel supported as individuals, see the big picture, and are resilient in the face of challenges. In this pandemic era for education, gameful learning can help both individual learners and the larger school system be more resilient, emphasizing goals and progress over daily routines. In an era when we have come to recognize systemic racism and inequality, gameful learning provides an approach that focuses on learners as individuals, offering a way forward towards more equitable schooling. The ideas behind gameful learning aren't new, but we need them in education now more than ever.

Acknowledgments

We thank the University of Michigan Office of the Provost and Center for Academic Innovation for their support of gameful learning and GradeCraft. We also thank the many colleagues, instructors, and students who have helped us refine our ideas through their own gameful learning experiences. The first and second authors disclose that they have a financial interest in GradeCraft. The ideas expressed in this paper are those of the authors and not necessarily those of the University of Michigan.

Resources

To support teachers seeking to implement gameful learning, we developed GradeCraft, a tool that can replace gradebooks and assignment systems typically found in the LMS. You can explore GradeCraft at https://gradecraft.com/.

Examples of gameful courses can be viewed at www.gamefulpedagogy.com/.

References

Bogost, I. (2011, August 8). Gamification is bullshit [Blog]. *Video Game Theory, Criticism, Design*. www.bogost.com/blog/gamification_is_bullshit.shtml

Brookhart, S. M., Guskey, T. R., Bowers, A. J., McMillan, J. H., Smith, J. K., Smith, L. F., Stevens, M. T., & Welsh, M. E. (2016). A century of grading research: Meaning and value in the most common educational measure. *Review of Educational Research*, *86*(4), 803–848.

Collins, A. (2017). *What's worth teaching? Rethinking curriculum in the age of technology*. Teachers College Press.

Davidson, C. N. (2013, January 7). Why students gripe about grades. *HASTAC*. www.insidehighered.com/views/2013/01/07/essay-how-end-student-complaints-grades

Deci, E. L., & Ryan, R. M. (2000). The "what" and "why" of goal pursuits: Human needs and the self-determination of behavior. *Psychological Inquiry*, *11*(4), 227–268.

Gee, J. P. (2003). *What videogames have to teach us about learning and literacy*. Palgrave Macmillan.

Guskey, T. R. (2010). Lessons of mastery learning. *Educational Leadership*, *68*(2), 52–57.

Guskey, T. R. (2013). The case against percentage grades. *Educational Leadership*, *71*(1), 68–72.

Kapur, M. (2016). Examining productive failure, productive success, unproductive failure, and unproductive success in learning. *Educational Psychologist*, *51*(2), 289–299.

Kendi, I. X. (2019). *How to be an antiracist*. One World.

Kirschenbaum, H., Napier, R., & Simon, S. (2021). *Wad-ja-get? The grading game in American education: 50th anniversary edition*. Maize Books.

Kohn, A. (2019, June 16). Why can't everyone get A's? *The New York Times*, 8. www.nytimes.com/2019/06/15/opinion/sunday/schools-testing-ranking.html

Landers, R. N., Auer, E. M., Collmus, A. B., & Armstrong, M. B. (2018). Gamification science, its history and future: definitions and a research agenda. *Simulation & Gaming*, *49*(3), 315–337.

Malone, T. W., & Lepper, M. R. (1987). Making learning fun: A taxonomy of intrinsic motivations for learning. In *Aptitude, learning, and instruction: Cognitive and affective process analysis* (Vol. 3, pp. 223–253). Erlbaum.

Perkins, D. (2008). *Making learning whole: How seven principles of teaching can transform education* (1st ed.). Jossey-Bass.

Rigby, S., & Ryan, R. M. (2011). *Glued to games: How video games draw us in and hold us spellbound*. Praeger.

Rose, T. (2016). *The end of average: How we succeed in a world that values sameness*. HarperOne.

Roy, R. van, & Zaman, B. (2017). Why gamification fails in education and how to make it successful: Introducing nine gamification heuristics based on Self-Determination Theory. In M. Ma & A. Oikonomou (Eds.), *Serious games and edutainment applications* (pp. 485–509). Springer International Publishing. https://doi.org/10.1007/978-3-319-51645-5_22

Salen, K., & Zimmerman, E. (2003). *Rules of play: Game design fundamentals*. MIT Press.

Shepard, L. A. (2000). The role of assessment in a learning culture. *Educational Researcher*, *29*(7), 4–14.

Shute, V., & Ventura, M. (2013). *Stealth assessment: Measuring and supporting learning in video games.* MIT Press.

Star, S. L., & Ruhleder, K. (1996). Steps toward an ecology of infrastructure: Design and access for large information spaces. *Information Systems Research, 7*(1), 111–134. https://doi.org/10.1287/isre.7.1.111

Thomas, D., & Brown, J. S. (2011). *A new culture of learning: Cultivating the imagination for a world of constant change.* CreateSpace.

Wiggins, G., & McTighe, J. (2005). *Understanding by design* (2nd expanded ed.). Association for Supervision & Curriculum Development.

2

Videogames, Feedback Loops, and Classroom Practice

Sandra Schamroth Abrams and Hannah R. Gerber

Introduction

Game-based learning (GBL), which has been part of educational literature and practice for over 15 years, has focused on the role of digital and nondigital games in helping students to hone "decision-making, innovation, and problem-solving," and to understand the "'procedural logic' or meta level of game design" (Johnson et al., 2011, p. 21; see also Squire, 2011). Digital and nondigital GBL approaches support agentive and collaborative learning and help students to develop skills necessary for economic and academic futures (Abrams, 2017; Abrams & LaRocca, 2020; Gerber et al., 2014; Johnson et al., 2011; Whitton, 2012), and GBL paves the way for fine-grained and holistic examinations of gaming and learning vis-à-vis student interaction, instructional practices, and system designs (among other dimensions). Although GBL has been mistaken as gamification (and vice versa), as Plass, Homer, and Kinzer (2015) explained, one particular distinction between the two is the element of redesigning learning activities in light of student needs and engagement. Additionally, Gerber (2014, 2017) has indicated that GBL, as opposed to gamification, includes elements of playful interaction with content that aids learners in the development of intrinsic motivation toward a given topic.

This chapter builds upon digital GBL (also known as DGBL) to examine how and why videogaming can support learning in and beyond the classroom. Looking to the features of videogaming—namely the feedback system that is an inherent part of the meta-level of game design *and* that plays a key role in the process of decision making and problem solving—we introduce and address how the *feedback loop* (Abrams & Gerber, 2013, 2021; Gerber & Abrams, 2018) can be used to engage adolescents in meaningful learning experiences. This especially is relevant given that, in the last 10–20 years, there has been extensive scholarship examining how adolescents' out-of-school literacy practices are known to influence their in-school and out-of-school meaning making (cf. Abrams, 2009a, 2010, 2011; Alvermann, 2011; Hull, 2003; Hull & Schultz, 2002; Ito et al., 2010).

When we consider adolescents' out-of-school practices, in general, and videogaming, in particular, we are drawn to our understanding of the feedback loop, or interconnected in-game and post-game data that enable the player to assess and (re)direct game play to improve or maintain performance.

The term, feedback loop, has been associated with the inner-workings of games (Salen & Zimmerman, 2004), or cybernetic systems that enable the machine to "communicate" if-then procedures, consequences, and turn-taking: "Within a game, many subsystems regulate the flow of play, dynamically changing and transforming game elements. . . Feedback loops can be tricky to grasp, but they offer a crucial way of understanding how formal game systems function" (Salen & Zimmerman, 2004, p. 218). Such a view of feedback through the lens of game design helps to identify the necessary procedures to progress through a game.

Videogames also build upon a cybernetic system, or a regulatory system that uses data to manage and/or control information and individuals within and surrounding the system (Lanier, 2018). Cybernetic systems account for practices in and around the game and the ways players appropriate and re-imagine game information and artifacts which "feed the game from the inside out, bringing meaning to the game through their circulation within culture" (Salen & Zimmerman, 2004, p. 552). Artifacts can run the gamut from in-game belongings and handiwork (e.g., what a player acquires or builds through game play, such as with gathering resources and potions in a role playing game (RPG), like *Skyrim*, or building structures in *Minecraft*) to beyond-game creations (e.g., stories, images, or guides that build upon or extend understandings of game-related storylines, characters, and achievements, such as with the creation of fanfiction[1] and machinima[2]). Although beyond the scope of this manuscript, the advent of beyond-game creations, also known as paratexts (Apperley & Walsh, 2012), can be worthwhile investigating, especially with regard to classroom practice (for more, see Black, 2007; Gerber & Price, 2011; Lammers, 2012; Neimeyer & Gerber, 2015).

The Feedback Loop and Meaning Making in and Beyond the Classroom

At the turn of the century, both of us began wondering about how youth make meaning as they play videogames, and the topic became a focus of our doctoral studies, our dissertations (Abrams, 2009b; Gerber, 2008), as well as subsequent studies and publications. We have contemplated how the feedback loop creates a framework to understand formative assessment (Abrams &

Gerber, 2013), and we have considered how the framework informs video-game environments and library-based programs (Abrams & Gerber, 2021; Gerber & Abrams, 2018). In this chapter, we look to the feedback loop to discuss videogames and meaning making, and we offer practical information to support instructional activities inspired by digital game-based feedback.

Activities in a classroom often are tied to student achievement, which can be defined in myriad ways. We understand achievement to be synonymous with meaningful experiences that are iterative, reflective, and interest-driven in nature. In what follows, we introduce the feedback loop with respect to videogaming and meaning making, as well as classroom practices, and we address the connections to iterative, reflective, and interest-driven learning.

The feedback loop addressed in this manuscript specifically attends to a system that provides key information related to success and failure. More specifically, four overarching features offer, inspire, and evoke feedback, response, and action: (1) objectives and rules, or how and why the game is played; (2) progress bars, or real-time information about progress; (3) in-game maps, or visuals of a player's (and, often, opponents' or team members') in-game location(s); and (4) leaderboards, or post-game scoreboards (Abrams & Gerber, 2013, 2021; Gerber & Abrams, 2018). These non-hierarchical and interdependent aspects of the feedback loop can have applications beyond the screen. Across all of our recommendations for practice, ongoing reflection is central to student meaning making.

Objectives and Rules

Objectives and rules attend to the purpose and function of most digital and nondigital games. Objectives often can include short- and long-term goals that encourage offensive and/or defensive moves. Rules dictate actions of "acceptable" play, including but not limited to, how and when, players can move, act, respond; which tools players can use, when, and how; which moves, if any, are restricted; and so forth.

Videogaming and Meaning Making

In research that we have conducted across the years, we have noticed that objectives and rules in videogaming shape players' interactions with multiple texts, resources, and other players. For example, in prior research (Abrams & Gerber, 2021) we have examined how players' negotiations of objectives and rules spurred partnerships and friendships that, in turn, helped players to renegotiate objectives and rules (e.g., trying to turn a two-player game into a six-player game by creating a turn-taking rule structure). This type of interaction and negotiation underscores the type of autonomy typically found in videogame play.

In the Classroom

When students examine and reflect on objectives and rules—in order to think through what is and is not working for a given situation—then students have the autonomy to chart their own path for learning. This might be as simple as teachers asking students to reflect weekly on their personal learning objectives and to establish revised and/or new goals for the following week. Likewise, any rules that become superfluous can be revised or removed.

Practical Applications
We suggest that teachers provide ample time and space for students to reflect on their own learning and revise accordingly vis-à-vis a series of peer conferences and self-evaluation strategies (Abrams & Gerber, 2021). Teachers can set up workshop stations and provide initial guiding questions that foster reflection, such as the following: "How have you personally contributed to meeting the learning objectives set forth by your team/groupmates?"; "What progress have you made toward your personal learning objectives?"; and "How well have you stayed on target for meeting the set weekly objectives?" Students should be encouraged to keep a running record of these reflections, as well as revisions to their personal learning objectives. Equally important is for students to review these reflections to achieve an ongoing, holistic view of their progress.

Progress Bars
Progress bars are visual displays of players' discrete, in-the-moment actions through game play. Depending on the game, such in-the-moment information might include the players' scores; task-based accomplishments; time, opportunities, or turns remaining; the degree of strength or weakness; the degree of players' (via their characters') health; the types of powers, weapons, or moves available; and the number of lives remaining. As we have argued, "In this way, progress bars provide players with ongoing data about their game play status through words, numbers, colors, symbols, sounds, and so on, which, in turn, help players make real-time, in-game decisions" (Abrams & Gerber, 2021, p. 20).

Videogaming and Meaning Making
Our research reveals that youth often are keenly aware of the progress bars in videogames, and rightfully so: In order to reflect on their progress, players pay attention to important information, such as their lives, their abilities and powers, and their time remaining in the game. It also is common for onlookers to examine the progress bars and offer players real-time information, such as, "Hey, you only have one life left now," or "Cool! You now have extra ammo!" In other words, just as progress bars provide important details that immediately impact game play, so, too, do they create a source of conversation among game players and bystanders.

In the Classroom
Integrating progress bars in the classroom is not as simple as using stars to indicate student success, especially in light of our research, which suggests

that progress bars become conversation starters for reflection upon progress. However, if those stars indicate work accomplished towards a final project, thereby offering formative feedback that is ongoing, then that is a start towards a larger initiative to use the ethos of the feedback loop, in general, and progress bars, in particular, in the class. Videogames include mile-marker feedback, and, in the classroom, this type of feedback can be related to short- and long-term goals. Teachers can create steps or levels to an assignment and then ask students to review the project's criteria and articulate what they need to do to "level up." Also, we recommend that there be as many opportunities as possible for students to work with and learn from one another by engaging in conversation about their individual and group progress.

Practical Strategies

Although a first inclination might be to help youth keep track of their grades, we argue that it is far more important for youth to be cognizant not only of their achievements, but also of *what they still need to do and the resources they will need to meet their goals*. Students need to develop the skills to take stock of these mile-markers and milestones. We suggest creating space for students to engage in iterative thinking and learning by continuously returning to their work—hopefully viewing it as a work-in-progress—and collaboratively determining next steps and the materials needed to meet their objectives. Although we recommend teachers help students to engage in daily iterative review, at the very least, we recommend creating opportunities for students to have weekly self and group check-ins. Doing so will support students' self-directed learning that privileges the process of learning.

In-Game Maps

In-game maps support players by providing real-time information about in-game locations, as well as location information of their teammates and opponents. Akin to travelers using landmarks to navigate direction and organize resources (e.g., when to refuel, when to take a break), players can use this location-based information to achieve their short- and long-term objectives.

Videogaming and Meaning Making

In-game maps can appear in different forms, including, but not limited to, a racing track, an outdoor field, a room in a building, and a corridor in a maze. Sometimes a compass is visible, and often other players' positions are noted. Regardless of the setting, the in-game map helps the players to know where they are at any given time, and, thus, is similar to a dynamic version of the "you are here" star on a shopping mall map.

In the Classroom

The in-game map can help students become self-driven learners who look at their work in relation to the associated responsibilities and deadlines (which also are related to objectives and rules). In game-maps also can be coordinated with progress bars; the daily or weekly check-ins used for progress bars can include a section for students to note how their short-term accomplishments map onto the larger picture of the particular assignment or task. Even asking students to see how long it takes them to complete their homework can help a teacher explore further students' trajectories and needs and if and how some students might need to review one level and others advance to another (i.e., differentiated instruction).

Practical Strategies

Given that the feedback loop components work in concert, the in-game map offers real-time information about where students are in relation to their project and/or learning trajectories. Unlike the progress bar, the in-game map helps the students to visualize where they are in terms of a particular task or project's completion. Take, for instance, a research project. The concept of an in-game map would help students consider: Are they at the beginning and need to engage in research? Are they rounding the corner to the middle and need to begin synthesizing? Have they gone off track and need to rethink and revise their work? Are they close to the finish line and need to engage in another round of peer review? These questions are but one way to concretize the concept of the in-game map in the classroom.

Leaderboards

Leaderboards typically provide post-game information, such as high score, player rank, and other statistics, and players often use this information in formative and reflective ways to make future in-game decisions that will support success.

Videogaming and Meaning Making

Across our observations of gamers, we have noticed a variety of ways that players use the leaderboard to help them reflect upon their progress. A leaderboard can provide a player with powerful gaming statistics about individual performance (e.g., self-statistics) and about game play in general (e.g., in comparison to other players), by providing information, such as total points, assists, and kills they have within a specific game, or even over time. Players then can use this information to reflect upon future moves to improve their own game play.

In the Classroom

Data can be powerful when used to help guide reflection, and leaderboard data are no exception, especially when they are used as a form of formative assessment. When students critically reflect upon their progress over time, they can glean important insights into their strengths and challenges. However, we offer a word of caution: Reflection should not be a superficial activity; rather students need the time to (1) examine and reflect on the data; (2) identify new and recurring strengths and challenges; and (3) plan their next course of action knowing well that that, too, will be progress- and process-oriented.

Practical Strategies

We suggest that teachers work with students to identify (a) what work will be assessed and (b) how it will be assessed, and we suggest that these criteria be tied to students' personal learning objectives (see Objectives and Rules section). Similar to game leaderboards that have a discrete amount of information, there should not be more than a handful of measurements used to track and gauge progress. We suggest teachers work with students to determine three-to-five areas of activity or performance. Although the simplest measurement could be one's grade or GPA, we suggest that other areas be included, such as (a) collaborative work, (b) critical thinking skills, (c) innovation, and (d) presentation. Then students can track their accomplishments and performance at key "ending" points (e.g., end of the day or end of the week). These measurements might change every semester, every grading period, or even every unit, but there should be some logical bounding of and rationale for the measurements, and students should have ample time to track progress and make changes in a meaningful way.

Conclusion and Implications

When learning through the feedback loop, students engage in the powerful practices of self-reflection. This does not always happen, however. Like videogame players who look to feedback loop components—objectives and rules, progress bars, in-game maps, and leaderboards—to advance in a particular game, students can build upon feedback loop features to engage in iterative, reflective, and interest-driven meaning making in the classroom. Across our recommendations are important partnerships between students and teachers and students and their peers. Videogaming is a social activity, and we contend classroom learning could be and should be as well.

In many ways, the feedback loop supports evidence-based awareness of progress, resources, and needs. Through an iterative and reflective examination of their individual and group performances and accomplishments, students can gain a deeper awareness of their meaning-making practices. Although iteration and reflection often go hand-in-hand, guidance for both will help to build and sustain ongoing and meaningful practices. It is important to understand *the purpose* of reflection and the methods and resources available. Thereafter, there are operational details—how teachers will support iterative, reflective, and interest-driven meaning making in the classroom. Here are some questions to help teachers brainstorm their approaches:

◆ How and when will you create time and space for students to reflect on their progress to identify what they need to modify and/or maintain to succeed?

- ◆ How will you support an evidence-based awareness of progress and needs?
- ◆ How and when will students identify and communicate what needs to be/what has been accomplished? Where and how will these observations be recorded?
- ◆ Likewise, how and to whom will students communicate their plan to meet the objectives?
- ◆ How will you help facilitate ongoing self- and peer-feedback? How will you then help students to connect this feedback to their progress (and vice versa)?

These questions are intended to inspire pedagogy and practice that are informed by the ethos of the feedback loop. By engaging in reflective practice guided by the feedback loop, students can take ownership of their learning and engage in powerful meaning-making practices.

Notes

1. Fanfiction is a type of work (e.g., writing, art, and video) that involves the creation, modification, and/or extension of an original text (e.g., storylines, characters, and settings). Fanfiction often is written online within a community of other fanfiction writers; however, it also can be written in isolation.
2. Machinima is a portmanteau of the words, machine, and cinema. Machinima creators often use software to capture scenes from videogames, and they overlay these captured scenes with a storyline and/or commentary.

References

Abrams, S. S. (2009a). A gaming frame of mind: Digital contexts and academic implications. *Educational Media International*, 46(4), 335–347.

Abrams, S. S. (2009b). *Real benefits from virtual experiences: How four avid video gamers used gaming as a resource in their literate activity* [Doctoral dissertation]. Proquest.

Abrams, S. S. (2010). The dynamics of video gaming: Influences affecting game play and learning. In P. Zemliansky & D. Wilcox (Eds.), *Design and implementation of educational games: Theoretical and practical perspectives* (pp. 78–90). IGI Global.

Abrams, S. S. (2011). Association through action: Identity development in real and virtual video game environments. *Teachers College Record Yearbook*, 110(1), 220–243.

Abrams, S. S. (2017). Cooperative competition, reflective communication, and social awareness in public high school math classes. In Y. Baek (Ed.), *Game-based learning: Theory, strategies and performance outcomes* (pp. 357–370). Nova.

Abrams, S. S., & Gerber, H. R. (2013). Achieving through the feedback loop: How videogames can help us understand authentic assessment and meaningful learning. *English Journal*, 103(1), 95–103.

Abrams, S. S., & Gerber, H. R. (2021). *Videogames, libraries and the feedback loop: Learning beyond the stacks*. Emerald.

Abrams, S. S., & LaRocca, T. (2020). Play in the making: Developing a range of literacies through making and game-based activities. In J. Rowsell, C. McLean, & J. Marsh (Eds.), *Making futures: Maker literacies and maker identities in the digital age*. Routledge.

Alvermann, D. E. (2011). Moving on/keeping pace: Youth's literate identities and multimodal digital texts. *National Society for the Study of Education*, *110*(1), 109–128.

Apperley, T., & Walsh, C. (2012). What digital games and literacy have in common: A heuristic for understanding pupils' gaming literacy. *Literacy*, *46*(3), 115–122.

Black, R. W. (2007). Fanfiction writing and the construction of space. *E-Learning*, *4*, 384–397.

Gerber, H. R. (2008). *New literacy studies: Intersections and disjunctures between in-school and out-of-school literacies with adolescent males* [Unpublished doctoral dissertation]. University of Alabama.

Gerber, H. R. (2014). Gamifying education: Perils and promises. *Internet Learning*, *3*(2), np.

Gerber, H. R. (2017). How gamification misses the mark: Playing through failure. *English Journal*, *106*(6), 88–90.

Gerber, H. R., & Abrams, S. S. (2018). The feedback loop, meaning making, and your library's (videogaming) programs. In *Level up! (voice of youth advocates)*. Library Press.

Gerber, H. R., Abrams, S. S., Onwuegbuzie, A., & Benge, C. (2014). From Mario to FIFA: What case study research suggests about games-based learning. *Educational Media International*, *51*(1), 16–34.

Gerber, H. R., & Price, D. (2011). 21st century learners, writing, and new media: Meeting the challenge with game controllers. *English Journal*, *2*(101), 68–73.

Hull, G. A. (2003). Youth culture and digital media: New literacies for new times. *Research in the Teaching of English*, *38*(2), 229–233.

Hull, G. A., & Schultz, K. (Eds.). (2002). *School's out! Bridging out-of-school literacies with classroom practice*. Teachers College Press.

Ito, M., Baumer, S., Bittani, M., Boyd, D., Cody, R., Herr-Stephenson, B., & Tripp, L. (2010). *Hanging out, messing around, and geeking out*. MIT Press.

Johnson, L., Smith, R., Willis, H., Levine, A., & Haywood, K. (2011). *The 2011 horizon report*. The New Media Consortium.

Lammers, J. C. (2012). "Is the Hangout . . . The Hangout?" Exploring tensions in an online gaming-related fan site. In E. R. Hayes & S. C. Duncan (Eds.), *Learning in video game affinity spaces* (pp. 23–50). Peter Lang.

Neimeyer, D. J., & Gerber, H. R. (2015). Maker culture and *Minecraft*: Implications for the future of learning. *Educational Media International*, *52*(3), 216–226.

Plass, J. L., Homer, B. D., & Kinzer, C. K. (2015). Foundations of game-based learning. *Educational Psychologist*, *50*(4), 258–283. https://doi.org/10.1080/00461520.2015.1122533

Salen, K., & Zimmerman, E. (2004). *Rules of play: Game design fundamentals*. MIT Press.

Squire, K. (2011). *Video games and learning: Teaching and participatory culture in the digital age*. Teachers College Press.

Whitton, N. (2012). The place of game-based learning in an age of austerity. *Electronic Journal of e-Learning*, *10*(2), 249–256.

3

Minecraft and Socially Situated Student Learning

Katie Salen Tekinbaş and Krithika Jagannath

Introduction

Would you know what to do if you and 15 of your students were trapped in a mine (or underwater, in a volcano, or ice dungeon) with only an iron axe and 10 pieces of beef jerky to go around? Do students in your class have the skills to build a shelter, forage for food, and repair the radio in time to call for help before the mobs arrive?

This chapter explores the use of *Minecraft* to create a rewardingly intense, team-based learning experience for students. *Minecraft* is a popular sandbox-style video game with a multiplayer mode that allows players to interact with each other inside a Lego-like virtual world. In the game, players can build an almost infinite number of unique creations out of cubic blocks, mining the world for raw materials and combining them to form new materials and tools. The game has two modes: Creative and Survival. Survival mode, the original game mode in *Minecraft*, challenges players to collect resources, build structures, battle mobs, manage hunger, and explore the world in order to survive, thrive, and "complete the game" (Survival, n.d.). In Creative mode players have access to unlimited resources and player avatars cannot die or be damaged by other players or creatures in the world. It is hugely popular among students, particularly those in middle and high school.

Minecraft is a platform used extensively by Connected Camps (Connected Camps, n.d.), a non-profit organization that runs online enrichment programs for students in topics like game design, coding, paleontology, biology, astronomy, and more. The programs are taught inside of *Minecraft*—students login as *Minecraft* avatars—and are led by college-age students whom Connected Camps hires and trains to be near peer, virtual educators. The online programs are designed to be social, hands-on, and engaging. They are also designed to take advantage of some of what games do best: drop students into worlds where they must communicate, problem solve, and overcome conflict together.

The opening example is taken from a Connected Camps' program called Survival Lab. During the program, teams of students explore a survival map containing different kinds of challenges: fix a broken radio from scavenged parts in order to call for help; create a stable food source; and protect the basecamp from waves of creatures that explode in close proximity. Players must plan, make decisions, and collaborate on their quest to survive and thrive in a perilous landscape. To do this they must prioritize and persevere. They must be able to communicate and resolve conflict. Each session brings a new challenge, and with it, a chance to flex problem solving, conflict resolution, and communication skills.

Connected Learning

To "get under the hood" of Survival Lab to understand how it uses *Minecraft* as a socially situated learning platform, it is important to understand the kind of learning the program has been designed to support. Survival Lab is an example of connected learning—learning that is fostered over time through a combination of elements that support students in developing interests, relationships, skills, and a sense of purpose (Ito et al., 2013). We highlight four key features here:

1. *Interest-based*: Survival Lab taps into students' love of *Minecraft* by situating the program and its activities within the game, and by designing learning activities that leverage their varying levels of experience and expertise.
2. *Clear pathways and roles for participation*: As they get more involved, students can contribute in varied ways. In the case of Survival Lab, this might mean leading a group to establish a base camp or being part of a team that is documenting the areas' flora and fauna. Learning happens in a social setting—students use in-game chat and third-party voice-chat applications like TeamSpeak, Skype, and Zoom to coordinate and plan, make friends, and complete challenges together.
3. *Near peer-mentor model*: Affinity-based mentorship centered on a shared interest in *Minecraft* allows Survival Lab's online counselors to support students in developing both technical and social emotional know-how. Youth connect with mentors around shared activities and meaningful projects, co-creating *Minecraft* worlds together.
4. *Shared norms and values*: Counselors facilitate community agreements as part of every program, working with students to define and refine norms and values—guidelines that are revisited as part of any conflict resolution process. Through careful moderation they model how to be friendly, constructive, and welcoming.

Survival Lab offers players the chance to take risks and have fun in the company of a supportive and expert learning community. In the following sections we highlight two core principles organizing Survival Lab's design: challenge and improvisation.

Design Challenge and Improvisation

Survival Lab takes place inside of *Minecraft* and its program design relies on the flexibility afforded by its sandbox-style game play, as well as on many of the game's mechanics, like the ability to collect resources and combine them to form new kinds of materials and tools. Resources within Survival Lab are intentionally limited, leading to kinds of play that can be competitive (when players compete for finite resources) or cooperative (when players share resources to help them complete a challenge). Counselors design scenarios within the game that leverage the need to find, share, and use resources, either individually or collectively.

Following is a snapshot of one version of Survival Lab, designed and run by counselors at Connected Camps. Note the emphasis on activity design that encourages both teaming and competing, and which challenge players to meet both short- and long-term goals.

Setting: One group has survived a plane crash and is now lost in a landscape rich in ore but waterless. These are the survivors. The other group is made up of cadets in training as Rangers, who must race against the clock to locate and extract the survivors using a limited set of tools. These are the rescuers. Day 2 begins . . .

Rescuers: Your group survived yesterday's plane crash and the first night by scavenging the wreckage for food and supplies to build a shelter. At dawn you set out in groups of two to survey the landscape. You and your buddy locate an abandoned mine that looks rich in ore, a resource needed by the group if they are to survive another night. You return to the group and lead them into the mine just as it collapses. Cave in!

To survive you and the other camps will need to work together to meet both short- and long-term goals. This includes:

♦ Establishing a base camp inside the mine
♦ Surveying the damage
♦ Finding a way out of the mine
♦ Protecting your team from mine-dwelling mobs

Survivors Day 2: You are in a bit of a pickle. The food won't last forever and you don't know when the rescue team will arrive, if ever. Staying near the crash will allow better visibility.

Your Ranger leader back at the tower sends instructions: Make a better camp at the plane crash. Clear out the area around the plane and start prepping. Document what you can while working to survive. Create a Scientist Tent with a wall of item frames. The natural rocks and flora in the area will be collected and named appropriately.

Your goals include:

♦ Building a better base camp
♦ Farming to create a stable food source
♦ Building a shelter to survive the night
♦ Creating a Scientist Tent to document the area

Players can only reach their goals by coordinating their efforts with others, maintaining their own health, and managing their time. Each day of survival ends with nightfall and the reemergence of the mobs.

In addition to creating challenges for players, counselors also respond, often in real time, to events in the game. During sessions, counselors act as virtual dramaturges, adding to existing challenges or creating spontaneous new ones. In one instance, after players completed a challenge sooner than expected, one of the counselors made it rain. The second counselor summoned lightning, striking the rescuer's base camp destroying many of the supplies that had been scavenged from the plane wreckage. Beyond creating drama and excitement the improvisation led to a new host of problems for players to solve together. It reinforced the need for players to rely on their wits and expertise, and ultimately on each other.

Anatomy of the Program

While the content of Survival Lab may vary each time we run it, many structural features remain the same. These include the overall structure of sessions, strategies for building community, managing behavior, and resolving conflict.

Session Structure

Survival Lab is typically run in 90-minute sessions, but the session structure can be adapted for class periods of shorter lengths. Sessions follow a consistent format, which is outlined in Table 3.1. All activities take place in *Minecraft* with students concurrently logged into Zoom. Participants communicate through video and voice chat via Zoom, and through text chat in *Minecraft*.

Building Community and Managing Behavior

Survival Lab's game-based setting allows it to lean into structures of challenge and conflict inherent in the game. *Minecraft*, like all games, incorporates conflict as a key element of game play. In multiplayer survival mode players must compete over resources and learn how to work together. Players experience conflict as they work within the constraints of the world: The game allows

TABLE 3.1 Structure of a Typical Session in Survival Lab

Activity	Duration	Description
Welcome and check-in	1–5 min	Session welcomes include a short opening exercise to build and reinforce relationships and to check in around student feelings and community climate.
Community agreements	1–5 min	Explain and/or review community agreements. In the first session of a program, counselors facilitate the creation of community agreements with students. Those agreements are reviewed and revised as needed.
Mini-lesson	5–15 min	A group discussion, presentation, and/or group activity that introduces the day's guiding question/theme and provides concrete information to be used as part of the session's activity(ies).
Activity	10–50 min	Students: engage in a hands-on activity. Counselor: individual check-ins with students to answer questions and provide support.
Post-activity share and reflection	5–10 min	Share and reflect on the activity.
→ 2nd mini-lesson	5–15 min	In some sessions, there may be two mini-lessons. This lesson should build on or expand the first mini-lesson. It could also be the result of a group discussion about topics your students would like to explore.
→ 2nd activity	10–50 min	Students: engage in a hands-on activity or match play. Counselor: individual check-ins with students to answer questions and provide support.
→ Post-activity share and reflection	5–10 min	Share and reflect on the activity.
Closing	5–10 min	A group discussion to share and reflect on the day's session and activities. We use "glows and grows" with students to highlight session activities. Give a brief overview of the next session and inform students of any tasks they need to do before then.
Exit ticket	1–5 min	Quick poll or chat prompt that gives students a way to reflect on a key takeaway, share something they are proud of, give a shout out to classmates, etc.

some things (upside down mobs) and disallows others (blocks cannot be broken by swords). When *Minecraft* is played on a multiplayer server, as in the case of Survival Lab, social conflict is inevitable. This is especially true when players are trying to work together. Conflict is both a present and necessary aspect of cooperative efforts: Players may agree on the goals, but be in conflict over how to reach them.

Survival Lab's online counselors act as arbiters, community managers, teachers, role models, curators, and enforcers (Seering, 2019). They handle misbehaviors and guide the community, but do so in partnership with technical tools called plugins, which can include automated moderation tools. Some *Minecraft* plugins automatically remove, mute, freeze, or temporarily ban players; others, which are focused on grief-prevention, keep players from destroying other people's builds, stealing items, spamming, or chat trolling. Deciding on the kinds of plugins used on a server is a key design consideration for any educator interested in using *Minecraft* for classroom or enrichment purposes. Many wonderful guides to setting up a *Minecraft* server are available online for free.

Resolving Conflict

Counselors at Connected Camps are trained to support student-led problem solving. Rather than swooping in and solving problems that arise between students during play, they do their best to turn ownership of the resolution over to the players (Slovak, Salen, Ta, & Fitzpatrick, 2018). This encourages students to see each other's perspectives and generate their own solutions. For example, if a student's proposed solution seems clearly inappropriate ("I will hit him back"), rather than rejecting such a solution from a position of authority, the counselor can either probe for an alternative solution ("that is one option, what else could you do?"), guide the student to think through the consequences ("how do you think he will react then?"), or ask the other player whether that would resolve the situation successfully from his/her/their perspective ("would this solve the problem?"). This shift from a more authoritarian role to one of mediator or coach can be empowering for both students and counselors. It enables all involved to spend their energy and time on developing possible solutions rather than fighting over "what happened".

The underlying philosophy of this approach is that conflicts are a normal and inevitable part of daily life that cannot be eliminated. It is rather how conflicts are managed—not their presence as such—that determines if they are destructive or constructive. Learning to see conflict as an opportunity to be creative in its resolution leads students to feel more optimistic and confident when conflict does arise. Rather than walking away from a problem they engage in ways that not only resolve the conflict but strengthen social bonds.

Online-Only vs. Hybrid Formats

While Connected Camps most frequently runs Survival Lab in an all virtual format: students login from home and interact with their virtual counselor (educator) and classmates via Zoom and a shared *Minecraft* server, they also run programs where students are co-located in a physical setting (like a classroom or library). In this hybrid model, it is the Connected Camps counselor who is fully online—counselors interact with the students in *Minecraft* as they would in the all-virtual model, and supplement communication with the class via Skype. In the hybrid model the classroom teacher, librarian, or other in-room adult plays an important role in providing social and learning support for their students and also helps to keep kids on task, while the Connected Camps counselor plans and facilitates the activities in *Minecraft*. A recent case study of a hybrid Connected Camps program conducted in partnership with the Seattle Public Library revealed that virtual meetings between the in-room educator and the Connected Camps' virtual counselor before and after every session were beneficial for both educators. The educators met to check in before the sessions, debrief about any events that had transpired among students in the room and in *Minecraft*, and frequently test the technology setup. Such regular conversations may help both educators build rapport and a shared understanding for coordinating their actions within the hybrid sessions.

Figure 3.1 shows how student desks can be configured to allow them to see the virtual counselor, each other, and any in-room facilitators.

The hybrid model comes with some benefits. The presence of an in-room educator, for example, allows for the integration of in-room rituals—warm-up games, ice-breakers, or mini-games—to foster social connection among students. In-room facilitators might suggest and facilitate routines or check-ins so that students (who might not know each other) can get to know each other as they wait for the virtual session to begin. Further, when the facilitation team is distributed (e.g., in-room and virtual), the in-room facilitator can serve as

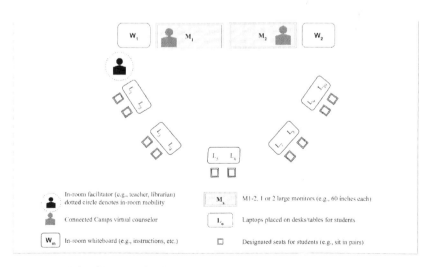

FIGURE 3.1 Hybrid *Minecraft* Classroom

Source: Image courtesy of Katie Salen Tekinbaş ©

the "eyes and ears" for the virtual facilitator, sharing information on in-room dynamics, which can be hard for the virtual counselors to pick up on.

Conclusion

This chapter has explored some of the ways that multiplayer *Minecraft* can be used as a platform to engage students in learning that is socially situated and interest-driven. We've emphasized the critical role played by social structures such as norms and values, and discussed the role played by near peer mentors who design and facilitate activities where students collaborate and compete to manage resources, overcome obstacles, and defeat angry mobs. In the case of Survival Lab, the rescuers did manage to rescue all the survivors, while learning a thing or two about solving problems together.

References

Connected Camps—Summer Camps and Afterschool Labs in Minecraft. (n.d.). Connected Camps. Retrieved September 29, 2020, from https://connectedcamps.com/

Ito, M., Gutiérrez, K., Livingstone, S., Penuel, B., Rhodes, J., Salen, K., Schor, J., Sefton-Green, J., & Watkins, S. C. (2013). *Connected learning: An agenda for research and design*. Digital Media and Learning Research Hub.

Seering, J., Wang, T., Yoon, J., & Kaufman, G. (2019). Moderator engagement and community development in the age of algorithms. *New Media & Society*, *21*(7), 1417–1443. https://doi. org/10.1177/1461444818821316

Slovak, P., Salen, K., Ta, S., & Fitzpatrick, G. (2018). Mediating conflicts in *Minecraft*: Empowering learning in online multiplayer games. In *Proceedings of the 2018 CHI conference on human factors in computing systems*. Association for Computing Machinery Digital Library. (pp. 1–13). https://doi.org/10.1145/3173574.3174169

Survival (Game Mode). (n.d.). *Minecraft* Wiki. Retrieved September 29, 2020, from https://*Minecraft*. fandom.com/wiki/Survival_(Game_Mode)

Minecraft and Transformative Teaching

Douglas Kiang

It was raining hard, as hard as I had ever seen. By the time I caught up to my student, she had sheltered in a hole underground, but I knew she would not last the night. I offered her what remaining food I had: some chicken, some carrots, and a steak. She was starving, but I knew she would not just accept the food as a gift. So, we agreed that I could use her mine to craft resources that I needed, and that way we would help each other. Then, I made a fateful decision. Against her advice, I ventured outside in the fading light to gather more food, and got jumped on by an enormous spider, shot at by a skeleton, and chased into the shallow water of the river by three zombies. As I fell into the water, arms outstretched with arrows in my back, I saw these horrified words fly by my computer screen in chat.

"OMG! I think I just got Mr. Kiang killed!"

Community

She did not kill me, of course, and the only thing that was hurt was my pride. I was playing on a *Minecraft* server that I set up for my students and dying on the server only meant a long walk back, and possibly losing everything I had recently gathered. But I found that my latest demise had some meaning. The kids knew that I cared enough about them to give up my last bit of food. This lesson in community was a powerful model to my students that they could help each other and take risks to help each other survive. Although most of my students thought I was foolish not to have waited until daylight to go outside, they were impressed and resolved to live up to my example of citizenship.

Being a citizen means being part of a community. What is the role of community in learning? What does community look like in a time of global pandemic, when so many of us are sheltering in our own holes and socially distant? These are questions I have explored through the world of *Minecraft*, a virtual world made of blocks, and interactive fiction, a virtual world made of words. But my exploration began with the powerful experience of teaching a course completely online.

Distance Learning

In 2014, I taught an online course for the first time for the Global Online Academy (GOA)—a consortium of private schools developing online courses and offering reciprocal course credit. We were told that students in online courses tend to lose motivation quickly if they are not made to feel part of a community. We were encouraged to build activities that got students to know one another just as well as they know the teacher.

In planning for my online course, I scheduled FaceTime sessions for the kids, who came from all over the world, to chat with each other. I made random pairs and told them to video chat about specific things: one week, it was about their favorite food, and the next week they might explain the most challenging question from the homework. They were not thrilled about these contrived talks, but they did them. We were able to do one chat each week for the first quarter which meant that by the time we hit independent project time, they had each chatted with about half the class.

What opened my eyes to the power of these online sessions was the fact that in a follow-up survey, the kids responded that they only felt comfortable working with students that "they already knew." When asked to define "know" they referred to kids they had previously chatted with, even if it was just a 30-minute chat three weeks ago about a contrived topic. My takeaways from this experience were: encouraging kids to collaborate early on builds trust, and a short personal connection can have a long lasting benefit for students.

I decided to try to bring these lessons into my face-to-face classroom by using *Minecraft* as a "virtual ropes course" to introduce kids to each other right from the start. If a pair of kids go into the mountains and bring me back an iron axe, I know right away that they have had to spend several hours watching each other's back, going into dangerous areas, and developing the technology to smelt raw iron ore into bars to make an axe. It is a tangible artifact representing hours of teamwork.

Games like *Minecraft* act as a catalyst for discussions about government, rules, and laws, and act as a crucible for discussion about which actions help a community grow and thrive. Everything I learned about teaching online became an unexpected benefit later, when I found myself having to teach all my classes online during the COVID-19 pandemic.

Minecraft as a Catalyst for Powerful Discussions

Minecraft is a virtual world made up of blocks. Kids can build any structure they can dream up, and a never-ending landscape of mountains, deserts, oceans, and forests extends in every direction. When kids play together on a *Minecraft* server, they can see each other and work together to build or explore as a group.

The first challenge for any group is how to live together as a community. Some students argue in favor of a strict system of rules, and penalties for breaking them. Other students argue that rules are not needed, because a *Minecraft* server can be set up to prevent actions that are not allowed. For example, if I build a house, the system knows that I "own" those blocks and can be configured to prevent other people from breaking them. This often leads to a great discussion of censorship, and internet filtering. Should we be allowed to make mistakes, and face the consequences, or should we use technology to moderate our behavior? What if I invite you over to work on my house with me? Can any system anticipate every situation? Talking about the rules ahead of time helps us to think about the problems any new community might face.

The guiding statement behind our *Minecraft* community is challenging students to "build a self-sustaining community that reinforces trust between individuals and rewards pro-social behavior." It is a vision that all students know by heart. As you take actions in this world, I tell them, constantly measure the decisions you make against that statement. Ask yourself, does what I am about to do reinforce trust between the members of our community? Is it pro-social? I take it seriously, and so do the kids.

For example, one of our fifth grade teachers uses *Minecraft* each year as they study the history of the Pilgrims coming to the New World. Together, they draft the "Minecraft Compact" whose rules will guide their behavior and provide a way to settle disputes once they are all online on the same *Minecraft* server, sharing the same resources.

This experience gives students some valuable personal context when they read the actual Mayflower Compact. They are often surprised that the Pilgrims faced many of the same problems and asked many of the same questions. What is the proper role of government? What is the balance between individual freedoms and the rights of the community? Together, they build houses, construct a city, and teach each other the skills they need to survive. *Minecraft* is more than a game to these fifth graders. It is a simulation, a learning environment, and a morality play all wrapped up in one incredibly engaging, shared experience.

A vigorous debate occurred in one of my classes over whether we should ban the use of TNT, a *Minecraft* block that can destroy large areas of the world. In a couple of seconds, someone can level an entire mountain, or destroy a building that took weeks to create. But TNT doesn't destroy anything that could not also be demolished by hand, block by block. It just does it a lot faster. So why do we need it? Is the risk that someone will misuse it worth the benefit to those who use it responsibly?

In another class, debate broke out on our own server and I had students on either side of this debate arguing passionately, and articulately, for their side. Some said, "Ban it! No one needs explosives that powerful." Others said, just as passionately, "No! I have the right to use it responsibly!" In the middle of the night, I received the following e-mail, in all caps: "BAN THE USER! NOT THE MATERIAL!!!" Every student had an opinion. When I pointed out the numerous parallels to our national debate over gun control, internet filtering, and regulation of hazardous substances, the conversation spilled over into the real world. "I did not really know that much about those issues," one student admitted. "But I feel like I'll definitely pay more attention to them now."

Minecraft creates the environment conducive to rich classroom discussion. Most of the learning takes place outside the game as kids make sense of the decisions they have made in the game and think about how they affect others in the community. Even though the 21st century classroom has changed, good teachers are at the heart of this change, because it allows us to help students to make meaning of the issues that arise while they are interacting with others in the game world.

Minecraft Creative Mode: Virtual Project-Based Learning

We were stuck inside at Grandma and Grandpa's house. It was pouring rain and my two children, Malia, and Michael, were each browsing their devices at the dining room table, sitting alone together.

"Guys," I announced suddenly. "I have a challenge." At the sound of this, their ears perked up. There is something about a challenge that elevates it beyond simply a "task" or a "job." A challenge implies "I bet you can't do this," and none of us can resist that kind of challenge.

"I wonder if you could build this house in *Minecraft*?" I asked. "Of course, you probably can't," I continued. "Minecraft doesn't have diagonals or curved lines. It would be hard to get it to look right."

My parents' house is a modern house mostly on a single floor, with hardwood floors, lots of glass, and a flat roof. We had been staying there for the past several days, but it had mostly been a place to see the relatives. Now the house started to develop its own character. Ten-year old Malia disagreed with me. "No Dad, Minecraft does have curved lines. You just have to place the blocks in the right places and make it big enough." (The centerpiece of the house is its kitchen and dining area, which is shaped like a Nautilus shell with a graceful, curved arc made out of glass panes leading to the study.) "I'll show you."

She opened the laptop and started up *Minecraft* in Creative Mode, which gives you an infinite supply of every type of block in the game. Then, as if she were sketching in a notebook, Malia quickly picked up and placed blocks in a shell shape on the ground. Within a couple of minutes, as a proof-of-concept, Malia had placed glass blocks in the rough shape of the kitchen. Looking at it, we could see that she was right. The glass blocks did not have to be curved themselves. By placing them in a mathematical pattern on the floor, they assumed the shape of a graceful curve.

"How did you know where to place the blocks?" I asked Malia.

"I just looked at the kitchen," she said. Sure enough, even the wall of the kitchen was made of flat glass blocks. They were smaller, but they still approximated a curve. I had just never noticed them before.

Malia continued, "I separated the first blocks by one. Then two, then three. Then to make the curve spread out more, I used a separation of five to one. Then eight to one. Then . . ." she counted. "Thirteen." she announced. "Then you reach the end of the counter."

I stared at her. "Do you know what that sequence is?" I asked her. "What sequence?" she said. "1, 1, 2, 3, 5, 8, 13 . . ." By this time, my 12-year-old had returned with reference photos he had taken of the rest of the house with his camera phone. "Oh, that's the Fibonacci Sequence," Michael said. "It's a famous sequence of numbers in mathematics. You see it in nature, architecture, and Algebra when you get to the high school."

"Hmm. No kidding?" she said, but her brow was already furrowed in concentration as she looked at the next room. "How should we do this part of the living room?"

Over the next day, the three of us worked together in Creative Mode, modeling the rest of the house. We took photos, measurements, matched colors, and debated. It made us look at the house in a completely different way, and notice details we had never noticed before. Michael and Malia chatted with their grandparents about the artwork on their walls and asked them why they had chosen certain elements of the house. They spent a fair amount of time taking turns on the computer, each doing a different room, but it was purposeful work, based off of real-world experiences and investigations.

By the end of the winter break, we had a *Minecraft* model that looked modern and sleek, perfectly matching every detail of the house. I was surprised that once it was built, Michael and Malia went off to play in different parts of the actual house that they had discovered, rather than in the *Minecraft* model. The process of building the model was even more fun than exploring the finished model. They knew every detail of the model, now it was more fun exploring the thing in real life.

I was reminded of this by the recent COVID-19 mandated stay-at-home lockdown that forced all of us to stay indoors. As teachers, we know the value of a powerful model for illustrating concepts, and we know how motivating a good project or challenge can be for kids. As we think about how to translate face-to-face lessons into stay-at-home lessons, perhaps there is something that can be learned from using reality simulations such as *Minecraft* to provide powerful models for the study of mathematics and science.

Many teachers use *Minecraft* Creative Mode to model real buildings. They use Google Earth to zoom in to the building, get an overhead view, even walk through the building itself. As they model the building, they develop questions that can then be posed to real experts, either on-site at the building or at academic research institutions or that research can answer. By the time the students actually visit the building, they are able to explore it in a much more knowledgeable way, and then return to the model and improve it.

Joining a Community of Learners

My students learn best when they are supported within a community of learners. One of my cherished father-son bonding moments came when I was 14, and my dad taught me how to shave. When my son was born, in the back of my mind I looked forward to the time when I would be able to teach him how to shave, too, as the ultimate father-son bonding moment. So, when my son finally started to sport some stubble, I remember asking him one day if he wanted to put aside some time for the shaving lesson.

"Dad," he told me. "I already know how to shave."

"Wha-a-at?" I sputtered, barely able to contain myself. "Who—?" I wanted to know who had encroached upon my territory, stolen my job, ruined the ultimate father-son bonding moment.

"I went on YouTube," he responded.

I searched for "learn how to shave" on YouTube and was astonished to find that there are nearly 800,000 dads on YouTube, all willing to teach my son how to shave. My kids can search for information themselves and do not look to me for all the answers. It makes sense. Anytime my son has wanted to learn anything, he has turned to the vast network of learners on the internet.

My daughter wanted to make a costume for Halloween this year. She wanted to be a character from a video game. So, we searched on Etsy, a web site for crafters and do-it-yourselfers. Sure enough, we found the exact costume she was looking for. I was ready to whip out my credit card and purchase it, but my daughter studied the screen carefully, and remarked, "You know, if they can do it, I can do it."

So, this turned into a mini-adventure as she found plans and patterns online, and we combed craft stores for supplies. She bought craft foam and gold spray paint, and mini jewels and hot glue. She printed out patterns on our printer, then cut them out of craft foam. She spray painted it gold and used hot glue to attach mini jewels to it. She braided her hair to match the character's hair style.

My daughter has never done any of these things before. This was the largest project she had ever taken on, but with the right motivation and the power of a whole community online, she was able to support her own learning and make a gorgeous costume. In the end it did not end up costing us any less than if we had bought it from Etsy, but I told myself the process of building it was a fantastic learning experience for her.

This generation of learners is used to going online and finding the answers to problems they encounter. It makes sense when you consider that most of these kinds of problems are unique. If you are solving the same problems every semester or doing the same kinds of problems out of a textbook over and over, there is less need to be innovative in your thinking. But if what you are trying to do is create a stable to keep your horses from escaping, and the stable has to be fairly small because of the particular terrain on your island, you might need to search through patterns and video tutorials on the internet until you find an example that you can build, or combine aspects of different designs until you find something that works.

When kids play *Minecraft*, they are part of a huge network of learners and builders who are sharing what they know online. Most people who learn *Minecraft* turn to online resources to get started, and later return to share and comment on other's creations. You can read about some of these resources at the end of the chapter.

Minecraft Makes a Student-Centered Classroom

What makes games like *Minecraft* addictive? We often hear the word "addictive" used in the pejorative, in the sense that someone is so attracted to something that it takes over every waking moment; when one is not engaged in the activity, one is thinking, craving, dreaming about the next session. Putting aside the clinical definition of addiction, in which one engages in risky or dangerous behavior to further the addiction, we might think of addiction as simply the dark side of engagement. Wouldn't we want our students to be as engaged in learning? What if they were addicted to learning? If all they could do outside of class was see connections, think, and dream about ways to do more, plan more, engage more with the curriculum? That's the positive side of being addicted to science, or literature, or history. We can learn many of the secrets game designers know to make learning as addictive as gaming.

When asked why *Minecraft* is so "addictive," one student says,

> Because you never run out of things to do. Because even while you are doing one thing, it's giving you more ideas of other things you want to do. So, it's like an endless list of tasks you have to complete.

In some ways, this sounds like work! But the key difference is that the student chooses what to do next. Work is still getting done, and there is still learning going on, but by choosing to do these things, the student feels a sense of ownership over the tasks. Each *Minecraft* player has a personalized list of things to do that are important to them.

Choice plays a powerful role in learning. We might have a long list of tasks we want our students to complete, but the order in which they do them may not be as important. For example, we don't necessarily need to learn history chronologically, even though it is often taught that way. Instead of making all students learn everything about the First World War, then the Great

Depression, then the New Deal, then the Second World War, and so forth, many teachers teach history thematically, and link learning to the present day.

For example, you might start by looking at the current economic malaise. What are some of its causes? What are some solutions? Then, come up with a theme, perhaps Global Collaboration, and then look back at key events in history and analyze them within the context of that theme. You might ask them to collect a list of resources that are aligned with that theme.

> *Big idea*: History
> *Essential question*: Does history repeat itself?
> *Challenge*: Create more jobs in our community

By providing some choice in how students proceed with their learning, you can create a "sandbox" environment where students are free to create and build artifacts that demonstrate their own learning, in the same way that *Minecraft* provides players with an endless list of tasks to accomplish. As one student put it, "Minecraft doesn't end until you run out of ideas. And because you never run out of ideas, the game just goes on and on." Suppose we substituted "learning" in that statement: "Learning never ends until you run out of ideas. And because you never run out of ideas, learning just goes on and on." That is our goal.

Challenge as Learning

What is the best way to motivate students to take learning into their own hands? Give them a challenge! Challenges are a great framework to structure students' explorations in a way that is open-ended and collaborative.

You might be familiar with TV shows that frame an entire show around a specific challenge: cook a meal that includes three bizarre ingredients; prove that the Archimedes heat ray was a myth; or hold a charity event in Manhattan that raises $100,000. The entertainment value comes from seeing how each group addresses that specific challenge. Many of the solutions are unique, and most of them are successful. The real learning occurs when you see how each group approaches the problem. But the idea of coming up with unique solutions to solve a challenge is firmly rooted in popular culture. Kids love a challenge, and they are accustomed to having to be resourceful to meet it.

As a general structure, challenges provide a way for students to frame their learning around a particular challenge that is actionable and that is meaningful to them. Unlike many project-based assignments, where the teacher decides what the solution will be and challenges students to mobilize around that particular solution, challenge-based learning asks students to work together to design their own solutions to problems that they are currently facing. Challenge-based learning is also a flexible framework. I have changed and adapted the process to fit everything from a six-week exploration to a single-period class. Once kids learn the strategy, they will find ways to use its structure to solve problems and meet challenges they come across in their own lives.

What Is the Big Idea?

A challenge-based learning starts with a big idea. The Big Idea is a broad topic that offers many different entry points for discussion and action. Some examples might be Community, Energy, Democracy, or Education.

> *Example*: Community

The Big Idea should generate several essential questions. In my class, we generate lots of essential questions on the board and then each group of students picks one essential question to focus on.

> *Example*: How do we create and sustain a community? How do we maximize health? Wealth? Influence? How do we measure happiness?

The Challenge

From the essential question, students form a challenge that is concise, and asks them to create a specific solution that will result in concrete, meaningful action.

> *Example*: Create a self-sustaining community in *Minecraft* that reinforces trust between individuals and rewards pro-social behavior.

Guiding Questions

Now that students have articulated a challenge, what are all the things they need to know to design a solution? Drawing up a list of guiding questions helps to focus the learning as well as provide tasks for the different group members to accomplish.

> *Examples*: What rules should there be? What are the consequences for breaking those rules? What *Minecraft* server plug-ins are available? What does a community provide for its citizens?

Guiding Activities

Now that we have guiding questions, what kinds of activities will lead to answers to those questions? Much of the learning in a challenge-based learning project comes in this phase.

> *Example activities*: Look at charter documents from historical communities, such as Colonial Jamestown, Dutch settlements in the West Indies, or the Pirate communities in the Caribbean. Conduct a survey of students in your school community. Interview a sociologist.

Solution

The solution to the challenge is actionable, appropriate, and informed by the data you collected from your guiding activities. Documentation of the project should be ongoing, and feedback can inform the development of the project as a whole.

> *Example solution*: Create a new world in *Minecraft* using options that are appropriate to the charter documents of the community. Allow a pilot group of students in to test the server out and give feedback about what privileges and permissions seem fair. Adjust the rules and the kind of support offered for new players before opening the server up to the larger school community or the world.

Conclusion

Minecraft is an incredibly powerful tool for learning. The way that students learn and share their discoveries in *Minecraft* mirrors the kind of engaged, participatory, autonomous learning we would want them to do in school. It is a crucible for ethical decision-making, and the combination of the *Minecraft* world and the classroom community is one in which students can take powerful actions, and with guidance from a teacher, process the effects of their behavior on others.

Resources

Reddit

One *Minecraft* community is the subreddit /r/Minecraft, on the popular crowd sourcing web site Reddit. This is a large message board where users share screen captures of their latest work or ask questions of others about the best way to get skeletons out of your mine or create the most efficient automatic wheat harvester. Many of the explanations are given cooking show-style, with videos or recipes that provide step-by-step instructions. Users can comment on each other's posts and "upvote," or validate, posts or comments that are particularly valuable.

Minecraft Wiki

Minecraft does not have a user manual. Instead, most players go to this online resource for information on every aspect of the game. One of the most valuable features of this site is the set of tutorials for mining, farming, smelting, enchanting, combat, and every other aspect of *Minecraft* that you might possibly want to know. It is a moderated wiki, which means that information must be verified as accurate before it is added, so the quality of the information is extremely high. The *Minecraft* wiki is also updated whenever

Minecraft is updated with new features, new explanations, and examples. You can begin your search for how to set up a *Minecraft* server here: https:// minecraft.gamepedia.com.

YouTube

Many *Minecraft* users have turned to YouTube as a place to share their work. The most popular *Minecraft* videos are shared on dedicated YouTube channels, and updated regularly. Most students, however, tend to just search for videos they are looking for. It is a particularly helpful place to go for information on how to use redstone, a technical aspect of *Minecraft* that replicates electronic circuits and logic gates. Once students have started building creations of their own, or modifying and improving existing designs, they can start using YouTube to share their work and receive comments of their own.

5

The Whole Enchilada, a Game for Teaching Mathematical Fluency

Kate Litman

My Quest to Enjoyable and Successful Teaching

My teaching journey began in 2005, when I joined the Teaching Fellows program in New York City. I secured a teaching placement in a very regimented and successful K-8 school in the Bronx. The position was so unlike my colleague's in the Fellows that we used to say my school was in "Bronxchester" because I was not experiencing the instability and constant change that runs rampant in the New York City Department of Education. After six years of diligently teaching seventh grade from a textbook—*Impact Math*, to be specific—I was bored and frustrated and wanted to be part of an innovative learning community. I did not want to be asked what page in the textbook I was on every week of the year. Nor did I want to fight battles with administration over taking more than one field trip a semester. Finally, falling behind the technological wave that was slowly cresting in the late aughts did not make me comfortable. I knew there was a school community out there that was inspiring and exciting, and where creativity was the norm rather than the exception.

After a grueling interview process, I finally secured my spot at Quest to Learn (Q2L) as the founding eighth grade math teacher. Quest to Learn is a specialized public school in New York City, founded by the Institute of Play, and based on three pedagogical principles: game-based learning, systems thinking, and design thinking. I know that these phrases sound like jargon to the uninitiated, but they lay the groundwork for some truly revolutionary teaching. Game-based learning is the simple belief that children are inherently motivated to learn when playing, and if a school could capture the joy and spirit of game play in the curricula, then academic success and deep learning would certainly follow. Systems thinking is the belief that everything is interconnected. In a dynamic world, school, community, or game, there are parts of the system that connect, and when one component or interaction is modified, then the outcomes and feedback in that system change. Quest to Learn challenges students to notice, analyze, hypothesize, and experiment with systems to find leverage points and opportunities to effect change. Lastly, the school uses design thinking—which is a problem solving protocol—to design new games, optimize school systems, and structure a week-long student challenge called "Boss Level."

The Quest 2 Learn Model

The founders of Quest to Learn were visionary leaders. They anticipated the social media learning networks that we now take for granted. They bolstered "empathy" as one of the core values of the school long before it became a popular buzzword in education circles. However, starting my teaching career at Quest felt simply overwhelming. Overnight, I transitioned away from a school that valued standardized testing and a pacing calendar to a school where my only limits were my own imagination and time. It was a steep learning curve to integrate these new foundational concepts into my practice. I remember crying under my desk that first winter because a project was going awry. A week later I was co-teaching a design challenge at the Museum of Modern Art (MoMA), dancing in a flash mob, and beside myself with joy. The highs were high, and the lows were . . . under my desk. It took three years before some of the processes and techniques started to click, and I'm so glad I had the patience and perseverance to adapt to these methods. I have never looked back.

Game-based learning is integrated into Quest to Learn curricula in three distinct ways: "Missions" and "Quests," "Boss Level," and digital or analog games. Put simply, a "Mission" is like your Unit Plan and your Quests are the mini units or lessons that support the main objective of the Unit. Missions often contain a story-like component where kids are taking on the role of a scientist, detective, or entrepreneur to tackle some problem or task. Quests are the embedded experiences and challenges that help you progress in your Mission. As a teacher, the task of planning a Mission and subsequent Quests is daunting—but it's essentially the same process as any backwards design planning routine. The true challenge is identifying a Mission context that is compelling enough to hook the students and flexible enough to encapsulate all the learning goals you want to integrate. This process is not for the faint of heart.

Boss Level is a week-long design challenge where kids compete and use the design cycle to create something incredible. Every year 6th graders compete in a Rube Goldberg Competition in the winter and Cardboard Carnival in the spring. Other grades get to choose different Boss Level experiences hosted by individual teachers. A high school student may compete in a "Restaurant Wars" style challenge or they may develop an app that educates others about the process of gerrymandering. Eighth graders have created visual illusion galleries and developed escape rooms. Boss Level is a super flexible framework that could be adapted at any school looking to create an exciting and engaging week of instruction that differs from the norm. However, this too is a lot of work for the teacher and there needs to be administrative support built into the plan.

Lastly, at Quest to Learn we integrate literal games—both analog and digital—into the curricula. We believe kids learn best through play. Therefore, teachers are empowered to design games and experiences that evoke that sense of play to maximize learning and engagement simultaneously. Games evoke different types of learning and feedback that are crucial to learning. We have codified 7 Principles of Game-Like Learning that we reinforce and reference at Quest to Learn:

- ◆ Everyone is a participant
- ◆ Failure is reframed as iteration
- ◆ Everything is interconnected
- ◆ Learning happens by doing
- ◆ Feedback is immediate and ongoing
- ◆ Challenge is constant
- ◆ Learning feels like play.

These principles are powerful tools for students. My favorite principle is "feedback is reframed as iteration." When a teacher grades a paper or gives verbal feedback to a child indicating they are wrong—there are consequences. Perhaps the student feels discouraged, mislabeled, or misjudged. When a game indicates that a player is not successful, the immediate thought is "I need to try again." The player takes the knowledge gained during play to revise their strategy, try new techniques, and test out hypotheses.

The most useful game a teacher can play is one that aligns with the curriculum and current standards. However, there may not be a useful game to teach the "Distributive Property" or the "Rock Cycle." This is when a skilled teacher can take a learning goal and turn it into a game. When designing a game, we start with the basic design cycle:

1. Empathize
2. Define the problem
3. Iterate
4. Prototype

5. Playtest
6. Communicate.

There is power to game play because the mode of learning can reinvigorate a stale topic that students are either frustrated by or find boring. As a teacher, you need to select a learning goal that is compelling and important. Ideally, the student needs and teacher needs will overlap. I wanted students to be able to quickly convert between different representations of fractions, decimals and percents and eventually add fractions correctly using mental math. I am going to walk you through the design process of a game called *The Whole Enchilada* and explain the pedagogical and technical decisions made along the way.

Designing a Math Game That Matters

As a middle school math teacher, I needed a game to reinforce fraction concepts and increase fluency between multiple representations like fractions, decimals, percent, and non-routine fraction images. It is easy to imagine a standard worksheet where kids fill in the blanks of a table with multiple representations. Not only is this method boring but it begs the question: how do you get that learning to stick? Students needed a game to make the standard rote learning associated with these topics more engaging, competitive, and fun. At this point in the design process, I have defined the problem and empathized with my user. The next step is to iterate or brainstorm.

At Quest to Learn, many of our good ideas come from adapting the core mechanics of other games. I experienced a flash of inspiration when playing the game *Swish. Swish* is a card game with transparent cards containing different colored balls and hoops. The goal is to layer cards so that the balls "swish" into the various hoops based on color. You deal out 16 cards in a 4 x 4 grid and yell "swish" when you've made a match. You can rotate and flip the cards to make these matches and the more cards you combine—the higher your total. I realized that I could copy some of the mechanics of this game to reinforce fraction, decimal, and percent concepts.

Brainstorming can be an overwhelming step for teachers. It's easy to get bogged down with options or paralyzed with technical details or fail to reach consensus with your peers. When designing *The Whole Enchilada*, I had a slight advantage because I could envision how game play would work: students would be combining cards to make a set or "whole." I was working with my curriculum developer Leah Hirsch and Arthur Eisenbach who wanted to use the deck for another type of game in the 7th grade. We had to decide on what fractions, decimals, percent, and images to use and more importantly . . . how many of each card we needed to include so the game would be playable. The worst outcome would be a game board of 16 cards where there were no possible moves.

We started listing fractions and equivalent fractions which could be the basis for the deck, and these are the cards in the finished deck (Table 5.1):

TABLE 5.1 Fraction Cards for *The Whole Enchilada*

Fractions	Decimals	Percent	Images
1/2, 2/4, 3/6, 4/8, 6/12	0.5	50%	×5
1/3	0.33	33.3%	×3
1/4, 2/8, 3/12	0.25	25%	×5
1/6, 2/12	0.16	16.6%	×2
1/8	0.125	12.5%	×2
1/12	0.083	8.3%	×1
3/4, 6/8, 9/12	0.75	75%	×3
2/3, 4/6, 8/12	0.66	66.6%	×3
2/12			×2

We rejected fractions like 3/8 or 5/8 and focused mainly on fractions that could share a least common multiple of 12. We considered including routine fractions like 1/10 and 1/5 and their equivalents but ultimately rejected them in order to emphasize and reinforce the rather non-routine 1/6, 1/8, and 1/12 and their equivalencies.

To push students to learn new representations rather than play a basic matching game with equivalent values, we decided the main goal of the game would be to combine multiple representations into one whole. In other words, students must use at least two different representations to make a valid move. A student cannot combine two ½ pictures, but they could combine 50% and a ½ picture for a 2-point move (Figure 5.1). We decided on the somewhat whimsical nature of the title—*The Whole Enchilada*—because as middle school teachers we feared the inevitable jokes about "holes" and had to make a title so ridiculous we would essentially circumvent any inappropriate humor with our own title.

After deciding on the content of the cards we divided up the formatting work and decided to do a basic paper prototype. The prototype would immediately help us to playtest the game with a small group of kids and witness whether the game play was compelling and enjoyable with just the right amount of challenge. I need to emphasize that we did not immediately print and laminate 10 sets of the game—rather we invested a conservative amount of time to create this prototype with the playtest in mind.

Scoring Examples

2 points

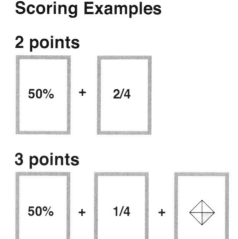

3 points

4 point moves are possible

FIGURE 5.1 Scoring Examples for *The Whole Enchilada*

Source: Image courtesy of Kate Litman©

At Quest to Learn, playtesting is a crucial step in developing a game. I've seen playtests where a teacher has dramatically under-estimated or overestimated students' readiness to play a game. Likewise, I've seen playtest where unnecessarily complicated directions are immediately streamlined and simplified to enable play. In other words, it is quite hard for a teacher with years of experience to magically place themselves in the role of student and get a reliable measure of how challenging or obvious a game might be.

A typical playtest involves bringing a small group of students together, explaining the rules of the game, and watching the game play unfold. Playtests occur during a student lunch period or some other flexible time in the schedule and is seen as a reward in the Q2L community. This process lets students know that their needs are a priority and their opinions matter. Playtests are so common at Q2L that I forget that this is not normal practice in other schools, but it can truly reveal gaps in game play and typical points of contention, and kids occasionally have brilliant suggestions to make games more fun. We generally give students feedback forms like so (Figure 5.2):

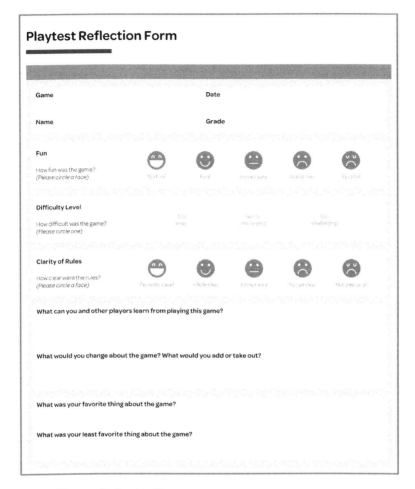

FIGURE 5.2 Playtest Reflection Form

Source: Image courtesy of the Institute of Play and Connected Learning, used with permission of Katie Salen Tekinbaş and The Institute of Play

Originally, we wanted kids to call out "whole enchilada" when they saw a move, but we realized that this mechanic would create unnecessary speed stress on students who might already feel anxiety dealing with fractions, decimals, and percent. We realized that we could modify the game based on student readiness; if groups were advanced, they could play with the original mechanic—but all groups would start playing by taking turns and play would continue clockwise from the youngest player. We also realized that it was possible to stack the deck—or rather shorten the deck—for groups that needed more remediation and add in the non-routine fractions like 1/6, 1/8, and 1/12 during the 2nd or 3rd day of game play. In an ideal setting, I could imagine the deck of *The Whole Enchilada* growing over the course of a fraction unit and game play happening multiple times over several weeks.

At Quest to Learn we call the period when we teach the game a "roll out." The easiest way to roll out a game is called the "fishbowl" where students circle up around the teacher and a few key players who watch an abbreviated version of the game. Another popular method is for teachers to play an example round on video so that all the components of the game and moves are clearly visible for all to see. Finally, it is game time!

Game-based learning is a hot topic in education circles, and it is often misunderstood. Sites like Gimkit and Kahoot represent "gamification" of traditional content where students are essentially answering multiple choice questions in a gamified environment. True game-based learning occurs when content is introduced, reinforced, or enriched through play itself. In *The Whole Enchilada*, students must convert fractions into decimals or percent or vice versa and then combine to make a whole. Here is an example game board (Figure 5.3):

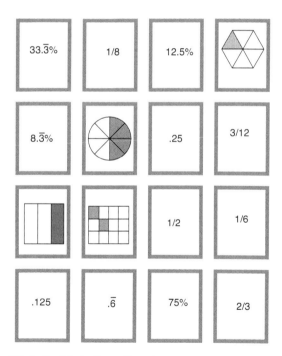

FIGURE 5.3 *The Whole Enchilada* Game Board

Source: Image courtesy of Kate Litman©

One student may approach a move by converting all values to fractions. For instance, the circle that is half green represents 1/2 and the 1/2 fraction would combine to make one whole because 1/2 + 1/2 = 1. Another student might approach this game by converting to decimals. For instance, .25 is a decimal and

75% is equal to .75. Therefore, .25 + .75 = 1. The more sophisticated a student's mental math, the more points they could earn. For instance, $1/8 + 12.5\%$ combine to make $1/4$, $3/12$ is $1/4$, and the green half circle is $1/2$. If we combined all of those cards you would get the following 4-point move: $1/8 + 12.5\% + 3/12 +$ half circle = 1. The more students practice and play the game, the more challenging the game becomes. However, there is a low bar to start game play because there are enough benchmark fractions like $1/2$ and $1/3$ peppered through the deck to give students some easier options. Not only do students learn through their own moves, but they are anticipating the moves of their peers, and having to find alternate cards when one of their planned cards gets used.

The Whole Enchilada reinforces the principle "learning happens by doing" because students need to attempt combinations every time; they make a move, and their peers are scanning those moves for accuracy. Furthermore, "feedback is immediate and ongoing" because not only do peers check your moves but you are learning by the combinations and examples set by your opponents. I use these principles as a guiding reference for every activity—even if it is not a game—because these principles ensure that students are taking ownership over learning and that the learning is student-centered not teacher-centered. Quest to Learn is a pioneer in game-based learning, but it is possible for any dedicated teacher to take the steps laid out in this chapter and design their own enjoyable and engaging learning game.

Resources

Connected Learning Alliance https://clalliance.org
An exceptional group of educators dedicated to promoting interest-driven learning that connects youth to the larger world outside school. The website has a wealth of resources including profiles of top educators, case studies, podcasts, videos, up to date research, publications, and much more. You can subscribe to their newsletter.

Quest to Learn http://www.q2l.org
Website of the pioneering school located at 351 West 18th Street, New York, New York 10011.

Quest to Learn: Developing the School for Digital Kids (The Catherine D. and Catherine T. MacArthur Foundation Reports on Digital Media by Katie Salen Tekinbaş, Robert Torres, Loretta Wolozin, Rebecca Rufo-Tepper, and Arana Shapiro (The MIT Press, 2010).
This report outlines the learning framework of the Quest to Learn school in detail with many practical examples that can be adapted by other schools.

Whole Enchilada Game Set https://bit.ly/WholeEnchiladaGameSet
You can order the game designed by Kate online.

6

Level Up Science
Design Thinking, Games and Project-Based Learning

Ashley Phillips, Diana "Dee" Weldon, Erin Milsom,
Sarah Fiess and Lindsay Portnoy

Imagine for a moment this unlikely scene: it is a cold day in November and 25 high school seniors have rolled up to a nearby middle school where they will effectively and enthusiastically teach 8th graders about the periodic table. It really happened! The 12th grade chemistry students under the guidance of teacher Diana "Dee" Weldon and student teacher Erin Milsom used inspiration from tabletop games such as Twister, Battleship, Guess Who?, and Jenga to bring meaningful learning to the younger students about the meaning and significance of ionization energy, electronegativity, atomic radius, ionic radius and chemical reactivity, and how they are reflected in the periodic table. This kind of high-engagement learning is a regular part of the education provided at Tech Valley High School, a program dedicated to authentic project-based learning. It's not just play to these students; they do real design work to create meaningful experiences where they take on the role of a teacher.

Studies (Zeiser, Taylor, Rickles, Garet, & Segeritz, 2014) show that adolescents learn best when they:

♦ Are faced with solving unforeseen problems and overcoming unpredicted obstacles.
♦ Work collaboratively on team-based projects.
♦ Take responsibility for their own learning.
♦ Understand how their learning fits into their futures.

Students are more likely to retain what they have learned as they have opportunities to work on complex problems, beyond repetition and review. These basic principles guide the project-based learning model embraced by Tech Valley High School in Albany, New York.

Tech Valley High School (TVHS) has been a unique venture in the Capital Region of New York since its inception. It was opened in 2007 as a joint venture of Capital Region Board of Cooperative Educational Services (BOCES) and Questar III BOCES as a four-year, comprehensive regional high school program. It was strategically developed in partnership with area businesses and two BOCES in the region. BOCES programs range from vocational to special education to payroll and IT services; they are formed when two or more districts share services (and costs) for similar needs. In the case of TVHS, two regions joined together to create a program dedicated to project-based learning. TVHS currently serves students in 30 school districts throughout their region and provides training and support for the districts that participate in their program.

From the beginning, it has been structured as a STEM (Science Technology Engineering Mathematics) school with an instructional model that prepares students for college and careers in the region's high-tech economy. Another key element of its creation is its founding as a laboratory for educational innovation to be shared with schools and educators across the region. Our shared goal is to prepare students for the 21st century workplace through project-based learning. The key goals outlined for student achievement at TVHS include:

◆ Students will learn in an innovative and professional environment fostered by the use of technology and project-based learning.
◆ Students will receive an education that is rigorous, academically rich and focused on character development, exceeding New York State's learning standards.
◆ Students will acquire global awareness and strengthen their commitment to the region.
◆ TVHS students will become lifelong learners who embrace entrepreneurial values.

Project-based learning (PBL) offers students multiple opportunities to apply their learning in new situations where the answer is not obvious and where they must solve unforeseen problems and overcome unpredicted obstacles. PBL requires teachers to cover fewer topics in greater depth with the goal of developing a deep understanding of subject matter that scientists, technology companies and business leaders in Tech Valley say is needed in our high school graduates. Learning at TVHS requires students to master the subject matter necessary for traditional state Regents exams but also requires them to develop the skills to meet the rigorous requirements of working in a technology-rich, intellectually complex and personally challenging world.

Project Based-Learning Approaches

Hands-On
Content in every class is taught through PBL that engages students in every facet of their education. PBL is a research-driven, effective way to address learning standards by emphasizing rigorous, real-world applications and connections.

Student-Centered
Students at TVHS take an active role in their own education. The control for learning is shifted from the passive style of teacher-directed learning, to the active style of student-engaged learning. PBL provides students of all ability levels with an environment to explore and understand content on a deeper level by investigating and responding to a complex problem or challenge.

Collaborative
The majority of TVHS coursework is completed through a collaborative process that teaches students how to lead, manage and support team goals. TVHS students need to be open-minded and ready to work with business leaders, educators and other students in a professional, collaborative learning environment.

Getting Started With Gaming
The game design projects at TVHS began with a professional partnership between TVHS School Outreach Coordinator Sarah Fiess and Dr. Lindsay Portnoy, a cognitive scientist and co-founder of the educational gaming company Killer Snails. These two educators developed a one-day workshop for teachers in the Albany area called "Level-Up Design Thinking" (Figure 6.1).

Attendees practiced using design thinking to create innovative learning experiences in the classroom. In alignment with the hands-on principles of PBL at the school, teachers not only planned for how they might accomplish this instruction in their own classrooms, but also worked collaboratively with environmental science students in the school as they embarked on a similar project.

The teachers began their exploration by playing several simple card-based games and asked the questions:

- ◆ What was the goal of the game?
- ◆ What is something you like about this game?
- ◆ What is something frustrating about this game?

Lindsay purposely selected games that were familiar or simple to learn so that teachers and students alike could play several in quick succession and analyze

FIGURE 6.1 Level-Up Design Thinking Workshop Flyer

Source: Image courtesy of Sarah Fiess

them. The games in the workshop included War and Pig (AKA Spoons), using a traditional 52-card deck, and the card games Anomia and Slapzi. When analyzing, players noticed things about speed of play, house-rules and set-up. Next, they began to ask questions about how elements of the game could be potential solutions for teaching (Figure 6.2).

For teachers, this became a rapid-fire brainstorming session. A math teacher quickly adapted War to incorporate a variety of facts in a fluency

Prototype

Guiding question: what is the goal of your game and how will you know if it's working?	
What content is taught in your game and how is this content taught through game play?	
This game is modeled after *(circle one)* Slapzi/Pig/War because….	
What is the goal of the game?	
What are the rules of the game?	

FIGURE 6.2 Rethinking Games Through the Lens of Design Thinking Guide Form

Source: Lindsay Portnoy, PhD © Used with permission of the author

review challenge. An art teacher used the concept of Slapzi to plan a game that incorporated artistic techniques with dozens of works of art.

Following a productive morning with teachers, Sarah brought the educators into a live turn-key session with 10th grade students in Ashley Phillips' Environmental Science class. This became the entry event for Ashley's "7 Billion and Counting" project. Teachers and students collaborated to play the games and notice the potential mechanics, objectives and principles of each that could be adapted to teach players about the pressures of a growing population on our planet. Having an authentic audience and the engaging aspect of the games was one of the main hooks in the project (Figure 6.3).

Students later engaged in a Game Mechanics Hackathon where they explored more simple games to unpack and adapt the rules/constraints of them. These included games with card-draw mechanics, dice, spinners and bells. For example, students tried changing the mechanic of a familiar game like Candyland from draw-cards to roll-a-dice. An already unexciting game somehow got less fun! At least in traditional Candyland, students found that there was the unpredictability of getting a special card. Students also discovered that using colors was good for little kids who could not yet read or count.

Despite being deeply engaged in elements of game design, students needed to learn the content of the project before they could effectively adapt a game. This project specifically addressed agriculture in terms of feeding a growing human population (human nutritional requirements, types of agriculture, genetic engineering, irrigation, pesticides). The students studied

FIGURE 6.3 Students in Ashley Philips' Environmental Science Class at Play

Source: Photograph courtesy of Tech Valley High School used with permission of Illia M. Haggerty, Melinda Darling, and Joy Jensen

human population dynamics and impacts of population growth by reading excerpts from Michael Pollan's *The Omnivore's Dilemma* (2007) and watching the Peabody-winning film *King Corn*, (Woolf 2007) in addition to individual and group research (Figure 6.4).

Frontloading the product for learning (a game) and getting students to refine as they learned new information was critical to the success of this project. Playtesting and repeated iteration helped many teams improve their game design. For example, one team used the feedback of their board game to change the spacing on the board (there were too few spots resulting in very

1. **Population Biology Concepts**
   - Population Ecology
   - Carrying Capacity
   - Reproductive Strategies
   - Survivorship
2. **Human Population**
   a. **Human population dynamics-**
      - Historical population sizes
      - Distribution
      - Fertility rates
      - Growth Rates/Doubling Time
      - Demographic Transition
      - Age-structure diagrams
   b. **Population Size**
      - Strategies for sustainability
      - Case studies
      - National Policies
   c. **Impacts of Population Growth**
      - Hunger
      - Disease
      - Economic Effects
      - Resource Use
      - Habitat Destruction
3. **Agriculture- Feeding a Growing Population**
      - Human Nutritional Requirements
      - Types of Agriculture
      - Green Revolution
      - Genetic Engineering
      - Crop Rotation
      - Deforestation
      - Irrigation
      - Sustainable Agriculture

FIGURE 6.4 "7 Billion and Counting" Concepts Outline

Source: Courtesy of Ashley Philips©

quick game play) and the clarity of the questions asked. Introducing the criteria for success on the first day is typical of instruction in a PBL classroom; Ashley accomplished this by using her rubric to clarify the constraints of the assignment and what success looks like (Figure 6.5).

7 Billion and Counting Rubric

Essential Question: *How can we create an entertaining game that educates others about the science behind feeding a growing human population?*

KEY

Mastering	Demonstrates exceptional performance. The work is complete, correct, and high quality. Work shows evidence of analysis, synthesis, and evaluation.	85–100%
Developing	Meets the minimum criteria. The work is partially complete, partially correct, or of mediocre quality. Work shows evidence of knowledge, comprehension, and application.	65–84%
Emerging	Below performance standards. The work is missing or entirely incorrect.	0–64%

Learning Outcome	Indicators of Success
Knowing and Thinking (100 points)	<ul><li>The game builds understanding of at least four subtopics from the provided list (bullet points)</li><li>The game includes a strategy to win that reflects a population science concept (such as building the largest population or strategies for maintaining a sustainable population)</li><li>The mechanics of the game simulate/model the effect of various factors on population</li><li>The game makes use of counters or other game piece to visualize the effects of changing population size factors</li><li>All science content is accurate and matches cited resources</li></ul>
Score (%)	0 - - 25 - - 50 - - 60 - -65 - - 70 - - 75 - - 80 - - 85 - - 90 - - 95 - - 100

FIGURE 6.5 "7 Billion and Counting" Rubric

Source: Courtesy of Ashley Philips©

Comments	
Communication (100 points)	• The Rule Book explains game play in a way that allows a new player to easily understand how to play • The Rule Book provides thorough description of the population science concepts underlying the game and how the game mechanics relate to these concepts • Writing is well edited, with no spelling errors or grammatical errors • References are provided
Score (%)	0 - - 25 - - 50 - - 60 - - 65 - - 70 - - 75 - - 80 - - 85 - - 90 - - 95 - - 100
Comments	
Technology and Information Literacy (100 points)	• Game components are designed with a high level of aesthetic appeal • Data from playtesters was collected and used to revise and improve the final design • Game design makes use of original artwork from team members (digital or by hand) that helps convey the scientific concepts
Score (%)	0 - - 25 - - 50 - - 60 - -65 - - 70 - - 75 - - 80 - - 85 - - 90 - - 95 - - 100
Comments	
Collaboration (100 points)	• Group contract has a team goal and individual goals. • Pacing chart 2-3 updates per week and is complete and detailed. • Pacing Chart includes links to student's work. • Each team member has an active, meaningful, contributory role on the team. • Benchmarks and the final project are on time and complete. • Warnings are given to members who do not complete their assignments on time, uphold class and team norms, or otherwise fail to contribute to the success of the project.
Score (%)	0 - - 25 - - 50 - - 60 - -65 - - 70 - - 75 - - 80 - - 85 - - 90 - - 95 - - 100
Comments	

FIGURE 6.5 (Continued)

Students tested their prototypes multiple times throughout the project. This feedback and iterative design process helped them greatly improve the strength of the game design and the content taught within the game over the course of the project. The first round of testing came from playtesting by peers in the class through a "Critical Friends" process of "likes and wonders." Students can offer each other effective feedback (beyond "I like the colors") because they are all familiar with the criteria for success. They can ask probing questions such as, "I wonder if students who are using this game to learn new information would know the answer to this question."

One game that very successfully taught the content used an "Apples to Apples" type mechanic where a question card is played that introduces a problem related to population growth. For example, "What are the best national policies that should be used to fix overpopulation?" Players then choose a solution card from their own hand and are given a chance to defend why it is the best solution to the question. One player serves as the judge to decide who wins the round.

Another team created an entirely original game after they tried to modify a pre-existing game. This led to more need for playtesting and resolving glitches in game play. Their game is called Pressing Issues. For example, they wanted each card to influence the population but realized writing the effects on the card led to players just reading this instead of reading the card and trying to predict the impact. This was fixed by putting the impact on the back of the card and not allowing players to view it until after deciding (Figure 6.6).

As described by the game's designers Sophia Haggerty and Ashton Jensen,

> Our game, *Pressing Issues* is all about making decisions based on environmental and economic issues we face today. It urges the player to pass or deny policies based on their background knowledge of environmental science, with all the decisions you make resulting in the impact of your country's statistics.

Near the end of the project, Ashley shared the prototype games with a class of junior and senior Advanced Placement (AP) students in another district. The more advanced students playtested the games and gave written feedback on each game. Their teacher used it as an introduction to the unit (they had not yet covered the content). His students asked why empowering women (a solution card in the deck) with better jobs and education would reduce population growth. This sparked a rich class discussion. The teacher even requested a copy of the game for his students to play every year.

Likewise, Ashley has repeated and refined this project inviting students to self-assess with a single column rubric. She includes much of the same content on her original rubric but invites students to self-report whether they think they were exceeding expectations or not successful in meeting the content goals of the project.

PRESSING ISSUES™: A Reader's Manual

Ages 11+
3-6 players

Intro

Pressing Issues™ is a game all about learning how to manage a country. While you play, you must decide which policies that you will enact to help your country's statistics stay as stable as possible.

Players are given the choice to accept or deny policies that they are presented with. These policies all have consequences which they must apply to their statistics scorecard. The goal of the game is to maintain the closest average to 50% at the end of all of the rounds. This game is meant to teach some of the nuances of the different topics of Environmental Science.

Set-Up

To start the game, shuffle all of the rainbow cards together, including the Wild and Event cards. Place the stack at the center of the table. Every player will get one scorecard each, which they will write their names at the top of. The youngest player chooses a Country card first, all of them should be face down. Once everyone has a Country card, fill in the statistics given into the Round 1 section on your scorecard. You are now ready to begin the game!

How it Works

Each round consists of all players either accepting or denying a policy. Once the cycle finishes, the second round will start. The four statistics which players monitor are Population, Resources, Economic Standing, and Sustainability.

The first player to decide on a policy has 15 seconds to choose whether or not they want to accept or deny it. It is crucial that they do not look at the back of the card before accepting/denying. Based on the description on the front of the cards, they will make a decision based on their knowledge of Environmental Science. If the card is accepted, the card is flipped over to reveal the statistics on the back. The player must add or subtract the statistics from their current ones. If the policy is denied, the card is placed at the bottom of the deck, without the statistics being revealed. The game advances to the next player.

If a player has already denied two policies, the third policy must be accepted as a penalty, regardless of the topic. If a Wild card or Event card is drawn, the topic will apply to all players. These cards cannot be skipped. Drawing a Wild or Event card ends the player's turn.

How to Win

Once all the rounds are finished, all players will need to add up their points from the last round in all categories and find the average. The player with the average closest to 50% wins. If at any point during the game a player exceeds 100% or drops below 0%, that player's game will end. The **Bonus: any player which has received the Zoomfloom buff will be able to add or subtract 5% from their averaged score.**

FIGURE 6.6 Pressing Issues™, A Reader's Manual Game Rules

Source: Sophia Haggerty and Ashton Jensen©. Printed with permission of the game's designers

Around the same time that Ashley was going ahead with her second time through the game-design project, Diana "Dee" Weldon had a chemistry intern student teaching in her classes. Erin Milsom took the concept of a game and ran with it. Like Ashley, she identified a suitable audience for learning the content. In this case, she chose a school in a neighboring district with about 45 8th graders who were learning about atoms in their physical science course. The senior chemistry students whom she taught were charged with a more sophisticated understanding of the principles of the periodic table, which they would outline in a Literature Review for a teacher.

Project: Periodic Table Game

Essential Questions

♦ How does the organization of the periodic table reflect the atomic structure of its elements?
♦ How are periodic trends explained by electron configuration and nuclear charge?
♦ How can games be used to teach middle schoolers about the periodic table?

Product

♦ Periodic table game.
♦ Periodic table game instructions.
♦ Literature Review for middle school teacher.

Like Ashley's students had, Erin's students worked through game mechanics and adapted games that would be familiar to middle schoolers (even if the content were new). Designing the games to be kid-friendly led the designers to make decisions eliminating certain elements from the choice cards in Periodic Table Guess Who? "We needed to make sure to have about an equal number of metals, metalloids, noble gasses, etc." reported Montanna Higgins, "So we eliminated a lot of the elements from the middle of the periodic table. It was important to us that the students learn the characteristics of the most common elements."

One of the cleverest iterations of the chemistry game project was a game where students created "Bachelor" cards and challenged the players to find the most likely "match" to create a molecule. This allowed students to gain new learning around electron configuration and nuclear charge—which atoms would be most likely to pair up. Erin found that like many PBL projects, the lift at the beginning can put planning pressure on the teacher, but once underway, the learning flows because the success criteria have been outlined from the beginning.

The repeated success of the game-design projects at TVHS owes much to Lindsay Portnoy who introduced a great structure for iteration and adaptation, but also to the teachers who committed to playtesting and repeated opportunities for design thinking even when it took precious class time away from content instruction. Ultimately, the students who created the games were able to come away with deeper understandings of the concepts that they presented because they were able to work through complex ideas with a deceptively simple frame.

Resources

Game On? Brain On!: The Surprising Relationship between Play and Gray (Matter) by Lindsay Portnoy, PhD. Dave Burgess Consulting Incorporated, 2020.
This book uses vignettes, practical examples and toolboxes to show teachers how to use games and playful experiences to promote deep learning.

Designed to Learn: Using Design Thinking to Bring Purpose and Passion to the Classroom by Lindsay Portnoy, ASCD, 2019.
A guide to the five elements of design thinking by a cognitive scientist and game designer. The book offers many examples, practical strategies and tools for teachers to use in the classroom.

Reference

Zeiser, K., Taylor, J., Rickles, J., Garet, M. S., & Segeritz, M. (2014). Evidence of deeper learning outcomes. (*Report #3 Findings from the study of deeper learning: Opportunities and outcomes*). American Institutes for Research.

7

Cellverse
Using Virtual Reality to Learn about Cells from the Inside Out

Meredith Thompson, Cigdem Uz-Bilgin, Chris Angelli
and Rebecca Webster

Introduction

Think back to biology class and imagine a cell. If you were asked to draw a cell, you would probably draw a circle, a nucleus (the brain of the cell), and the mitochondria (the "powerhouse" of the cell). You are not alone. We have asked hundreds of people, children, teens, and adults, to draw cells and the same picture often emerges: circle, mitochondria, and nucleus.

The limited view is challenging as a basic understanding of biology becomes even more essential for everyday decisions. We must consider whether to use a direct to consumer (DTC) genetic test, whether genetically modified organisms (GMOs) are dangerous, and understand the importance of an annual flu vaccination. The rapid rise and global spread of COVID-19 has transformed biology from a required course in school to a requirement for navigating everyday life. We must understand how personal choices such as handwashing, facemasks, and social distancing contribute to a worldwide battle with a highly infectious disease. We have to understand how therapies or vaccines are developed and tested for efficacy. We have to know enough about biology and science to navigate the "infodemic" that has accompanied the pandemic, and to be able to know what to believe and what not to believe.

Biology Knowledge Is Developed in Schools

Biology knowledge is typically developed in biology classrooms in schools, and biology education remains rooted in minimally interactive websites and textbooks (Vlaardingerbroek, Taylor, & Bale, 2014; Thompson et al., 2020). One example is how high school students learn about cells. Students continue to learn about cells using oversimplified, two-dimensional schematics in biology textbooks that portray cells as static, circular, and mostly empty. These materials misrepresent the complex and dynamic environment of the cell, reducing a fascinating and fundamental aspect of life to a vocabulary lesson about cell organelles. Students express their knowledge about cells through defining organelles or replicating the simplified models with objects found around the house. The common "create a cell from pasta or common household objects project" reproduces and reinforces cells as sparsely populated circles with meticulously organized organelles.

Technology Can Help Students Better Understand Cells

How can we bring the cell to life in a way that is understandable by novices as well as advanced students? Websites, simulations, and movies all help students understand cells. What if you could learn about cells by going inside one? Simulating the environment of a cell in an interactive way is possible using virtual reality (VR). In this case, VR refers to a virtual environment that the user is immersed in using a headset and hand controllers. For many years VR was too expensive to be feasible for K12 education, but decreasing costs make VR more viable as a learning tool. Here we explore how VR could be applied to learning about cells.

Cellverse: Using Virtual Reality to See Inside a Cell

The game started with a grant from Facebook Oculus, as one of a set of grants for education based VR experiences. We considered several different topics but settled on cell biology as the topic for the game, since it is an important topic in biology. The Education Arcade and The MIT Game Lab at MIT designed and programmed *Cellverse*, an interactive game about cellular biology as part of the CLEVR project, aimed to bring collaborative efforts into VR. Our three goals were interactivity, authenticity, and collaboration (Thompson et al., 2018). We aimed to make an interactive experience that was as authentic of a representation of a cell as possible for a team of players: an explorer in VR and a navigator on a tablet. We had a working game that was tested by both experts and adults (Wang et al., 2019). We were preparing to bring it into classrooms in the fall of 2018. However, midway through the project, there was a breakthrough in scientific knowledge about cystic fibrosis: a cell called an "ionocyte" was the root cause of CF. As a result, we had to completely redesign the cell environment to maintain authenticity and did not have a chance to finish the collaborative part in time. In this chapter, we describe the single player version of the game.

What Would It Be Like to Play *Cellverse*?

The goal of *Cellverse* is to explore, diagnose, and select a therapy for a virtual cell. As a player, you are introduced to the narrative through a low-tech comic strip, as shown in Figure 7.1. You are students interning with a scientist named Dr. Blob. Your role is to help determine what type of cystic fibrosis a young patient has and then determine the appropriate cure. Time is of the essence. You are given a VR headset and the game begins.

When you first enter the virtual cell, you are in a projection, which is less dense than the more central part of the cell. You immediately see FR3ND, a robot-like character who accompanies you throughout the game. FR3ND shows you how to move forward, how to select organelles, and how to call up a virtual clipboard to learn about and collect samples of the organelles (See Figure 7.2).

After completing the tutorial, you start the inquiry. Your goals are listed at the bottom of the dashboard. Step 1 "look for the organelle with translating, bound ribosomes". Step 2 "Check for signs that translation stops early", either by "sampling the CFTR amino acid chain to determine its length" or "sample a codon on the mRNA chain to check for early stop codons". Step 3 "verify your evidence, determine the CF type and select a therapy".

FIGURE 7.1 A sample of the introductory comic for the game narrative

Source: Image courtesy of Meredith Thompson© MIT

FIGURE 7.2 Virtual clipboard and FR3ND in microscale view of *Cellverse*

Source: Image courtesy of Meredith Thompson© MIT

You and FR3ND set out on your journey by pressing the "A" button on the hand controllers, navigating out of the projection and towards the center of the cell environment. It is a dense thick jungle of organelles, twisted filaments, and floating proteins, much different than the cell diagrams you remember from the textbooks. Luckily, this is not a quiz! You do not have to remember all the organelles—you can point to an organelle and pull up a clipboard that will tell you the name and function of the organelle. If you take too long to find the organelle with the ribosomes, then FR3ND will offer hints to guide you to the Rough Endoplasmic Reticulum (RER).

Once at the RER, FR3ND suggests moving closer to the organelle and selecting the "B" button on the hand controller to activate the nanobot and see a nanoscopic scale of the process of translation at the RER. You transport into the "nano view" and suddenly you are in an environment that is buzzing with activity. tRNA (dark blue) are flying around like a flock of seagulls, while long green snake-like chains of mRNA wind through the ribosomes (red) as shown in Figure 7.3. The RER now appears to be a gigantic wall with ribosomes coming together at window-like translocation channels. The green mRNA moves through the ribosome, and tRNA matches an amino acid for each triplet set of nucleotides. These "codons" are translated into amino acids that move through the RER and are folded into proteins on the other side.

FR3ND suggests trying to go through the translocation channels on the RER. When you do, you see a truncated amino acid chain that is a result of an early "stop" codon in the mRNA. You gather a sample of mRNA and a sample of the amino acid and verify your evidence. Once verified, you review the five classes of CF. An early stop codon means it's class 1. You have figured it out! Now you can help the patient!

FIGURE 7.3 Dashboard in nanoscale view of *Cellverse*

Source: Image courtesy of Meredith Thompson© MIT

Getting Teacher Feedback on the Game

We began designing the game in June 2017 and had an initial cell environment in the fall of 2017, which we shared with Chris Angelli of Somerville High School. Chris thought that the game would be a useful way to explore the cell even without the larger narrative, and that both his biotechnology and AP biology classes would benefit from trying the game. In the spring of 2017, we brought *Cellverse* to the Greater Lawrence Technical School (GLTS) and gave a demonstration to teachers and administrators, including biology teacher Becky Webster. Even at the early stages of the game, both Chris and Becky were intrigued by the premise of the game and the different approach to the commonly taught topic. Becky appreciated the authenticity of the cell organelles and the density of the cell as represented in the game and was excited for first years to have that mental model of cells early on in their high school career. Gene therapy is a topic Becky covers with her seniors, and the focus on a specific type of cell (a ionocyte, which is a type of lung cell) and the context of cystic fibrosis were valuable links to that topic; the virtual cell environment could help trigger seniors' memory about cell structure that they learned in their first year.

Trying the Game Out in Class

During the fall of 2019, we tried the game out in both Chris' and Becky's classrooms (Thompson, Kaser, & Grijalva, 2019). In September, Becky Webster's biology classes at GLTS, and first year and senior students were able to try the game. In October and November, we visited Chris Angelli's senior level biotechnology class at Somerville High School. Both Becky and Chris had separate lab tables with space for us to set up the laptops and VR headsets. Between two and five researchers set up five stations and cycled students through the game. However, we found that the WI-FI connection was variable at both schools. At GLTS we had to get special permission from the technology support coordinator, while in Somerville we ended up connecting the laptops to the network using wired ethernet cables. The research staff made sure all equipment was sanitized before students put on the headset or held the hand controllers, and helped students get into VR and monitored the VR experience. The extra help in starting and monitoring a VR experience is a luxury that many teachers do not have.

We had students create cell drawings both before and after they played the game. The post drawings included more types of organelles and a more realistic number of organelles in the cell. We also conducted five question mini-interviews with students after the game to learn how they felt during the game and how it was different from other learning experiences. We interviewed 154 high school students between 14 and 19 years old. Students were Hispanic/Latino (n=93), White (n=36), African American (n=7), and Asian (n=3). We recorded and transcribed the interviews, and then coded them. Most of the students who played *Cellverse* liked the VR experience. Students described three ways that the VR experience was different from other ways they had learned about cells: interactivity, presence, and attention. Students enjoyed the interaction afforded by the game and perceived it as a "hands-on" interaction with a cell. Students talked about touching, going through the cell environment and past the organelles. One student described, "You actually have to be like hands on with it. Like you actually got to see it", while another said, "I like diagrams of cells [they] picture it very simply, [when actually] like everything's right next to each other all touching when they are complicated. So, it's cool to be able to see the different sizes and then go to see some different perspectives of them". The vocational students in particular described a preference for tactile learning, and the ability to see and experience organelles in the first person through VR. Playing the game took a lesson with limited interactivity and abstract concepts or organelles and cells into a concrete experience (n=47). Second, students felt present in the cellular environment (n=111). When students moved into the crowded middle of the cell or from micro to nano level, many reacted by saying "Cool" or "Wow" or "Oh", evidence of being highly engaged in the experience. They described being able to go around the organelles or events in the cell (translation process) and being able to see them from different perspectives. The game created the illusion of being in the cell and really trying to find what is wrong with the cell. VR gave students the ability to do the impossible and allowed students to make a deep connection with the material.

Another important feature of VR technology is that it has the capability of focusing the users' attention. One student noted that "you're forced to see the environment" while wearing the head mounted display (HMD). Being immersed in the game focuses your entire attention on cells, removing all other distractions that can occur in the classroom (n=38). Students also mentioned, "It's better [than images] to be honest, because you could like you could actually like see it and like, look around, like, you're kind of like, you're forced to like see the environment" and

> I think this is a really good way to teach so because like on paper so people don't really pay attention to what they're doing. But when they are looking through a headset, and moving things around learning, virtually, make contact physically contact them within themselves. You actually pay attention, you read things because you have to, like reach your goal and finish the game.

Designers can also leverage this capability to guide the user to attend to specific parts of the game through drawing the users' attention to different parts of the game. In *Cellverse*, the non-player character (NPC) FR3ND was designed to prompt the student to find different organelles or try moving through the cell in a particular way to find clues in the game.

As VR is still an emerging technology, theories about how learning happens in VR are also emerging. Seymour Papert introduced the idea of constructionism, or the learning that happens through interacting with materials and other people and building projects (Papert & Harel, 1991). We believe the combination of presence, embodied learning, and interactivity in an authentic environment could enable "virtual constructionism". *Cellverse* allowed students to interact with abstract concepts in ways that were like actual objects to be perceived as "hands on". While *Cellverse* did not have students specifically build in VR, students' perceptions of the virtual environment as "real" could be leveraged that way in the future.

There are a few caveats to consider with the game. For many of the students, this was the first or second time they had been in VR (n=131), and the resulting novelty effect of VR is a factor in how the game is received by students, and something we keep in mind as we review the results. The students only played the game for 40 minutes, and it was not possible to see its long-term effect on students' experiences and performances. The game lasted 30–40 minutes, and by the time the students completed the game, they were ready to get out of the headset. We had very few cases where students felt nauseous. Students who did feel nausea were able to calm their stomach by getting out of the VR headset and closing their eyes. We also offered peppermint or ginger candy, two remedies for calming nausea. We saw changes in their knowledge of organelles through cell drawings, and of knowledge through a posttest about a week after they played the game (Thompson et al., 2020); however, we are still not sure of the long-term effect on students' experiences and performances. Some students who were not experienced game players described navigation problems and difficulty getting oriented in the environment (n=29). They suggested more clear instructions or a map that shows where the player is in the cell. As mentioned before, a two player game with an explorer in VR and navigator on a tablet was part of our original game design, but that was not finished in time for the study.

Time was also an issue. Both Becky and Chris prepared other materials for the class during the game days. Chris' classes were a longer block and had fewer students, so the study took about four days. Becky classes were 45 minutes long with up to 25 students in them, so running each student through the single player game took about six days of class time with five setups running. Alternate setups could include a fishbowl setup with one student explorer and the view on a larger screen for the rest of the class could capture some of the interactivity in a shorter amount of time. Having four or five groups with one "driver" viewing the game in VR and three "back set drivers" viewing on a monitor or tablet is another possible set up. Despite the challenges, the students loved playing the game and wanted more time to understand the VR environment and solve the puzzle.

Conclusion

We learned a great deal from designing, revising, and testing the game in actual classrooms. In making the cell authentic, the team both learned a lot of biology and were reminded of the pace of scientific discovery. Testing the game in actual classrooms surfaced both the potential and the limitations of including VR experiences in schools. The level of realism students felt in their interactions with the game suggests that virtual reality games could be used to experience constructionist hands-on learning with virtual objects in virtual environments, a concept we've called virtual constructionism. In the future, VR experiences like *Cellverse* could allow a wider range of students the ability to create knowledge and understand complex systems by making abstract concepts concrete.

References

Papert, S., & Harel, I. (1991). Situating constructionism. *Constructionism*, *36*(2), 1–11.

Thompson, M., Kaser, D., & Grijalva, K. (2019). *Envisioning virtual reality: A toolkit for implementing VR in education*. Lulu Press, Inc.

Thompson, M. M., Wang, A., Roy, D., & Klopfer, E. (2018). Authenticity, interactivity, and collaboration in VR learning games. *Frontiers in Robotics and AI*, *5*, 133.

Thompson, M. M., Wang, A., Uz-Bilgin, C., Anteneh, M., Roy, D., Tan, P., Eberhart, R., & Klopfer, E. (2020). Influence of virtual reality on high school students' conceptions of cells. *Journal of Universal Computer Science*, forthcoming.

Vlaardingerbroek, B., Taylor, N., & Bale, C. (2014). The problem of scale in the interpretation of pictorial representations of cell structure. *Journal of Biological Education*, *48*(3), 154–162. https://doi.org/10.1080/00219266.2013.849284

Wang, A., Thompson, M., Roy, D., Pan, K., Perry, J., Tan, P., Eberhart, R., & Klopfer, E. (2019). Iterative user and expert feedback in the design of an educational virtual reality biology game. *Interactive Learning Environments*, 1–18.

8

Living in Media
Why Teach the World's most Controversial Video Game?

Paul Darvasi

In the spring of 2017, my high school English class played and studied *Grand Theft Auto V* (*GTA V*), the most recent installment of a video game franchise with a troubled past. When I first announced the plan, my seniors were delighted and a little incredulous that the taboo game that was typically enjoyed in the seclusion of their basements and bedrooms was now required reading. As you might imagine, including the world's most controversial video game in the curriculum involved some preliminary footwork. Letters were written, conversations had, promises made, suggestions received, tempers pacified, documents signed, and, following careful deliberations, rather miraculously, the experiment was allowed to proceed.

The *GTA V* unit was the subject of my doctoral research that sought to study how adolescent boys process their gameplay when filtered through a critical media literacy lens. During the unit, my students reflected on representations of gender, race, violence, and political ideology, and my dissertation ultimately narrowed to a consideration of how white adolescent boys make connections between race and place in *GTA V*'s virtual city. The experience provoked remarkably honest and animated discussions and, in many cases, shifted some worldviews. It also raised pressing questions about how schools might better address the reality of the complex media that suffuse the lives of teens.

Even when video games are not formally part of the curriculum, my students know that I am easily derailed by video game talk. Our discussions span new releases, graphics, narrative choices, characters, mechanics, strategy, and gameplay anecdotes. When I let them know that my doctoral work is on

GTA V, I am usually met with a barrage of questions: Why *GTA V*? You have a PhD in video games? What did you write about? Do we get to play *GTA V*? I barely manage a response before they break off into their own lively exchanges about the game. They share the intricacies of infiltrating a high security military compound to steal a fighter jet, recite a jingle from a parody commercial from the in-game radio they heard while racing in a stolen cab, or laugh at the episode of the sexually opportunistic yoga instructor. I try to settle them down with an informal poll: "raise your hand if you play or have played *GTA V*." A few hands proudly shoot up, but many raise uncertain hands while some visibly pause to consider the consequences of openly admitting they play, especially since they are younger than the recommended age. Maybe they cannot decide whether it is more embarrassing to admit that they play or that they do not play.

It has been seven years since *GTA V*'s release and, when I recently polled a class of Grade 10 students, three quarters of the hands went up. I have asked the same question in over a dozen different classes of adolescent boys and have never had less than half the class confess to playing. In the competitive video game market, where thousands of games jostle for control of consoles, computers, and mobile phones, *GTA V*'s commercial resilience is virtually unrivaled. My informal class polls are hardly rigorous or statistically significant, but they do hint at the game's staggering reach, particularly with young men. Since it launched in 2013, it has sold over 120 million copies with an estimated revenue of more than $6 billion, making it the third bestselling video game of all time (Kain, 2019). Copies in circulation are likely much higher due to the resale market and pirating. Its sprawling influence established it as a staple of male youth culture and, even before the release of *GTA V*, games scholars Ben DeVane and Kurt Squire described it as "one of the most dominant media franchises of the new millennium and a cornerstone media point for millions of today's youth" (2008, p. 264). Despite its enduring popularity, aside from sales figures, there is almost no data, demographic information, or empirical studies available about *GTA V*. An informal sweep of player forums and Steam gameplay charts indicate that offline *GTA V* players devote between 50 and 100 hours to the single player edition, while online players frequently log over 1,000 hours of gameplay, many reporting over 5,000 hours. These figures are not entirely reliable, but considering the game's scope and astronomical popularity, it's reasonable to estimate that tens of millions of adolescents spend hundreds of hours in the virtual city of Los Santos, a social phenomenon about which we remain largely in the dark.

Addressing the Media Elephant in the Room

GTA V's appeal stems from its magnitude of scope, photorealistic graphics, and edgy, open world play. And the game is no stranger to controversy. Players can undertake an array of criminal activities in an elaborate city simulation that *The Guardian* reviewer Keith Stuart called "a warped mirror of Los

Angeles" that is nothing less than a "monstrous parody of modern life." A layered narrative campaign unfolds across an urban playground where players can blow up meth labs, patronize strip clubs, blackmail celebrities, murder prostitutes, hijack luxury cars, torture terrorists, and manipulate the stock market to buy expensive clothes and luxury mansions. In a social climate where video games have been linked to mass killings, school shootings, misogyny, suicide, street racing, and addiction, no other mainstream video game franchise has generated more public outcry. It has been the target of lawsuits; it is frequently blamed for gun violence; it is condemned for its degrading representations of women, racial stereotypes, and celebrations of criminality; and it even caused a political firestorm in the U.S. Congress for sexually explicit content in the now infamous "hot coffee" scandal. Conversely, the *GTA V* playground also offers more benign activities, such as golfing, tennis, scuba diving, jet skiing, dancing, yoga, and cruising while listening to music from one of the dozens of radio stations. However, its penchant for headlines and massive sales have earned *GTA* the dubious distinction of being crowned the most controversial video game franchise in history by the *Guinness Book of World Records* (Moore, 2016). Clearly, not a shoo-in for high school English.

Understandably, schools are risk-averse, and a video game like *GTA V* that is saturated in violence and antisocial content is kept at radioactive distance. However, scholars like Chris J. Ferguson (2010) argue that schools may be short-sighted for ignoring violent games. On the contrary, there is a responsibility to provide the tools and outlets to help teens make sense of the complex media they consume. Adolescents inhabit a fragmented landscape of social media, fake news, pornography, sexualized music videos, persuasive algorithms, photorealistic interactive environments, psychologically addictive reward mechanisms, endless streaming, sexting, hacking, and data mining. They are frequently exposed to senseless violence, impossible body images, narrow gender scripts, misogyny, and racist stereotypes without guidance, constructive dialogue, or the space for reflection.

Our youth no longer live *with the media*, but *in the media* as they inhabit an environment carefully crafted to seduce hearts and minds, and with significant consequence to the development of identity, moral reasoning, and emotional regulation, to list a few (see, for example, Bijvank et al., 2012; Olson et al., 2008; Jansz, 2005). Unfortunately, schools are constrained and do woefully little to address the voracious consumption of media. But ignoring the elephant in the room abandons young people to a hallucinatory labyrinth that shapes developing views and attitudes towards interpersonal relationships, culture, politics, and society.

A Political Education: Popular Culture and Critical Media Literacy

Teaching with *GTA V* was rooted on the theories and practices of critical media literacy which, in barebones terms, encourages critical consumption of media. The approach invites students to look under the hood and consider how media are made, who makes media and why, and how media shape self and society. Video games, comics, TV shows, and films, among others, are media texts that become the grounds for inquiry into the relationship between culture, power, knowledge, and authority with attention to the social context in which they are produced, consumed, and studied. Supporters of critical media education believe that formal education must better support students to interrogate media representations of the social world and empower young people to critically read and produce media. The use of popular media such as video games as valid sites of scholarly and pedagogical work is not only timely, but relevant. It is an opportunity to meet our students where they are while providing them with the tools to become savvy consumers and, ultimately, more responsible citizens.

Critical media literacy can be framed as a type of political activism, particularly when it delves into questioning established power structures and drawing awareness to pressing social issues. However, the deliberate political agenda can be critiqued as a form of political indoctrination in a climate where teachers are encouraged to remain ostensibly neutral or undeclared in their political inclinations. However, media scholar Henry Giroux distinguishes between *political education* and *politicizing education*. Rather than forwarding a dogmatic political agenda, a *political education* is informed by the principles of democracy, and aims to create an equitable, reflexive, and inquisitive learning environment underscored by a sense of civic responsibility that interrogates oppressive instances of power. This political position is also what distinguishes *critical* media literacy from the relativist and apolitical approaches that typically characterize media education.

GTA V in the Classroom: Structure and Delivery

Our month-long drive through the mean streets of Los Santos aimed to expose and question implicit and explicit power structures in the game's content, production, and distribution. I also sought to extend the examination of power by diminishing my authority as teacher/researcher to make space for the student/participants to assume greater responsibility for the instructional design and research. Students were invited to provide regular feedback on how classes were structured, and we sat in a circle for every session to encourage equitable dialogue. Additionally, they were positioned as co-researchers and prepared with a rudimentary grounding in ethnography so that they could take effective field notes and film themselves playing, which would culminate in a summative autoethnographic report. All their work, which encouraged self-reflection and fulfilled the unit's learning objectives, also contributed invaluable research data.

Each class followed a similar template: we dragged our desks into an imperfect circle, read articles, and watched videos, and discussed a wide range of topics that broadly and narrowly connected to *GTA V* and/or the readings. For research purposes, I filmed each class. The all-boys group was small enough that no hand raising was required, and conversation flowed naturally and respectfully with very few exceptions. Students played *GTA V* at home, logging an average gameplay time of approximately 14 hours each over a 30-day period. All the students but one had previously played *GTA V*, and the one who had not played previous installments of the franchise had watched the entire game played in YouTube. Handouts, class outlines, announcements, assignments, links, and copies of the readings were posted on the class learning management system. During each class, students rotated note-taking duties, and the notes were placed on a Google Doc and shared with me and their classmates. We also set up a private Facebook group where students responded to prompts and voluntarily posted material. In addition to the final autoethnographic report, they were also asked to produce a counter-hegemonic media artifact in response to the game. It would be helpful to have a closer look at the unit's key instructional components.

The Facebook Group

Facebook has increasingly fallen out of favor with adolescents and has come under public scrutiny for its data sharing practices. However, it was still viable at the time of the study and our private Facebook group created a sprawling record of emergent discussions. The online group operated in the dialogic spirit of our circle of desks and asynchronously extended the conversation beyond the classroom walls. Formally, I posted seven separate prompts over the course of the month that ranged from requesting that students post screenshots with accompanying descriptions to inviting them to discuss a quote from a paper we read in class. Their responses to the prompts were a graded activity and informally, they posted videos, screenshots, quotes, and memes in a digital-age deployment of Paolo Freire's method of using culturally relevant artifacts to incite meaningful dialogue. These included interviews with hip-hop stars, *The Game Theory* videos, newspaper articles, and viral YouTube videos. The free and equitable flow of information in the space leveraged student knowledge and expertise and invited their interests and concerns to the instructional sphere. Many of the posts were later referenced and unpacked during our in-class discussions.

Counter-Hegemonic Media

Critical media literacy not only involves the analysis of cultural products but also encourages students to create media that address issues of gender, race, class, and power. Students produce their own media in response to media texts such as *GTA V* to present a counter-narrative that challenges values or assumptions in the source text. Ideally, the media they produce are derivative of the media they critique, meaning that the source text is reworked to transmit a counter-message. In the case of my students, many created counter-hegemonic videos and comics using *GTA V* footage and screenshots.

This approach can empower marginalized or misrepresented people and groups, but it can also allow for a dominant group such as the white male adolescents involved in the experiment to critically reflect on broader social realities from a standpoint of actionable complicity. The unit's instructional design followed the critical media literacy prescription that students should be exposed to critical readings, structured discussions, and media production that reveal the potentially damaging values and representations embedded in media texts. The existing and established culture of repurposing and modifying video games can make them into a type of culturally transformative play. Some examples of media that students might produce include machinimas, comic books, posters, screenshot photo albums, photo essays, Public Service Announcements (PSAs), podcasts, and music videos. The method is multifaceted and can include a *multiperspectival* critical approach that employs various technologies and yields diverse responses with the aim of transforming education and furthering democratic society.

Many of my seniors submitted projects that were memorable explorations of political issues in formats that empowered them to communicate their message effectively. These included comics that exposed how the game portrays masculine stereotypes, a narrative video that explored how a black protagonist might evade a life of crime, and a short film that acknowledged that players (like themselves) undertake a form of identity tourism when they play characters of color.

Grand Theft (Auto) Ethnography

The unit's cornerstone summative assignment was a structured 1,500 word autoethnography. Ethnography has traditionally involved a researcher carrying out a qualitative study of a particular cultural context. In the case of an autoethnography, the researcher and subject are one and the same and they study themselves within a cultural milieu they inhabit. Students were provided with an outline to structure their final report and were encouraged to include relevant portions of their gameplay fieldnotes, class notes, and supporting quotes from the scholarly articles we had read in class.

It is important to remember that an autoethnography produced by a high school student should not be held to the same standards and outcomes as those authored by a graduate student or a seasoned scholar. The mode is confessional, but fear and sensitivity to emotional, sexual, and psychological exposure is heightened in a high school setting. A gay student who has not come out to his peers or a student who likes to play video games while high on cannabis may be reluctant to confess these positions. Efforts were made to encourage transparency, and many of my students shared personal experiences, but the confessional aspect was mitigated by the setting and demographic. Furthermore, autoethnography distinguishes itself from autobiography because it does not merely tell a personal story but is a narrative supported by methodological and theoretical tools. My students did not have the experience, focus, or resources to structure their work with a sophisticated scholarly framework. They were instructed in the bare-bone rudiments of critical theory, but most turned to "hegemonic masculinity" as their "theoretical lens," and their accounts careened towards the naturalistic end of the spectrum. Finally, they were given the option to document their gameplay through diverse means, including video, pictures, and audio; however, most defaulted to written accounts. The flexible options in response to media permit students to report on their experience in their own terms, and they are more likely to provide additional emotional insight, veracity, and detail when empowered to articulate their stories through channels where they feel capable and proficient.

Positioning my students as co-researchers was most valuable from the instructional perspective. First, this was their first exposure to the methods and practices of academic research. They learned to distinguish between qualitative and quantitative methods, read scholarly articles, became acquainted with the broad issues and practices of ethnography, and developed a basic grasp of how theory and methods inform research. They also put into practice a cycle of observation and note gathering which was synthesized in a cohesive final product. When asked open-ended questions about what they felt they had learned in the unit, most included some mention of the research process itself. One even credited the classroom research for his improved understanding of *GTA V*, writing, "If it were not for playing the game in a research environment I may not have picked up on all the subtle pokes and prods at society." Involving my university-bound students as co-researchers, exposing them to the basic tenets of investigative practices, and making the research process transparent proved a valuable learning opportunity.

As a practicing teacher, I will use autoethnography again as an authentic and meaningful assessment, as its blend of research and self-reflective writing encourages self-awareness and social and emotional growth. I was also convinced and excited by the immense potential of conducting ethnographic and autoethnographic research to capture data in a complex virtual environment like *GTA V*.

Living in Media: The Exotic Familiarity of the *GTA V* Mediapolis

There is little debate that adolescents are saturated by media, but it was fascinating to uncover and document the extent to which it suffuses their discourse and shapes their views. Throughout the unit, students referenced an array of media in their discussions, writings, videos, and social media posts to contextualize and inspire their in-game activity, to substantiate their political views, and to contribute material for debate and discussion.

Although I shared articles, videos, and ideas to support the instructional and research objectives, the students were much more reliant on popular media, music, YouTube videos, and diverse *GTA* paratexts to articulate their views. Some examples include students comparing a location in the game to a Sting video, referencing *Paul Bart: Mall Cop* to illustrate a humorous take on hegemonic masculinity, and enlisting Bill Nye and *The Office* to discuss how gender is on a spectrum. They evoked a range of bands and musical genres from Lady Gaga to Hip-Hop to Vaperwave, and an incomplete list of games they referenced including *Madden*, *NHL* (or "chel" as it is popularly known), *NBA2K*, *Starcraft*, *Bioshock*, *Saints Row*, *Civilization*, *Skyrim*, *Mafia III*, *Call of Duty: Modern Warfare 2*, *Call of Duty: Black Ops*, and numerous *GTA* franchise titles. Reddit, YouTube, and Facebook were all used as sources of information on topics ranging from Feminism to the productive value of anger. One reported feeling like James Bond in the game, and another, who robbed a jewelry store, remarked that he felt like "I was actually in a Quentin Tarantino robbery movie. The only thing missing was 'Stuck in the Middle With You' by Stealers Wheel." There were many instances where their views and opinions were drawn from media: online player forums and *The Game Theorist* videos influenced their in-game experiments to determine whether the Los Santos police were racist, *Django Unchained* and *Dear White People* fueled a debate about cultural appropriation, Reddit provided the substance by which to critique other posts on Reddit, and *National Geographic* and *Rick and Morty* helped them envision a post-race future.

These scattered examples further buttress the notion that youth live in media, and help explain why players feel at home in the otherwise exotic world of *GTA V*. It is often missed that *GTA V* was developed in Scotland as a deliberate satire of American media-saturated culture. The virtual city of Los Santos is a referential pastiche that pulls widely from popular culture and contains a diverse media ecology within it, all the while representing a parody of Los Angeles, the world capital of media production. *GTA V*'s developers deliberately constructed Los Santos according to how LA is presented in media, drawing from films like *Boyz in the Hood*, *LA Story*, *Heat*, *Get Shorty*, *LA Confidential*, Hip-Hop music and media, previous *GTA* games, and the Rodney King riots, to name a few. Furthermore, *GTA V* not only operates as a referential nexus embedded in a broader media ecology, but it is also a media ecology onto itself. It contains in-game TV networks with hours of original content, a navigable Internet, multiple radio stations with extensive programming, news shows, billboards, video games, mobile phones, and even a social media company (Life Invader). The *GTA* gamespace, then, is not only familiar because the content is designed to satirically reference popular media, but its formal qualities echo the diverse media landscape outside the game, making it a fertile site to investigate the effects and consequences of the increasingly ubiquitous role of media.

Once the unit ended, I surveyed my students to gauge their views of the experience and determine what, if anything, they felt they had learned. A number reported an increased awareness and sensitivity to the material addressed in the unit. One stated that the study "opened up my eyes to many issues and made me see the world from many other directions. It has allowed me to see prejudices a lot more clearly," while another wrote that

> [t]his study made me think a different way, I got to see things like racism and sexism firsthand. I now realize that throughout society, it seems that we are drifting farther apart rather than together, and that we are moving farther from equal rights.

A few discussed how they would consume media differently therein, such as one who shared that the experience "has changed me. I'm definitely more aware . . . of race and violence in . . . everyday media than I was before. And it's opened my eyes a lot, which was great." In some cases, students reported a more generalized awareness of how media bear tangible consequences on society: "One viewpoint of mine was drastically changed by this study[:] I now see that improper representation in media isn't only about what is happening on the screen, but how that projects stereotypes and holds back real change." These comments were not cherry-picked, but roundly reflect the significant shifts in attitude expressed by most of the students at the end of the project. Applying a critical lens to relevant and timely media in an inclusive pedagogical environment can prove transformative and help reverse the potentially negative consequences of internalizing damaging representations.

Despite the success of using *GTA V* as a curricular centerpiece with my all-male class, the experience will not cleanly translate to other settings. The unit was crafted specifically with my students and my research in mind and would not likely yield the same results in other contexts. Rather than a template, I see it as a model to inspire educators to consider the use of diverse media in their practice, particularly if it plays a significant role in the lives of their students. The study unearthed the extent to which media in general and *GTA V* in particular impact the lives of my students, but also highlighted the need for a more robust engagement with media and digital literacy in formal education.

Whatever the merits of this exercise, it is unlikely that many teachers will be able to reproduce this instructional experience. In my case, my unique school, class, student demographics, and research ambitions created the circumstances that brought this unique project to fruition. My research focus was on the dominant upper middle-class white male category, but it may be even more valuable for racialized students to undertake a similar direction and think about how they are constrained by media representations. It is crucial that marginalized communities learn to critically consume and understand media, as they hold so much cultural and social sway and can catapult real change. Furthermore, rather than impose *GTA V* as the curricular centerpiece students can be offered options, as *GTA V* may not be relevant or interesting to all students. A unit might, for example, be designed around racial and/or gender representation where students can choose the media on which to conduct the analysis and apply lessons learned. This approach sidesteps the pitfalls of actively introducing contentious media into the curriculum, but still allows for each student to connect with the material in a way that makes sense for them. It is also ideal for teachers to keep in touch with their student's media consumption trends and habits. Media literacy must continuously evolve to keep pace with a landscape whose content and channels of delivery are in constant flux.

Finally, I add my voice to the growing choir that advocates for greater curricular space to be afforded the study of media. Perhaps the traditional English class would be better recast as a Communications class to reflect the skills, texts, and issues that affect the present and future of our youth, all of which have pressing sociopolitical implications. Furthermore, media texts must not only be used as sites for critical inquiry, but educators would also benefit from enlisting media to provide the theoretical and critical framework from which students conduct their critiques. Imaginaries formed in synthetic worlds like *GTA V* bear consequences for culture, society, identity politics, and individual social and emotional development, which is why it is crucial we better understand and support youth to critically process their gameplay experience. Moreover, a program of critical consumption and production can help alter cultures and practices within the game spaces and their contextual communities, and this can transform potentially pernicious media into a site for resistance and empowerment.

References

Bijvank, M. N., Konijn, E. A., & Bushman, B. J. (2012). "We don't need no education": Video game preferences, video game motivations, and aggressiveness among adolescent boys of different educational ability levels. *Journal of Adolescence, 35*(1), 153–162.

DeVane, B., & Squire, K. D. (2008). The meaning of race and violence in Grand Theft Auto: San Andreas. *Games and Culture, 3*(3–4), 264–285.

Ferguson, C. J. (2010). Blazing angels or resident evil? Can violent video games be a force for good? *Review of General Psychology, 14*(2), 68.

Jansz, J. (2005). The emotional appeal of violent video games for adolescent males. *Communication Theory, 15*(3), 219–241.

Kain, E. (2019, May 14). Putting grand theft Auto V's 110 million copies sold into context. *Forbes.* www.forbes.com/sites/erikkain/2019/05/14/putting-grand-theft-auto-vs-110-million-copies-sold-into-context/#7916cd762cac

Moore, R. (2016, March 4). 15 Most controversial games in history. *Screenrant. http://screenrant. com/most-controversial-video-games-ever/?view=all*

Olson, C. K., Kutner, L. A., & Warner, D. E. (2008). The role of violent video game content in adolescent development boys' perspectives. *Journal of Adolescent Research, 23*(1), 55–75.

Stuart, K. (2013, September 16). GTA 5 review: A dazzling but monstrous parody of modern life. *The Guardian.* www.theguardian.com/technology/2013/sep/16/gta-5-review-grand-theft-auto-v

9

Engaging History Through Student Authored Text Adventure Games

Joy Baker and Hap Aziz

Teachers understand the interesting and difficult place that middle school students find themselves in their individual academic journeys. Students in this age group are going through an often emotional and physical as well as cognitive maturation process. If you have taught middle school before, you know that your students are starting to take responsibility for their learning and education; this is when they start to own it (hopefully cultivating this ownership mentality to serve them as lifelong learners). You also know that middle school is a time of training, extending grace, and helping your students find their niche and comfort with who they are so they may succeed not only in the classroom but outside it as well.

Middle school history can be particularly challenging in finding ways of engaging students while implementing more creative and interactive ways to effectively evaluate their learning. Since today's students are open to, comfortable with, and accepting of computer technology for recreational pursuits, there is unexplored potential opportunity in using technology to engage students in the classroom. While the focus of this chapter is the use of technology to facilitate learning in history, you will find that the methodology presented here may also be used in other subject areas.

Critical Thinking and Creativity

As part of the typical course design process you must cover and map out your learning objectives. There are two critical questions to ask: what knowledge and experiences do you want your students to have by the end of the unit, and how do you maximize students' long-term retention of the information? Unfortunately, rote memorization of facts to be regurgitated (especially through drill and practice activities) is not particularly effective, yet it is still a fairly common practice in middle school classrooms. Standard assessments may not be indicative of actual content mastery, as students may suffer from test anxiety (at this age, they have not had the time to develop good test-taking strategies), and in the context of Bloom's Taxonomy, only lower-level thinking is being assessed. Game-based learning can help you craft teaching methodologies and assignments to foster higher-level thinking (HOTS).

Standard curricular tools available to middle school teachers do not often provide a sufficient framework necessary to encourage critical thinking skills or help develop creativity. However, leveraging technology can be effective in moving your students beyond remembering and understanding to a point of applying, analyzing, evaluating, and even creating their own learning artifacts. History is a rich and complex area of study. Students can learn about people, places, events, and dates for say the Korean War, or perhaps the Civil Rights Movement. They can even discuss the how and why of America's involvement in Vietnam. But how might you equip your students to evaluate historical decisions from a variety of viewpoints, understand cause and effect regarding historical actions, and then take the next step, imagining and thinking through alternative decisions and their possible outcomes? Training your students to research information, assimilate it, look for answers, navigate different perspectives, and move into drawing well-informed conclusions for themselves is an invaluable skill that will serve them over a lifetime.

The Power of Narrative

The use of narrative techniques is widely accepted as an effective method of promoting learning by connecting the student to the content being taught (Slater & Rouner, 2002). Additionally, the role of narrative methods in computer gaming has now been recognized as promoting meaningful engagement with players (Robertson & Good, 2003). Properly integrated into your lesson plan, narrative materials and activities can place the student into a position of understanding history from the perspective of the principle historical figures.

Some of you may be familiar with Choose Your Own Adventure (CYOA) story books. These books place the reader into the narrative by allowing the reader to make decisions regarding the path the story will take. At certain points in the story, the reader would get to a part of the story and then would be able to choose what the character did next, or where they went. Then the book would send you to the appropriate page that corresponded with the reader's choice in a simple branching scenario structure. Several such branching points exist, and there are multiple possible endings to the story.

Digital versions of CYOA books exist in the form of computer games. One such game titled "80 Days" (published by Inkle Studios in 2014) is based loosely on the novel *Around the World in 80 Days* by Jules Verne and was awarded the 2014 Game of the Year award by *Time* magazine. While CYOA games do not exist in sufficient variety to map directly to existing middle school curriculum, there are available authoring tools that can facilitate the development of custom-created CYOA games. One such tool is Inklewriter, developed by Inkle Studios and made freely to the public as a web-based authoring system. It is located at www.inklewriter.com.

Teachers could make use of Inklewriter to publish CYOA games to support any historical topic assignment, but if the intent is to foster student engagement through creative participation, consider the possibility of teaching your students how to author with Inklewriter. Rather than writing an eight-page paper on the Six-Day War in the Middle East, for example, they would analyze and evaluate the information they learned in class, and then apply it to create their own interactive story as their assignment artifact, removing the strict parameters and formality of a paper.

Introducing Students to Inklewriter

Inklewriter is a web-based authoring system for CYOA games. The system does not require any special hardware or software, and it will run well on any computer that can be used to surf the Internet. Students will be able to set up their own Inklewriter account for free, and their created games will be stored online. (Have your students provide you with the email address and password they used in creating their accounts. This will help you when it is time to review their work for grading.) When your students have finished creating their game, Inklewriter will publish the game so that it can be viewed publicly by anyone who has a link, and Inklewriter will automatically generate and provide that link.

The basic skills your students will need in order to author their stories in Inklewriter is the ability to type their text into text boxes provided by the Inklewriter interface and the ability to use the Inklewriter prompts to link the branching choices for their stories to the appropriate outcomes. The Inklewriter interface is easy to use and guides the students to the next steps.

Figure 9.1 depicts the interface your students will see.

Although Inklewriter is relatively easy to use, your students will need some in-classroom training and practice time before they will be ready to begin developing their story. You will want to plan for at least two of three class periods in which you teach your students how to use the program. Alternatively, you may have someone more familiar with using Inklewriter lead these class sessions. This could be another teacher, a guest speaker, or even some particularly skilled students. Some visual demonstrations coupled with actual in-class practice will provide your students with the requisite skills to succeed. (This will require that your students have access to computer or

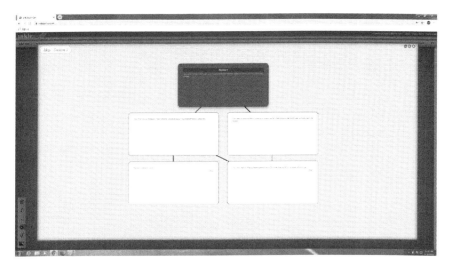

FIGURE 9.1 Inklewriter initial editing screen with initial story elements

Source: courtesy of Hap Asiz and used with permission of Inklewriter.

tablet devices to participate during the class periods.) There are extensive tutorials on using the system located on the Inklewriter website, and a Beginner's Guide to Using Inklewriter developed by the authors of this chapter is located here: https://hapaziz.wordpress.com/2017/04/12/beginners-guide-to-inklewriter/. Even if you decide to utilize an external Inklewriter resource, it will be greatly advantageous for you to become comfortable with the system to support your students adequately from beginning to the end of the assignment.

Designing the Assignment

After gaining some familiarity with Inklewriter, you may start considering what it will take to add a CYOA game assignment to your lesson plan. There are several questions to be answered:

◆ How much time will it take?
◆ How will you train the students on the program?
◆ How will you grade the artifact (making it measurable without squelching the creative aspect of it)?
◆ What are your objectives?

Developing the learning objectives for the assignment might be the most straightforward part of the process, as the academic goals for the assignment would not be completely different than those for a paper or a presentation. Here are three possible objectives assuming a unit topic on the Middle East:

♦ Students will be able to integrate historical content from previous Middle East research into a fictional game setting using the Inklewriter authoring software.
♦ Students will be able to describe and justify possible outcomes to past events in the Middle East based on alternative actions or decisions that key historical figures could have made.
♦ Students will be able to explain the historical impact of actual actions or decisions made by key historical figures.

Choose Your Own Adventure Game Rubric

Once you have your learning objectives for the assignment, you may consider the rubric. This part of your work will be more challenging, especially if you have little experience in game authoring with software. While providing a detailed outline of an appropriate game development process will not be covered in depth in this chapter, there are characteristics of the process that are similar to creating a presentation. Students will need to create a narrative framework or outline of their story. They will develop the branching points as it will fit into the narrative. Also, you'll want your students to create a simple "test game" in Inklewriter to help them develop their programming skills.

You should give your students enough structure to meet the objectives, but not so much that they don't have freedom to be creative. Keep the rubric simple, and don't get so technical that the students get lost in the rubric requirements, unable to engage in their story creatively. The following are six key components that will provide a good starting point.

Length

You should define a length requirement measured by the number of levels, segments, and choices provided in the Inklewriter program, and the length of the story content will follow. Figure 9.2 depicts these elements in Inklewriter.

Levels are the horizontal "rows" between the decision points or branches. In Figure 9.2, there are three levels. Segments are the individual blocks of text, and there are five in Figure 9.2. Choices are represented by the connecting lines between segments (there are five), and endings are the terminating segments (there are two). The "map view" shown in Figure 9.2 is an option within Inklewriter, letting students track their progress toward the length requirement.

Content

For historical fiction, the students must stay focused on accuracy. "No UFO's or unicorns" is a helpful statement when giving students creative liberty in historical fiction assignments. Once they decide on the event they will focus

FIGURE 9.2 Inklewriter map view depicting game choices and paths

Source: Courtesy of Hap Asiz and used with permission of Inklewriter.

on, they need to decide on characters. Consider requiring two historically accurate people in their story (a general, a soldier, a civilian, etc.). They may take liberty with the other characters, but the historical ones must interact with others as they would have during the event or time period. Students also should include historically accurate dates and places.

Interactions

Students should use at least three types of interactions with their characters and choices: an object interaction, a direction interaction, and a verbal interaction. For instance, an object interaction could be "John picks up the sword" or "John picks up the flare gun." The direction interaction could be which city they go to or which direction they go geographically. The verbal interaction is how the characters react to each other. "John got angry and yelled at Yamil," or, "John took a minute to calm himself and tried to explain the situation to Yamil." Using multiple interaction types helps bring depth and creativity to their stories.

Inklewriter Map Print-Out

This will help with grading, as you will be able to see the level, segments, choices, and endings numbers (as in Figure 9.2). For convenience in an online learning environment, you could simply view the map within Inklewriter, not requiring a physical print-out.

Bibliography

This could be submitted as a separate document or included at the end of their story. This supports the historical accuracy and interaction components of the objectives and drives the accountability students need when using videos and other elements from online sources.

Creativity

This encourages students to step away from the technical part and add more details and enhancements to the story. The students who were very tech savvy may add videos, art, pictures, and even animation. You need not weigh this item too heavily, so students focus more on the historical content elements.

Assignment Time Frame

Your students will need enough time to complete the assignment, and it is important to understand that Inklewriter will be new to most, if not all of them—not to mention game development as a process. To set your students up for success, consider the structure of the assignment time frame, and build in class time to learn and practice with Inklewriter. The following is a proposed four-week time frame that you may use or modify for your needs as appropriate.

> *Week 1*: During the first week you may spend one or two class sessions as an introduction to Choose Your Own Adventure games, Inklewriter, and the assignment.

> *Week 2*: During the second week (as well as the following weeks), the two class sessions dedicated to the assignment should be sufficient. You may have your students work on their assignments in class collaboratively or individually during both days, and you will be available to provide both Inklewriter and assignment support.

> *Week 3*: The third week should follow the same format as the second week.

> *Week 4*: The final week of the assignment is when your students may make final edits to their artifacts, and they may spend much of the session playing each other's games by sharing their laptop or tablet devices. During the last session, all work should be completed. Students may demonstrate their artifacts to the class by using a classroom monitor or projector. This should be done on a volunteer basis, with no demonstration exceeding five minutes.

Real-World Observations Regarding Engagement

The methodology described in this chapter was developed as a dissertation study and first implemented at the International Community School in Winter Park, Florida in 2014–2015. The following outcomes were derived from the study and may help you frame some expectations should you decide to include a similar activity in your classroom or other teaching and learning environment.

During the class sessions, most of the students were willing to expend a significant amount of effort in creating their game, becoming familiar with Inklewriter, the concept of Choose Your Own Adventure games, the integration of actual historical information within fictional settings, and so on. This effort is a characteristic of cognitive engagement (that is, processing of learning content, self-regulation strategies applied to content mastery, and the application of learning strategies). While performing the assigned tasks, the students demonstrated various self-regulation strategies, and they were thoughtful about their overall efforts.

Task planning was displayed by many students as they created outlines for their games. The planning was focused on what historical facts would be included in their game. Students used tools such as index cards and Post-It notes to visually depict the flow and structure of their games, and they spent much of their own time outside of class working on the assignment, a good measure of engagement. After their assignments were submitted, the students talked about what they felt could have been done better in creating their games, demonstrating ongoing engagement with the assignment.

A great part of the joy for the instructor was in seeing how much time and effort students spent in the classroom discussing clever fictional settings for their games. Some games incorporated elements of science fiction (as an appropriate narrative device), and fantastic inventions transported the main character from the present day back to the time of the Six-Day War. Other ideas were based on spy stories with top secret missions and impossible-to-break codes. Though some of students were not excited by the Middle East as a topic, they didn't avoid doing the research for their game. Again, this points out the level of interest the students had in the assignment.

An Engagement Observation Protocol (Aziz, 2016) for measuring student engagement was developed using the following 10 questions, which the teacher answered based on observing the participation and performance for each of the 14 students in the class.

1. This student often spends time outside the classroom working on the assignment.
2. This student researches or plays other interactive fiction (IF) games beyond assigned work.
3. This student works hard developing branching situations in his or her game.
4. This student is not hesitant at utilizing Inklewriter documentation.
5. This student repeatedly tests the playability of his or her IF artifact for technical functionality as well as game-play enjoyment.
6. This student seeks methods of improving or increasing the narrative pathways of the game artifact.
7. This student exhibits enthusiasm and shares verbal encouragement among the members (emotional engagement).
8. This student exhibits little or no signs of distraction or boredom and remains on task (emotional engagement).

9. This student discusses and plans game strategies and narrative paths for the game artifact well (cognitive engagement).
10. This student exhibits curiosity regarding ways to integrate assignment content on the Middle East into the fictional narrative framework (cognitive engagement).

By observing the student's participation and performance during class sessions, a picture of engagement was developed across the three domains of behavioral, emotional, and cognitive engagement. The first six items of the protocol are specific to behavioral engagement, with items 7 and 8 related to emotional engagement, and items 9 and 10 associated with cognitive engagement. For each question, the observation scoring was based on one of two possible answers:

1. Little evidence of this behavior.
2. Much evidence of this behavior.

The "Engagement Score" percentage is simply a score assigned to each student across the six observational questions regarding their behavior. If a student was scored as having exhibited much evidence of this behavior for five out of the six questions, the Engagement Score was calculated simply as $5/6 =$ 83 percent. The aggregate score for the group of students is calculated as the average score for all 14 observed students, resulting in 84 percent.

Table 9.1 (see the chapter Appendix) shows the scoring for the six questions related to behavioral engagement. (The Q prefixes denote the number of the corresponding question in the Engagement Observation Protocol, while the S prefixes denote the student being observed.)

While there are no comparative data available for these engagement scores, on the surface, engagement appears to be high. (Conversations at the end of the unit assignment confirmed this assessment based on student feedback regarding their experiences.)

Observing the Student Experience

Of course, all students are different, and there are class personalities as well that account for great variation in experience, but there are enough commonalities so that you might anticipate issues, questions, and levels of enthusiasm for your particular group of students. You can be certain that some students will be tremendously excited by the possibilities of the assignment from the beginning, while other students will need time to warm up to it. Still other students may never become enthusiastic, and they may even come back to you asking that you give them a paper or test as a substitute assignment.

One strategy that may help students along is to build a short story as a class. If you are able to display computer output on a large screen for the whole class, do so. Your students will be able to devote more attention to your example without being distracted by their own computer. In fact, Inklewriter provides an online tutorial that you can work through as a large group activity. (This tutorial is a good resource for the students to utilize should they run into their own difficulties while working on their assignment at home.) It will be most productive if you have a short story in mind, having the students simply decide on the choices to make.

Once your short example story is complete, you can introduce your students to the Inklewriter interface. The Map, Content, Write, and Read tabs are all tabs they need to be familiar with from the start, as these are the functions that will help them with organization and fulfilling the rubric requirements. After your students develop a basic familiarity with the interface, they will be more comfortable in sharing some of their story ideas, including key events and time frames.

Final Considerations

At the conclusion of the unit assignment, you will want to have a follow-up conversation with the class *en masse* about their experience. The students will be able to share what they liked or didn't like, what they found to be challenging, what parts of the assignment they would like to change, and so on. Ask your students what they thought of the assignment compared to writing a paper or making a presentation. If you can give this assignment more than once, you will be able to refine it based on your students' feedback, ultimately improving engagement over time. Ultimately, your level of comfort with Inklewriter (or some other similar development system) and your desire and ability to shepherd students through the game development process in addition to developing their assignment artifact will determine whether or not this is an activity you will find sustainable in your classroom. If your experience is anything like the authors' experiences, you could find yourself adding another instructional tool to your toolkit.

Appendix

TABLE 9.1 Behavioral engagement observations

	Q1	Q2	Q3	Q4	Q5	Q6	Engagement Score
S1	2	1	2	2	2	2	83%
S2	2	1	2	1	2	2	67%
S3	2	2	1	2	2	1	67%
S4	2	2	2	1	2	2	83%
S5	2	2	2	2	2	2	100%
S6	2	1	2	2	2	2	83%
S7	2	2	2	2	2	1	83%
S8	2	2	2	2	2	2	100%
S9	2	2	2	2	2	2	100%

	Q1	Q2	Q3	Q4	Q5	Q6	Engagement Score
S10	2	2	2	2	2	2	100%
S11	2	2	1	2	2	2	83%
S12	2	1	1	2	2	1	50%
S13	2	2	2	2	2	2	100%
S14	2	2	2	2	2	1	83%

TABLE 9.2 Emotional engagement observations

	Q7	Q8	Engagement Score
S1	2	2	100%
S2	2	2	100%
S3	2	1	50%
S4	2	2	100%
S5	2	2	100%
S6	2	2	100%
S7	2	2	100%
S8	2	2	100%
S9	1	2	50%
S10	2	2	100%
S11	1	2	50%
S12	2	2	100%
S13	2	2	100%
S14	2	2	100%

TABLE 9.3 Cognitive engagement observations

	Q9	Q10	Engagement Score
S1	2	2	100%
S2	2	2	100%
S3	2	2	100%
S4	2	2	100%
S5	2	1	50%
S6	2	2	100%
S7	1	2	50%
S8	2	2	100%
S9	2	2	100%
S10	2	2	100%
S11	2	2	100%
S12	2	2	100%
S13	2	2	100%
S14	2	2	83%

References

Aziz, F. I. (2016). *Understanding student engagement and experiences during the construction of interactive fiction in a middle school history course* [Doctoral dissertation]. University of Florida.

Robertson, J., & Good, J. (2003). Using a collaborative virtual role-play environment to foster characterization in stories. *Journal of Interactive Learning Research, 14*(1), 5–29.

Slater, M. D., & Rouner, D. (2002). Entertainment—education and elaboration likelihood: Understanding the processing of narrative persuasion. *Communication Theory, 12*(2), 173–191.

10

An Overview of Live Immersive Social Interactives and Their Educational Value for Grades 6–12

Randall Fujimoto

Real Life to Video Games

Digital Versions of Real Life

In the early days of video games, many games were simply attempting to create digital versions of real-life activities. *Pong*, the first commercially successful video game that was released in 1972, was based on real-life table tennis (Baer, 2005). Shortly after *Pong*'s release, the early text-based adventure game *Colossal Cave Adventure* (a.k.a., *Adventure*) was a game that emulated real-life exploration of caves inspired by the Mammoth Cave system in Kentucky (Wikimedia Foundation, 2020a).

In the 1980s and 1990s, the video game market came to life with the popularity of arcade gaming and first-generation console gaming. Many of the most popular games during this period were based on or influenced by real life, including *Missile Command*, which is basically a simple simulation of missile defense in a theoretical nuclear war, and *Paperboy*, a simulation game of delivering newspapers on a bicycle (Wikimedia Foundation, 2020b). Sports games are another example of video games mimicking real life. Early sports games, such as *Pole Position* (racing), *Track and Field* (Olympic sports), *Punch-Out!!* (boxing), and *Tecmo Bowl* (football), all tried to simulate real-life sports with as much fidelity as possible.

Digital Realism: Form and Function

Because of the constant improvements in graphics technology over time, we now have games that are often indistinguishable from real-life video. The rapid advance of graphics chips and processing speeds in consoles and computers has allowed game developers to create incredibly lifelike environments and characters. Playing games like *Red Dead Redemption 2, MS Flight Simulator 2020*, and *Forza Motorsport 7* makes you feel like you are navigating in a real world instead of a digitally simulated one.

While graphics technology was bringing lifelike appearance to video games, game designers were working on improving the gameplay to make games feel more like living in real life. Each year, sports games like *Madden NFL* and *NBA 2K* constantly improved not just the look of the games but also how players moved and acted to be more like real-life sports action. *The Sims* video game series started in 2000 with the first game primarily focused on fulfilling your avatar's simple needs, such as food, shelter, and entertainment. By 2017, with the release of *The Sims 4*, the gameplay had advanced to incorporate many more real-life qualities, including an emotion system that resulted in more complex conversations between avatars.

These improvements in the form (appearance) and function (gameplay) have made video games look and feel incredibly lifelike today. This realism has resulted in a more immersive experience, which has made players feel more like they are playing in a real-life world.

Video Games to Real Life

Throughout the history of media formats, there has always been the media adaptation from one format to another. Books, television shows, movies, and games are often adaptations from one of the other formats, and all of them often are adaptations or portrayals of real life. There are constantly evolving medium shifts that become popular at various times, such as the development of video games based on big-budget movies starting in the mid-1980s.

We have now started to see an increasing shift from digital video games back to new types of real-life games in the physical world. Real-life gaming experiences like puzzle hunts, paintball and lasertag games, and LARPs (live action roleplaying) have been around for many years, but generally they have been more for niche audiences. Recently, we have seen more real-life adaptations of video games that are becoming more a part of mainstream society.

Examples

Alternate reality games are real-world, multiplayer games that utilize various physical and digital media to progress through a narrative. They became popular in the early 2000s as a real-world experience of an adventure video game. NBC's *American Ninja Warrior* debuted in 2009 as a real-life, obstacle course gaming contest that resembles the gameplay of side-scrolling action video games. In 2015, a life-sized, in-person version of *Pac-Man* was featured in a Bud Light Super Bowl commercial. Augmented reality (AR) games, like

Pokémon Go and *Minecraft Earth*, use AR technology to bring in-person, real-life gaming to the masses.

Escape Rooms

In recent years, escape room games have become one of the most popular examples of gaming coming to real life, with around 2,000 escape rooms now operating in the U.S. (Spira, 2019). Escape rooms have their roots in puzzle-solving, adventure video games, such as *Myst* and the Sierra On-Line games from the 1990s. In an escape room, you are basically playing inside of a video game-like environment, trying to quickly solve puzzles and escape the room before the timer runs out. Escape rooms are now evolving to include narrative, actors, and new technologies, such as virtual and augmented reality, to make the gameplay even more immersive and like real life.

Immersive Theater

Although not actual gaming experiences, immersive theater productions are interactive events that place people in active, participatory roles. In contrast to traditional theater or movies where the audience sits back passively and absorbs content, immersive theater provides an interactive space where people feel they are part of the experience. For example, in *Sleep No More*, one of the most famous and popular immersive theater productions, participants actively follow around one or more actors to piece together a narrative that is unfolding simultaneously throughout a five-story building. Having the audience actively participate in a simulated environment can make immersive theater feel like a real-life gaming experience.

Live Immersive Social Interactives

Escape rooms and immersive theater are examples of a Live Immersive Social Interactive (LISI), which is a broader media category that encapsulates experiences that resemble video game-like experiences in real life. "Live" refers to the experience taking place synchronously in real time and in-person, either physically or virtually. "Immersive" means that participants feel a sense of immersion and engagement in the setting of the experience. "Social" implies that the experience features strong social presence and interaction. Finally, "Interactive" means that people are actively participating in the experience interacting with other people, characters, and/or the environment.

In addition to escape rooms and immersive theater, LISIs can encompass other current and future new media storytelling experiences, including transmedia/mixed-media productions, augmented reality (AR) interactives, virtual reality (VR) immersives, and location-based experiences. LISIs can be a physical, in-person experience and/or a remote experience that utilizes digital platforms such as AR and VR that provide live, social presence to the users.

Transmedia/Mixed-Media

Transmedia and mixed-media productions are ones that utilize a variety of media to immerse participants in evolving narratives. Alternate reality games (ARGs) are real-world, multiplayer experiences in which players play as themselves in a simulated world to progress through an emerging storyline. ARGs often utilize both physical and digital media to communicate clues and other gameplay that allow participants to view the real world as a gaming environment. *The Nest* is an immersive audio experience that utilizes actual audio cassettes to provide a narrative experience in an immersive-designed storage facility. Similarly, *The Demigods* is an audio experience at the Getty Villa in Los Angeles that immerses users into the world of the *Percy Jackson* book series. There are various ARGs that are specifically designed for education, such as *The Ward Game* that featured the storyline of the book *One Flew Over the Cuckoo's Nest* (Darvasi, 2016) and *Terrarium* that focused on learning about climate change (Center, 2020).

Augmented Reality

Whereas transmedia and mixed-media add media to create a video game-like experience in real life, augmented reality typically uses a mobile phone or tablet to add a gaming layer on top of the real world. Popular augmented reality games like *Pokémon Go* and *Minecraft Earth* allow players to navigate the real world to capture Pokémons or place *Minecraft* buildings. Various AR scavenger hunt apps, such as *Goosechase*, utilize QR codes, images, and videos to turn the real world into an immersive gameplay experience. *The Raven* utilizes AR audio glasses along with Bluetooth-connected lantern sensors to provide a narrative experience for users navigating through the immersive space.

Virtual Reality

The "L" in LISI refers to "Live," meaning that the experience takes place in real time and in-person, either physically or virtually. Therefore, LISIs include virtual reality experiences in which participants are in a shared VR space that provides social presence with other participants and characters. For example, *The Under Presents* is a VR immersive theater production that takes place in a shared virtual space occupied by both participants and actors. Another VR immersive theater production is *Chained: A Victorian Nightmare*, which integrates a physical, in-person setting in with the virtual production. Being in a shared virtual environment together with other real-life people can make VR have similar social presence as in-person experiences, especially when they can incorporate real-life sensory experiences, including touch and even smell.

Location-Based Experiences

LISIs can be designed for a particular location, from an individual room or building to an entire plot of land. *Meow Wolf's House of Eternal Return* is a converted bowling alley in Santa Fe, New Mexico, that features over 70 rooms of interactive, explorable art wrapped up in a narrative experience. *AREA15* is an immersive space located in Las Vegas that contains 40,000 square feet of interactive art and experiential experiences. *Star Wars Galaxy's Edge* is a 14-acre, immersive experience at Disneyland and Walt Disney World that's been described as "essentially a giant video game" (Carey, n.d.). *Evermore Park* in Utah is an 11-acre, immersive theme park where participants can "interact with characters, go on quests, and become a part of the world of Evermore."

Other location-based experiences include *Can You See Me Now*, which is a game played in a real-life city space that is overlaid with a virtual city viewable through handheld devices. There are also 3D projection technologies, such as the *BEAM Interactive Projector Game System* and the *Lightform AR Projector*, which can turn rooms and other physical locations into location-based LISIs.

Educational Benefits

The use of LISIs for educational purposes has vast potential because of the format's design flexibility, ability to cover content, and underlying foundation on well-established learning principles.

Design Flexibility

To bring a game-like experience to users, LISIs can utilize a wide variety of physical and digital media, including images, video, art, audio, and live actors. LISIs can also utilize both physical media and digital media together, like the *Chained: A Victorian Nightmare* production which uses a physical setting and VR, with live actors present in both. Educational LISI designers can make use of this wide variety of media to create deeper and more engaging learning experiences.

Like a video game, LISI designers have the flexibility to use various settings, characters, interactive elements, and storylines. However, unlike a digital video game, LISI designers have the freedom to also use physical media and real-life people to create unique designs that can engage users in ways different from a video game experience. This flexibility can help educational LISI designers to utilize classroom or other school space to bring a video game-like experience to students.

Content

LISIs can cover practically any academic content area, from basic literacy and numeracy skills to science, humanities, and any other subject matter. The design flexibility of LISIs allows educational LISI designers to use characters, settings, narratives, and gameplay in myriad ways to engage learners in content and cover required learning objectives. LISIs can provide deeper and stronger learning than traditional classroom learning environments because of their ability to immerse students in a contextual learning space. An example of an educational LISI is *Manzanar Immersive*, which is an immersive theater and escape game hybrid experience about the history of Japanese-Americans during World War II.

In addition to subject matter content, LISIs can also help participants learn and develop important life and learning skills. LISIs can promote social-emotional learning by providing opportunities for participants to become immersed in situations in which they need to interact with others in meaningful ways. LISIs can help students develop teamwork, communication, and other 21st-century skills in addition to various soft skills, such as empathy and grit, and character skills/values, such as kindness and humility.

Educational Rationale

The primary reason that LISIs can be effective learning experiences is their inherent foundation on well-established learning principles and theories.

Active Learning

Games can be effective as a learning medium because, unlike other instructional media such as books or videos, games require active participation. Active participation promotes active learning, which can provide higher order thinking and deeper learning of learning objectives. Like educational games, LISIs can be good active learning environments that allow participants to deeply engage with learning content and situations. Educational LISIs can also feature collaborative, team-based learning activities that require active participation from each member of the group and promote teamwork and communication skills.

Situated Learning

In addition to being an active experience, LISIs are also situated experiences in which learning occurs in the context of a situation or story. Situated learning provides a stronger just-in-time learning experience in which learning participants "learn while doing" instead of the traditional "learn then do" (e.g., read the textbook, then take a test) approach used throughout much of education. LISIs provide context that gives participants a purpose to learn and makes the learning more meaningful than, for example, arbitrary worksheet questions about something meaningless to students.

Discovery Learning

LISIs can also provide a space for participants to explore and learn through discovery of content embedded in the experience. Discovery learning allows users to build on their previous knowledge and experience to construct new knowledge as they navigate through the LISI. The five core principles of discovery learning: problem solving, learner management, integrating and connecting, information analysis and interpretation, and failure and feedback, can all be featured in well-designed educational LISIs (Pappas, 2014).

Social Learning

Because LISIs are multiplayer experiences, they can provide good opportunities for social learning in which people learn from others. LISIs can support various social learning principles, including observational learning, roleplay, and identification through group gameplay, activities, and discussion opportunities (Swagatika, 2017). Also, because LISIs take place in live, real-time settings either physically in-person or in a virtual space, they can provide strong social presence that can make social learning even more effective.

Intrinsic Motivation

As an immersive, interactive, social experience, a LISI can provide intrinsic motivation that engages participants throughout the entire production. Four intrinsic motivators that LISIs can promote are: social, purpose, autonomy, and mastery (GameTrain Learning, 2020). Social motivation in LISIs comes from being a social experience in which participants help one another and enjoy the experience together. Story and goal-oriented gameplay in LISIs can give users a sense of purpose to progress through the experience. LISIs can provide a sense of autonomy to participants by providing various choices and exploratory environments. Finally, LISIs can give participants a sense of mastery as they complete various tasks and activities to progress through to the end of the experience.

Gameful Mindset

One of the most important reasons why LISIs have such educational potential is that they are primarily designed for today's gamer generation. Because of the countless hours playing games, young people's brains have literally been rewired to think and learn differently than in previous generations. Specifically, they have a "gameful mindset," which describes the ways that gamers think, learn, and live in the world, and is characterized by how they experience playing games. Those with a gameful mindset embrace failure, constantly iterate, expect continuous feedback, practice just-in-time learning, and seek flow experiences (GameTrain Learning, 2019). Educational LISI designers can integrate all of these characteristics to fully engage those with a gameful mindset.

The Future

Today, games are a major contributor to the digital media consumption of people in the U.S., where people spend an average of over five hours per day on a mobile or desktop device (Watson, 2020). With both adults and kids spending increasingly more time-consuming digital media, there is concern that people are spending too much of their lives glued to a device.

LISIs are becoming more popular in response to this overload of digital media consumption. LISIs provide opportunities for people to be socially present with other human beings instead of escaping into their digital devices by themselves.

In the future, we will undoubtedly see new types of LISIs that connect people together in new game-like spaces. Open-world games, such as *Minecraft*, have given rise to the anticipated creation of a metaverse, a persistent, shared, virtual world in which people have simulated, real-life experiences interacting with each other and the simulated world. There are a number of companies, including some game companies such as Roblox, that are working toward bringing a metaverse to the masses, similar to the plotlines of the books *Snowcrash* and *Ready Player One*.

There is great potential for future LISIs to not just entertain but also educate students in more engaging ways about any academic content or valuable learning and life skills. The effectiveness of future educational LISIs will rely on the creativity and world-building ability of designers, who might be professionals but could also be educators, students, or anyone else who has the desire to engage students through a new, interactive medium. Teachers can turn their classrooms—possibly with the help of their students—into LISI learning environments. Educational LISIs can also be used in after-school programs, libraries, museums, other educational organizations, and socially conscious businesses.

Most importantly, LISIs appeal to today's "gamer generation" of students, who approach learning with a gameful mindset. These students need engaging and meaningful experiences to show them that learning is not a burdensome task but something enjoyable and stimulating, just as learning is in a video game.

Resources

Breakout https://breakoutgames.com/.
A site dedicated to escape rooms around the country and online. The escape rooms are 60-minute collaborative experiences with a blended model of solving puzzles.

Projects/Productions

Can You See Me Now? *Blast Theory*. www.blasttheory.co.uk/projects/
can-you-see-me-now/, 27th, M. A. A., Adams, M., 6th, J. la C. M., &
Courq, J. la. (2020, May 14).
A game of chase played online and on the streets. Online players compete against performers on the streets. Tracked by satellites, Blast Theory's runners appear online next to your player on a map of the city. On the streets, handheld computers showing the positions of online players guide the runners in tracking you down. Created in collaboration with the University of

Nottingham's Mixed Reality Lab. This game helped pioneer the use of GPS in outdoor games.

Chained: A Victorian Nightmare. *MWM Interactive.*
www.becomechained.com/.
A Virtual Reality adaptation of one of Charles Dickens' masterpieces, *A Christmas Carol.* Players experience the world Dickens created, and maybe, after playing, they will read the novel as well!

About Meow Wolf House of Eternal Return. Meow Wolf: Interactive
Art Experiences. https://meowwolf.com/visit/santa-fe/about.
If you are ever in Santa Fe, New Mexico this interactive exploration of art is extraordinary.

The Nest. www.thenestshow.com/.
Immersive and Interactive Theater: Los Angeles.

> *The Nest* is an intimate, live experience for two audience members at a time, combining elements of immersive theater, narrative video games, serialized podcasts, and escape rooms into a new way to tell a story. Equipped with a flashlight, search through personal effects, explore your surroundings, and listen to audio cassettes to piece together the dramatic narrative of Josie's life.
>
> (from the home page)

Immersive Entertainment & Events Complex in Vegas. *Area15.*
(2020, October 7). https://area15.com/.
An interactive space in Las Vegas that features a wide variety of immersive experiences.

Manzanar Immersive. (n.d.). http://japantownproductions.com/manzanar-immersive/
In Virtual Manzanar Immersive, up to six people connect through Zoom to interact with the story, actors, and the other participants. The experience lasts approximately one hour, including a short debriefing session at the end of each experience.
Percy Jackson Audio Tour: The Demigods. *Getty Museum.* www.getty.edu/education/kids_families/percy_jackson/.

The McKittrick Hotel https://mckittrickhotel.com/about/.
Located in the Chelsea region (West 27th Street) of Manhattan in New York City, this hotel plays home to several immersive theatrical performances produced by Emursive and Punchdrunk (a British theater company).

The Under Presents. *Tender Claws*. https://tenderclaws.com/theunderpresents.

A multiplayer adventure that brings together immersive theater and Virtual Reality now available at home or school on STEAM for virtual headsets: https://store.steampowered.com/app/1232940/The_Under_Presents/.

References

Baer, R. (2005). *Video games: In the beginning*. Rolenta Press.

Carey, B. (n.d.). We visited Disney's Star Wars land and this is what we saw. *CNET*. www.cnet.com/news/star-wars-galaxys-edge-everything-you-need-to-know-about-disneys-newest-theme-park-food-drinks-rides/

Center, L. (2020, June 24). Alternate reality game: A Labyrinth offers a model for new media in a distanced age. *In Practice: The Official University of Chicago Arts Blog*. www.uchicagoartsblog.art/archive/2020/5/27/alternate-reality-game-a-labyrinth

Darvasi, P. (2016, January 17). *The Ward Game: How McMurphy, McLuhan and MacGyver might help free us from McEducation*. www.ludiclearning.org/2016/01/17/the-ward-game-how-mcmurphy-mcluhan-and-macgyver-might-help-free-us-from-mceducation/

GameTrain Learning. (2019, March 18). *Gameful Mindset*. http://gametrainlearning.org/articles/gameful-mindset/

GameTrain Learning. (2020, July 9). *Motivation in Game-Based Learning*. http://gametrainlearning.org/articles/motivation-game-based-learning/

Pappas, C. (2014, Oct. 8). *Instructional design models and theories: The Discovery learning model*. https://elearnin gindustry.com/discovery-learning-model

Spira, L. (2019, August 10). Three years of Room Escapes: The growth of the US market. *Room Escape Artist*. https://roomescapeartist.com/2017/07/30/three-years-of-room-escapes-the-growth-of-the-us-market/

Swagatika, M. (2017, March 15). *6 Important Principles of Social Learning: Process: Learning: Psychology*. www.psychologydiscussion.net/learning/social-learning/6-important-principles-of-social-learning-process-learning-psychology/3309

Watson, A. (2020, March 23). Topic: Media use. *Statista*. www.statista.com/topics/1536/media-use/

Wikimedia Foundation. (2020a, July 26). Colossal Cave Adventure. *Wikipedia*. https://en.wikipedia.org/wiki/Colossal_Cave_Adventure

Wikimedia Foundation. (2020b, October 14). Golden age of arcade video games. *Wikipedia*. https://en.wikipedia.org/wiki/Golden_age_of_arcade_video_games

11

Don't Split the Party
Using Games to Enhance Social-Emotional Learning Strategies

Jonathan Cassie

Whether played in a digitally mediated space like those offered by video games or face-to-face across a tabletop, roleplaying games provide a uniquely useful tool to educators interested in developing the social-emotional learning (SEL) skills of their students. The Collaborative for Academic, Social and Emotional Learning (CASEL) defines social-emotional learning as

> the process through which children and adults acquire and effectively apply the knowledge, attitudes, and skills necessary to understand and manage emotions, set and achieve positive goals, feel and show empathy for others, establish and maintain positive relationships and make responsible decisions.
>
> (CASEL, 2020)

This chapter will consider the ways roleplaying games can contribute to healthy, positive development of students' capacity to demonstrate and deploy self-awareness, self-management, responsible decision making, relationship skills and social awareness in the interest of their long-term growth.

Research conducted since the early 1990s confirms that investment in the development of non-cognitive social-emotional learning skills has a demonstrable effect on outcomes for adolescents and young adults. A meta-analysis of 213 diverse SEL programs conducted in 2011 documented the benefits of social-emotional programming. This study showed that SEL programming significantly improved students' social skills and their positive social behavior as well as their academic performance (Durlak et al., 2011). Moreover, this study showed that students exposed to SEL programming had statistically significant reductions in emotional distress and conduct difficulties (Durlak et al., 2011). Taylor et al. (2017) showed that these gains endure, often into adulthood, with students who participated in SEL programming showing statistically significant improvement in academic performance. In addition, the 2017 study showed that students involved in SEL programs had stronger social and emotional skills and capacities and that these were the most significant predictor of sustained, across-the-board social and academic benefits (Taylor et al., 2017).

The genre of roleplaying games began with the publication of *Dungeons & Dragons (D&D)* in 1974. *D&D* laid out the fundamental structure of roleplaying games which all subsequent games follow, reflect or critique. The structure of roleplaying games, be they tabletop or online, centers on the relationship between three elements. First, every player interacts with the game environment through a character, generally created by the player and brought to life by the player. Roleplaying characters have certain physical and mental properties described and codified by the game system as well as an assortment of skills through which the character can manipulate and change the game environment through their decisions. Second, characters are immersed in a game environment which is described by the gamemaster (the individual in charge of description, managing the flow of the narration, enacting all characters in the game not under the control of players, adjudicating conflicts and making binding decisions when the rules of the game aren't clear). These game environments have conventionally been high fantasy settings inspired by the works of J.R.R. Tolkien and other fantasy authors, but in contemporary gaming, they can be virtually anything. Third, characters regularly interact with other characters in a group context. In tabletop roleplaying games, adventuring parties work together to solve problems, advance the story and learn together. In online games where a solo-play mode is a critical part of the game, the individual player interacts with the game world in a one-on-one fashion and joins groups to complete more difficult game content. Many of these groups are one-off groups designed to address a particular kind of content in game, but others, in the form of guilds, constitute long-term social structures within the game. Regardless of format, roleplaying games have the unique capacity to give young people an opportunity to practice SEL skills in a structured setting distinct from the "real world." This character-based practice in a game environment can have an impact on the players' development of SEL skills in their real lives, as evidenced by the feedback I received from interviews with parents and students connected to The Game Academy, a California-based education non-profit that runs summer camps and enrichment classes for students with the goal of advancing their social, emotional and economic success.

Self-Awareness

CASEL (2020) defines self-awareness as "the abilities to understand one's own emotions, thoughts, and values and how they influence behavior across contexts," going on to identify integrating personal and social identities, self-efficacy, a growth mindset, purposefulness, honesty and integrity as key elements of self-awareness. The act of taking on a character in a roleplaying game fundamentally engages these skills. The simple act of creating a roleplaying character obligates the player to consider their character's personal and social identity. In *D&D*, for example, players are required to generate a set of statistics that enumerate the character's Strength, Dexterity, Constitution, Intelligence, Wisdom and Charisma, all of which have an effect not just on how the character is conceived and would conceive of herself in their milieu, but also in the ways that character can best interact with the world. Most roleplaying game systems begin with a process like this, regardless of how they are structured, creating a framework in which the player can explore the aspects of self-awareness from the vantage point of their character. One particularly noteworthy character creation system is found in the game *Numenera* and a version of the game for noticeably young children called *No Thank You, Evil!* In these games, the character creation process leads you to writing a sentence that describes your character with the form: I am an [adjective] [noun] who [verbs]. It is simple, elegant and creates a context for enormously powerful development of character-based identity formation.

Young people are immersed in a cultural context where these notions are easily understood. Take the Marvel Cinematic Universe as an example. The character of the Hulk when we first meet him is powerfully described by his strength (formidable) and his constitution (he's tough and resistant to physical harm). Having said that, he's not especially dextrous (Hulk Smash!) or clever. This makes the revelation of his "Professor Hulk" persona in *The Avengers: Endgame* all the more delightful, because it shows his growth and change. One Game Academy parent, who I will call Ben, said of his daughter:

> the most interesting part of playing for her is creating a character. When she makes a new character, she wants to explore what that character can do in the world and how she will fit in with the other characters her friends are playing.

Another Game Academy parent, who I will call Rick, noted that, for his child,

> dealing with complex emotions is difficult. when he was much younger he would get angry and frustrated and that would lead to these bombastic outbursts . . . sometimes when he would be playing with groups, there would be times where a rule wouldn't be followed correctly or someone at the table would tell him that he was wrong and he would full-out lose it.

Another Game Academy parent, who I will call Alice, observed that her child "struggles with her sense of self-image. She's very hard on herself . . . but when she's doing gaming, she's creating character, and that character has strengths, and she has to exercise those strengths." Doing this from the lens of her character was the essential part of Alice's child's development. She noted that "she has the ability, through the character, to build her sense of self-efficacy." This is in keeping with the findings of Rosselet and Stauffer (2013), who showed that roleplaying games are a positive venue for children to develop their self-concept and explore their personal identity.

Self-Management

CASEL (2020) defines self-management as "the abilities to manage one's emotions, thoughts and behaviors effectively in different situations and to achieve goals and aspirations." Storytelling in a roleplaying setting can be both pleasurable and highly stressful at the same time. Learning to navigate this through the act of game playing can be deeply shaping of a young person's development. Wagner (2016) studied the play experience of 13 young children over the course of six roleplaying game experiences. The children, many of whom were given the responsibility of being the gamemaster, reflected on their experiences, noting that although their experiences were far from perfect from a viewpoint of self-management, there was definite progress. One child said:

> I would say that, learning how to gamemaster, people . . . begin to learn respect and learn how to respect their peers in different situations. I would say we have not reached the height of the place . . . but I think we are definitely on our way there.
>
> (Wagner, 2016, pp. 21–22)

Blackmon (1994) further supports this longer-term development of self-management skills, telling the story of one patient who was able to use *D&D* to become more familiar with his feelings and as importantly, be able to control them. Game Academy parent Rick observed that his child has developed an ability to recognize when an emotional outburst is coming and to deal with it. Rick said that

> he's had a great amount of growth. He's developed coping mechanisms to help deal with his frustrations. He's been involved in the Game Academy for four years and when he started playing, he would have an emotional outburst every game. Since then, I can count on maybe one hand now the times he's had an outburst. I've seen it maybe once or twice in the last two years.

Social Awareness

Games are uniquely social experiences and roleplaying games especially so. CASEL (2020)'s perspective on social awareness is that it is "the abilities to understand the perspectives of and empathize with others, including those from diverse backgrounds, cultures, and contexts." The expanding creative marketplace for "indie roleplaying games," generally written by a single author and representing a particular worldview about society and about gaming, has made for a roleplaying space that is uniquely suited to the development of social awareness. In particular, the work of Avery Alder has charted a strong perspective on the capacity for games to develop social awareness. She says: "I believe a few things pretty seriously: We are strongly moved and informed by stories. Stories can bring communities together. Stories reveal who we are" (Alder, 2020). Her games reflect this. In *The Quiet Year*, players play as a post-apocalyptic civilization emerging from a terrible crisis that has one year to restore itself to some level of order and dignity before the next challenge emerges. In this game of collaborative mapmaking, each individual player, on their turn, draws a conflict/conundrum from a deck of cards and then stipulates how the community is going to resolve that problem. As the community's decisions begin to shape the community's experience, there are regular opportunities for other players to redirect the community's efforts, turn them in another direction or deepen connection based on a shared commitment to a goal. Because the individual isn't the point of a game like *The Quiet Year*, players are immediately placed in a context where perspective-taking, empathy development and coming to understand diverse contexts is not just foregrounded, it is in fact the entire point.

Responsible Decision Making

It almost goes without saying that in roleplaying games, the only difference between a character who is still living and one who has shuffled off this mortal coil is responsible decision making. Recklessness in roleplaying games is frequently rewarded with the axe and the opportunity to re-roll a new character to join the adventuring group. CASEL (2020)'s definition of responsible decision making states that it is "the abilities to make caring and constructive choices about personal behavior and social interactions across diverse situations." One game that puts this dimension of social-emotional learning front-and-center is *This War of Mine*, which exists in both video game and tabletop board game formats. Game play and story in both formats are similar. The player or players take on collective responsibility for a group of survivors trying to endure a siege in the city of Pogoren, an analogue for Sarajevo during the Bosnian War. Because the city is experiencing a devastating civil war, shelter is in ruins, food and bandages are in short supply and the potential for violent assault is ever-present. Players have to make thousands of decisions over the course of the game to maximize the likelihood that the characters they are managing survive long enough for a truce to be declared, opening the city to relief. Because the survivors are cold, hungry, often injured and generally demoralized, the choices afforded the players are extraordinarily difficult to balance, sometimes obligating the players to provide food to a relatively healthy individual and deny it to a hungrier, sicker character, because the uninjured person is the only one who might survive a violent encounter outside of the shelter. Having to make decisions that are both clearly constructive, but also seem uncaring, presents players with a great opportunity to reflect on their own behaviors, their moral compass and how their decisions affect others.

Relationship Skills

Game playing of all sorts is quite effective at building "the abilities to establish and maintain healthy and supportive relationships and to effectively navigate settings with diverse individuals and groups" (CASEL, 2020). Every parent and student I interviewed from The Game Academy seconded this perspective. Parent Ben observed that because of his daughter's roleplaying experiences, she was able to build and sustain relationships even over a digitally mediated context like Discord. He said:

> The way she thinks about herself has been shaped by being part of the Game Academy. She found her niche, her community . . . where I see this most is in her ability to have friends online and make her own roleplaying games on Discord. She and her friends, they're building three to six different worlds with these friends and these stories are about adolescent angst. That's what my daughter is choosing to pursue.

Parent Rick noted that game play really helped his son notice and respect the needs of others. "He can see different types of characters and players in their fictional cultures and how those cultures have different ways of behaving and acting and celebrating. . . . roleplaying has definitely helped him understand different people and to build connection with them." Parent Alice said of her daughter:

> doing cooperative games like D&D where you have to work with people and where it isn't so much about winning but doing what's right for one's self and more importantly others, looking at the group and what's good for the group is what really matters. Gaming gives them the opportunity to practice relationship building and for a kid with social anxiety, it can really help create a safe space, if the gamemaster is doing a good job.

Social-emotional learning is central to the development of the whole child into a compassionate, capable adult who can exercise their rights and carry out their responsibilities in a democratic society. Ample evidence shows that programs that develop social-emotional skills pay huge dividends. Roleplaying games, whether they are played on a screen or on a tabletop, are one highly effective and capable way of developing social-emotional skills and ought to be a part of any school's approach to this topic.

Resources

While I cite five games in this article, all roleplaying games use similar play strategies and could impart similar benefits. *Dungeons & Dragons, 5th Edition*, the classic high fantasy game, is the most accessible of all roleplaying games and can be found virtually anywhere (even in mass-market retailers like Target).

Numenera and *No Thank You, Evil!* are published by Monte Cook Games and can be found at specialist game retailers or at www.montecookgames.com.

The Quiet Year can also be found at specialist game retailers or at Avery Alder's digital storefront: https://buriedwithoutceremony.com/the-quiet-year.

This War of Mine is both a videogame and a board game. They're similar enough to give the same feeling during play and different enough that both ought to be tried. The videogame can be found here: www.epicgames.com/store/en-US/product/this-war-of-mine/home, and the board game can be found at specialist game retailers or at Amazon. For those interested in discussing this theme, the podcast Game Level Learn can be found here: www.gamelevellearn.com/podcast/.

References

Alder, A. (n.d.). Retrieved October 07, 2020, from http://buriedwithoutceremony.com

Blackmon, W. D. (1994). Dungeons and Dragons: The use of a fantasy game in the psychotherapeutic treatment of a young adult. *American Journal of Psychotherapy, 48*(4), 624–632.

CASEL. (n.d.). Retrieved October 09, 2020, from https://casel.org/

Durlak, J. A., Weissberg, R. P., Dymnicki, A. B., Taylor, R. D., & Schellinger, K. B. (2011). The impact of enhancing students' social and emotional learning: A meta-analysis of school- based universal interventions. *Child Development, 82*(1), 405–432.

Rosselet, J. G., & Stauffer, S. D. (2013). Using group role-playing games with gifted children and adolescents: A psychosocial intervention model. *International Journal of Play Therapy, 22*(4), 173–192.

Taylor, R., Oberle, E., Durlak, J. A., & Weissberg, R. P. (2017). Promoting positive youth development through school-based social and emotional learning interventions: A meta analysis of follow-up effects. *Child Development, 88*, 1156–1181. https://doi.org/10.1111/cdev.12864

Wagner, B. N. (2016). *Roleplaying to develop self-regulation*. Retrieved September 30, 2020, from Sophia, the St. Catherine University repository website: https://sophia.stkate.edu/maed/157

12

Promoting Student Health and Well-Being with Digital Games

Claudia-Santi F. Fernandes, Tyra M. Pendergrass Boomer, Kimberly Hieftje, Andrew Evanko and Lynn E. Fiellin

Introduction

The Coronavirus Disease 2019 (COVID-19) pandemic transformed our nation's education system in a matter of weeks from a brick and mortar learning environment to an online one. Massive efforts were made by teachers with different levels of comfort in using technology to adapt their curriculum and deliver content virtually. What often takes years to craft in effective pedagogy using technology was done in record time. This transition created an increase of stress for many. The role of schools not only serves to deliver educational content to our youth, but also offers support services as well as promotes health and well-being throughout the school day. Many schools were and remain concerned about effectively serving the needs of students academically, emotionally, and physically (Lee, 2020). With the ubiquity of technology in today's society (Lenhart et al., 2008) and the promising approaches that focus on developing core competencies in social and emotional learning (SEL; see Figure 12.1; Dalton et al., 2020), is it possible that the silver lining in this shift is we, as a society, are forced to rethink learning? Are we able to serve students virtually in the same manner, if not better, by adapting pedagogy and creating systems of support online, such as increased access to healthcare services via telehealth, positive virtual learning environments, and more? If we address the digital divide first, are we able to effectively serve the needs of students?

With the value of relationship building at its core, this is possible and—in fact—there is evidence that various transitions are proving beneficial. Beyond

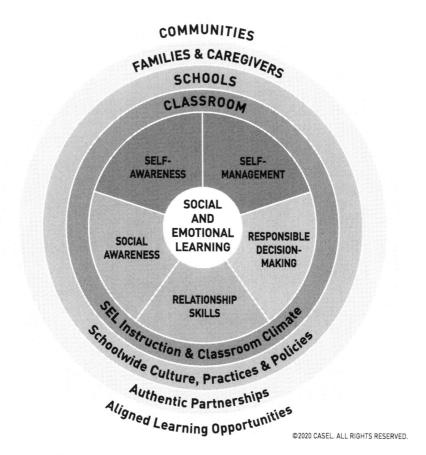

©2020 CASEL. ALL RIGHTS RESERVED.

FIGURE 12.1 CASEL's Core Social and Emotional Learning (SEL) Competencies

Source: ©2020 CASEL, all rights reserved, www.casel.org

COVID-19, we now have an opportunity to not only rethink learning in the age of technology but fully embrace it given the current pandemic. While we know that lives at home for youth can be complicated and that some families will require additional in-person supports, we recognize that online learning can provide considerable value and beneficial opportunities that otherwise would not be available. To support this transition, our digital, theory-, and evidence-informed interventions complement or offer standalone opportunities to help this shift and enhance positive youth development (Duncan, Hieftje, Culyba, & Fiellin, 2014; Duncan, Hieftje, Pendergrass, Sawyer, & Fiellin, 2018; Fiellin, Hieftje, & Duncan, 2014; Fiellin, Hieftje, Pendergrass, Kyriakides, Duncan, Dziura, . . . & Fiellin, 2017; Fiellin, Kyriakides, Hieftje, Pendergrass, Duncan, Dziura, Sawyer, & Fiellin, 2016; Hieftje, Duncan, & Fiellin, 2014; Hieftje, Duncan, Florsheim, Sawyer, & Fiellin, 2019; Hieftje, Duncan, Pendergrass, Sawyer, & Fiellin, 2016; Hieftje, Edelman, Camenga, & Fiellin, 2013; Hieftje,

Fernandes, Lin, & Fiellin, 2019; Hieftje, Pendergrass, Montanaro, Kyriakides, Florsheim, & Fiellin, 2018; Hieftje, Rosenthal, Camenga, Edelman, & Fiellin, 2012b; Montanaro, Fiellin, Fakhouri, Kyriakides, & Duncan, 2015).

While COVID-19 has paused much in our lives, healthy child and adolescent development continues and remains imperative—in fact, critical in every decision made moving forward. Prior to COVID-19, one in six U.S. youth aged 6–17 experienced a mental health disorder each year (National Alliance on Mental Illness) and many believe that there will be an increased need of support among youth due to COVID-19 (Liang et al., 2020). Prevention approaches typically focus on aspects related to the *Whole Child* approach as well as the *Coordinated School Health (CSH)* approach to promote well-being and healthy development among youth as well as increase protective factors and reduce risk factors (Baiden et al., 2019; Payton et al., 2000; Weisz et al., 2005).

The *Whole Child* approach is student-centered and focuses on a safe and supportive school climate where SEL is integrated into the fabric of a school by fostering skills, habits, and mindsets that enable healthy and positive youth development (Darling-Hammond & Cook-Harvey, 2018; Liew et al., 2010). The *CSH* approach is a system-based approach addressing eight components of the school as a venue for health promotion and disease prevention services (Lewallen et al., 2015). These approaches together, and expanded upon to better reflect current research and practice, are defined as *The Whole School, Whole Community, Whole Child Model (WSCC): A collaborative approach to learning and health* (see Figure 12.2; Lewallen et al., 2015) and include 10 components: 1) health education; 2) physical education and physical activity; 3) health services; 4) healthy and safe school environment; 5) counseling, psychological, and social services; 6) family engagement; 7) community involvement; 8) employee wellness; 9) nutrition environment and services; and, 10) social and emotional climate. Through a systematic, integrated, and coordinated approach, the *WSCC Model* addresses the physical and emotional needs of students. Research continues to corroborate that healthier students are better learners (Basch, 2011), and supporting students' mental health and SEL is a critical aspect of learning and general health (Durlak et al., 2011). While the majority of school-based approaches to address health, learning, and well-being rely solely on in-person school- and classroom-based implementation (Corcoran et al., 2018; Durlak & DuPre, 2008), there is clearly a dire need for online offerings and this includes digital games.

Digital games have a well-established role in health education and behavior change. The development and use of these "serious games," or games that are designed to educate, train, or change behavior as they entertain players (Stokes, 2005), has substantially grown over the past decade (Djaouti et al., 2011). Several systematic reviews have demonstrated the effects of serious games on improving a variety of health outcomes in youth including diabetes, asthma, physical activity, nutrition, medication adherence, eating disorders, sexually transmitted diseases, management of chronic disease, depression, and anxiety (Barnes & Prescott, 2018). To address health

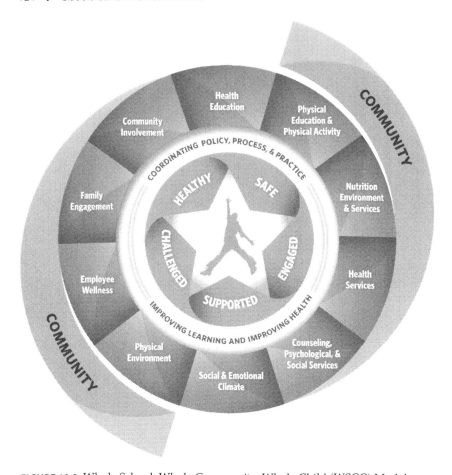

FIGURE 12.2 Whole School, Whole Community, Whole Child (WSCC) Model

Source: Reprinted with permission of The Centers for Disease Control and Prevention (CDC) and the Association for Supervision and Curriculum Development (ASCD)

outcomes, digital games offer opportunities for simulated role-play, which is known to be a highly effective approach for situated learning (Lave & Wenger, 1991; Shaffer et al., 2005). Role-play allows players to practice skills in an engaging way (Lieberman, 1997; Street & Rimal, 1997), and can influence healthy attitudes (Janis & Gilmore, 1965; Peng et al., 2006) and behaviors (Kohler et al., 2007). They can also offer a "hands-on" approach to learning, which allows for the acquisition and rehearsal of new skills that can then transfer to real-life situations (Kato et al., 2008). As evident, the benefits of digital games are numerous—digital games are able to create contextualized learning experiences that are meaningful to the player, thereby creating long-term retention of new knowledge and cognitive skills (Wouters et al., 2013).

The PlayForward Prevention Platform: Four Games for Health

Interest in digital games to promote health and well-being among youth is burgeoning because they are accessible, scalable, and seemingly impactful (although not all games have produced the evidence to support their efficacy). Although systematic reviews demonstrate the potential promise of videogame interventions in affecting a variety of health outcomes, there continues to be a great need for the development and rigorous testing of theory-driven digital game interventions (DeSmet et al., 2014). For over a decade, our play2PREVENT Lab at the Yale Center for Health & Learning Games has been a leading research lab in the design, development, and evaluation of digital games as health and behavioral interventions. Prototypes are first piloted for preliminary efficacy, acceptance, and feasibility, and then built out with feedback from youth to later conduct large-scale randomized controlled trials, the gold star in research, with the goal of measuring outcomes and identifying implementation strategies. As part of our PlayForward Prevention Platform, our evidence-informed digital games focus on topics such as smoking and electronic nicotine delivery systems (ENDS) use prevention, health advocacy, sexual risk reduction, and opioid misuse prevention while integrating necessary SEL competencies throughout storylines. All of our digital games align with SEL competencies, national health education standards, and components of the WSCC approach, and are designed by youth to engage youth. *PlayForward: Elm City Stories* was the first game launched, and it serves as the foundation for the development of our three other digital games: *smokeSCREEN*, *PlayTest!*, and *PlaySmart*.

PlayForward: Elm City Stories

PlayForward: Elm City Stories (*PlayForward*) is an original evidence-informed, role-playing videogame that was developed with funding from the National Institute of Child Health and Development and serves as the foundation for all games in the platform. *PlayForward* focuses on risk reduction and HIV/STI prevention in youth. *PlayForward* was designed and developed using multiple theoretical frameworks. The game includes storylines and skill-building opportunities around sex, drugs, alcohol, and positive decision-making, and has up to 16 hours of unique gameplay. In the game, the player uses an avatar to travel through time facing challenges and has the opportunity to experience how specific decisions yield certain outcomes, and then they have the opportunity to go back in time and make different decisions and see how those decisions have different outcomes. *PlayForward* was evaluated through a large randomized controlled trial with 333 adolescents (Fiellin et al., 2017). The primary outcome was delay of sexual initiation (vaginal/anal intercourse). Other outcomes included sexual health attitudes, knowledge, and intentions. Participants aged 11–14 years from 12 community after-school, school, and summer programs played the experimental game (*PlayForward*) or control games over six weeks. Through the randomized controlled trial, *PlayForward* demonstrated efficacy in improving attitudes and knowledge around sexual health, findings that persisted to 12 months.

smokeSCREEN

To combat the growing epidemic of tobacco and ENDS use (Creamer, 2020), our play2PREVENT Lab, with funding from Yale, Dartmouth's Center for Technology and Behavioral Health, USC Tobacco Centers of Regulatory Science (TCORS), and the CVS Health Foundation, developed *smokeSCREEN*, a web- and App-based digital game focused on smoking and ENDS use prevention in youth aged 11–16. *smokeSCREEN* addresses a range of challenges that youth face involving peer pressure and the use of tobacco products with a focus on combustible cigarettes, electronic cigarettes, and flavored tobacco. The game allows youth the opportunity to develop important skills related to refusing peers in risky situations involving tobacco products and ENDS. *smokeSCREEN* provides youth the opportunity to role-play and apply knowledge learned in the game in a "battle of the wits" with other game characters. The game takes 2–3 hours to complete and can be completed over several program or class sessions.

Several prototypes of the game have been pilot tested by our play2PREVENT Lab team (Duncan et al., 2018; Hieftje, Fernandes et al., 2019; Pentz et al., 2019). One study (Pentz et al., 2019) evaluated the short-term effects of *smokeSCREEN* on shifting youth knowledge, beliefs, risk perceptions, and intentions to use e-cigarette, cigarettes, and other tobacco products. According to this pilot study, brief exposure improved knowledge of e-cigarettes and tobacco products, risk perceptions of e-cigarettes and cigarettes, and beliefs about e-cigarettes and other tobacco products. And most recently, our team at the play2PREVENT Lab assessed the effectiveness of *smokeSCREEN* (Hieftje, Fernandes et al., 2019), aimed at improving positive beliefs and knowledge associated with smoking and ENDS use. Five hundred sixty adolescents between the ages of 10 and 13 were enrolled from school programs to play our game. They were assessed using measures in a pre- and post-survey on beliefs and knowledge about tobacco product use and ENDS use. Significant improvements were reported on questions related to their beliefs and questions related to their knowledge, especially related to ENDS use. Overall, participants enjoyed playing the game. Findings from this recent pilot study suggest that *smokeSCREEN* has a promising effect, and is enjoyed by youth.

PlayTest!

Another digital game in our platform is *PlayTest!*, a videogame intervention that aims to encourage youth between the ages of 14 and 18 to get tested for STIs and HIV in school-based health centers. The game incorporates evidence-informed concepts from prominent behavior change theories. In addition to the main storylines, there are also five mini-games built into the overall game that teach the players specific skills to practice. Our team currently completed a randomized controlled trial (RCT) of *PlayTest!* Measures included self-reported assessments knowledge, attitudes, and beliefs around HIV/STI testing and counseling. The primary outcome is whether a student utilizes the school-based health center to get tested for HIV/STIs. Currently, data analysis for the RCT is underway. With plans to continue to collaborate with school-based health centers, schools, and other educational settings, our team intends to share *PlayTest!* broadly once our evaluation stage is complete.

PlaySmart

Our most recently funded digital game is *PlaySmart*. With funding from the National Institutes of Health (NIH)/National Institute on Drug Abuse (NIDA)'s Helping to End Addiction Long-term (HEAL) initiative, our team is currently developing a digital game, *PlaySmart*, to address opioid misuse in older adolescents with plans to evaluate its efficacy through a randomized controlled trial beginning in Fall 2021. The goal of *PlaySmart* is to prevent opioid misuse in older adolescents by targeting their perception of risk. In addition, SEL competencies are threaded throughout gameplay interactions. The videogame intervention includes six relatable storylines, the content of which was informed by our focus groups with youth, those in treatment for opioid use disorder, treatment providers, prevention specialists, and key stakeholders at the national School-Based Health Alliance. Due to the strong correlation between mental health and substance use as well as findings from our youth focus groups, we also included in the game an emphasis on better understanding of mental health. Topics related to mental health focus on normalizing seeking help, recognizing warning signs of emotional distress in a peer, challenging one's own cognitive distortions, identifying coping strategies, and learning more about our brain's neuroplasticity to enhance one's growth mindset. Given the initiation of opioid misuse frequently occurs in adolescence and young adulthood (Lankenau et al., 2012), *PlaySmart* will focus on prevention strategies specifically, and has the potential to deliver a technology-/evidence-based prevention intervention to address opioids in adolescents (Compton et al., 2019).

Standards and Competencies

The aforementioned digital games offer a comprehensive approach to deliver health education, a key component of the *WSCC*. Health education "helps students acquire the knowledge, attitudes, and skills they need for making health-promoting decisions, achieving health literacy, adopting health-enhancing behaviors, and promoting the health of others" (Lewallen et al., 2015). All of our digital games in the play2PREVENT PlayForward Prevention Platform address the National Health Education Standards and offer an engaging and interactive delivery of health education curriculum to youth. While the content addresses health education, the process of learning aligns with CASEL's SEL core competencies framework (see Figure 12.1). SEL enhances students' capacity to integrate skills, attitudes, and behaviors to recognize and manage emotions, develop empathy toward others, practice responsible decision-making, and navigate challenging relationships (Weissberg et al., 2015). There are five core competencies that can be taught in many ways across many settings:

1) self-awareness, 2) self-management, 3) social awareness, 4) relationship skills, and 5) responsible decision-making. All of our digital games allow the player to practice these core skills repeatedly throughout storylines and mini-games. The use of digital games in conjunction with effective pedagogy offers a systematic approach to teaching core SEL competencies and health education that allows for differentiation and extends beyond the school setting.

Multi-Tiered System of Support and Evidence-Based Practices

Translating scientific discoveries from concept to practice takes an average of 17 years (Morris et al., 2011); however, theory- and evidence-informed approaches with implementation strategies (or effective pedagogy for our purpose) help facilitate the translation of evidence-based practices (EBPs; Bauer et al., 2015). According to the UNESCO's Rethinking Learning: A Review of Social and Emotional Learning Frameworks for Education Systems (Farber & Rivers, 2020), a sole focus on the classroom restricts the development of SEL and limits opportunities to apply skills and competencies to other contexts. To expand contexts and support a school-wide approach, we encourage our digital games to be delivered through a multi-tiered system of support (MTSS) that can be done virtually with concrete examples discussed later in this chapter. Delivery of school-based prevention interventions has shown success through the framework of a multi-tiered system of support (Shepley & Grisham-Brown, 2019). MTSS is a prevention framework that offers EBPs through the delivery of interventions in a tiered approach to meet all students' needs (Cook et al., 2015). A tiered approach allows for screening, progress monitoring, and problem identification (Kilgus et al., 2015). A *universal*/tier 1 delivers an intervention to all students and the expectation is that all students will receive the intended benefit of the intervention. For students who exhibit behaviors more "at-risk," a *selective*/tier 2 provides a more targeted group-based intervention. Lastly, an *indicated*/tier 3 is delivered to students who require a more intensive and individualized approach, such as one-on-one counseling. Incorporating digital games as EBPs adds an innovative approach that requires little training and provides support to educators in delivering a tiered approach virtually.

As part of a *universal*/tier 1 intervention, our digital games are accompanied by an Educator's Manual to provide support to educators in incorporating digital games in their classrooms use and now online learning environments. The Educator's Manual provides an introduction about the purpose of the manual, a summary of the game, an overview of curriculum including learning objectives, materials and preparation, content areas, and discussion points. The purpose of this manual is to support educators in delivering effective pedagogy to all students and support them in incorporating our digital game into their curriculum as well as meet the necessary standards. For example, educators download our *smokeSCREEN* Educator's Manual (see Figure 12.3) from our website and utilize it in their efforts nationally and

FIGURE 12.3 *smokeSCREEN* Educator's Manual

Source: Used with permission of Lynn E. Fiellin, MD© Yale University School of Medicine

internationally while they incorporate the digital game in their classrooms. This delivery is able to be done virtually. Our team is also working on creating curriculum units and lesson plans to complement the use of our games in the classroom, as educators indicated that they would find value from them.

Delivered universally, digital games can be a powerful tool for differentiation in the classroom as well. In addition to appealing to different learning styles and modalities, digital games such as the play2PREVENT PlayForward Prevention Platform as well as other platforms allow for students to move at their own pace while providing continuous feedback for the student and their instructor. For example, quiz-like digital platforms such as *Kahoot* or *Quizlet Live* are popular among educators and provide feedback in the form of scores that can be logged by educators and studied later to better identify students' specific needs and differentiate accordingly. The open-ended nature of these platforms offers an ideal platform for differentiation. *Kahoot* is often used primarily for reviewing before a major assessment such as a test, but can be individualized for each class or student by creating different games or quizzes. Instructors can also use it as a survey to gauge students' background knowledge of an event or their interest level in a topic. This function is particularly helpful at the high school or college levels, as you can ask students more open-ended, difficult questions. *Quizlet* is particularly useful as a homework reinforcement in terms of differentiation, as it is set up mostly as flash cards or quizzes. This feedback is helpful to educators as the field of education becomes increasingly data-driven over time. Since all of the feedback gathered from these games can be retained and studied by educators, they are then able to keep a log of how students have performed on such games over time and adjust their instruction accordingly, including tailoring it to specific students or cohorts who are struggling. Understanding perceptions of educator experiences using a variety of digital games offers an opportunity to address and integrate their needs into the development of additional digital games in our platform. As such, our team recognizes the value of games in providing feedback to teachers on student gameplay. For this reason, this feature will be considered as we strive to support teachers in universal delivery of games that allow for differentiation.

As part of *selective*/tier 2 interventions, digital games may supplement group-based counseling sessions. In schools with a mental health provider (e.g., school counselor, social worker, or behavior health provider in school-based health centers), our digital games may be used in group counseling sessions. As part of a *selective*/tier 2 intervention, a mental health provider would lead a group counseling session using a digital game as a discussion entry point. For example, *PlaySmart* addresses opioid misuse and normalizing seeking help for mental health. In this case, a mental health provider would be able to explore student experiences, if any, on the topic of substance use in a safe space as well as process more deeply the exploration of each storyline with their peers and a trusted adult.

As part of *indicated*/tier interventions, digital games allow students to practice role-playing within the game with a character who is a healthcare provider. This type of approach allows the player to develop their own sense of health agency. For example, *PlayTest!* Allows the player to engage with a healthcare provider at a school-based health center (SBHC) and ask questions about confidentiality as well as what to expect from getting STI/HIV testing. Although not all schools have SBHCs, this skill is critical as older adolescents typically transition from pediatricians to internists. It is important for youth to learn how to advocate for their health by asking questions, finding a good fit in healthcare providers, and seeking resources to meet one's needs in care.

Conclusion

Theory- and evidence-informed digital games, including those produced by our play2PREVENT Lab, offer an opportunity to scale up and deliver highly impactful and engaging interventions with fidelity (Duncan et al., 2018; Fiellin et al., 2014; Fiellin et al., 2017; Fiellin, Hieftje, Rosenthal, Camenga, & Edelman, 2012; Fiellin et al., 2016; Hieftje, Duncan, et al., 2019; Hieftje et al., 2016; Hieftje, Fernandes, et al., 2019; Hieftje, Rosenthal, Camenga, Edelman, & Fiellin, 2012a; Pentz, Hieftje, Pendergrass, Brito, Liu, Arora, Tindle, Krishnan-Sarin, & Fiellin, 2019). Additionally, they can be delivered outside the classroom setting given they are digital and translate to most platforms. There are many ways to incorporate digital games in the class. Successful implementation of digital games in the classroom works well when educators incorporate guided activities that can be led by students to enhance deep reflection, interactive discussions, and even project-based learning (Farber & Rivers, 2020). While the focus of our digital games specifically has been on health education and social and emotional climate (Fernandes et al., 2020), our Lab's long-term goal is to continue to build a platform of videogames that support educators, healthcare providers, families, and society in promoting long-lasting health and well-being among our youth. Technology is here to stay and we are living in a time where it is essential in order to feel a sense of normalcy, social connection, and belonging (Odgers & Robb, 2020). For this reason, concerted efforts must focus on the digital divide where youth and their families lack access to devices and technology, and ensuring that youth and their families who are disproportionately affected have access to devices and technology as we rely so heavily on them right now. First and foremost, remaining connected is a basic need, and digital games offer an opportunity to feel connected—socially, emotionally, and safely.

Resources

1. Free access to *PlayForward: Elm City Stories*

    a. Visit www.play2prevent.org/our-games/
    b. Click *PlayForward: Elm City Stories*
    c. Input contact information for access
    d. You will receive requested usernames/passwords approximately 24–48 hours after your request

2. Free access to *mokescreen*

    a. Visit www.smokescreengame.org/
    b. Click *Request Access* at top left of page (to the right of *mokescreen* title)
    c. Input contact information for access
    d. You will receive requested usernames/passwords approximately 24–48 hours after your request

3. *CASEL SEL Framework*: https://casel.org/sel-framework/

4. *Whole School, Whole Community, Whole Child (WSCC):* www.cdc.gov/healthyschools/wscc/index.htm
5. *smokeSCREEN* Educator's Manual: www.smokescreengame.org/for-teachers

References

Baiden, P., Graaf, G., Zaami, M., Acolatse, C. K., & Adeku, Y. (2019). Examining the association between prescription opioid misuse and suicidal behaviors among adolescent high school students in the United States. *Journal of Psychiatric Research, 112*, 44–51.

Barnes, S., & Prescott, J. (2018). Empirical evidence for the outcomes of therapeutic video games for adolescents with anxiety disorders: Systematic review. *JMIR Serious Games, 6*(1), e3.

Basch, C. E. (2011). Healthier students are better learners: A missing link in school reforms to close the achievement gap. *Journal of School Health, 81*(10), 593–598.

Bauer, M. S., Damschroder, L., Hagedorn, H., Smith, J., & Kilbourne, A. M. (2015). An introduction to implementation science for the non-specialist. *BMC Psychology, 3*(1), 32.

Compton, W. M., Jones, C. M., Baldwin, G. T., Harding, F. M., Blanco, C., & Wargo, E. M. (2019). Targeting youth to prevent later substance use disorder: An underutilized response to the US opioid crisis. *American Journal of Public Health, 109*(S3), S185–S189.

Cook, C. R., Lyon, A. R., Kubergovic, D., Wright, D. B., & Zhang, Y. (2015). A supportive beliefs intervention to facilitate the implementation of evidence-based practices within a multi-tiered system of supports. *School Mental Health, 7*(1), 49–60.

Corcoran, R. P., Cheung, A. C., Kim, E., & Xie, C. (2018). Effective universal school-based social and emotional learning programs for improving academic achievement: A systematic review and meta-analysis of 50 years of research. *Educational Research Review, 25*, 56–72.

Creamer, M. R. (2020). Tobacco product use among high school students—youth risk behavior survey, United States, 2019. *MMWR Supplements, 69*.

Dalton, L., Rapa, E., & Stein, A. (2020). Protecting the psychological health of children through effective communication about COVID-19. *The Lancet Child & Adolescent Health, 4*(5), 346–347.

Darling-Hammond, L., & Cook-Harvey, C. M. (2018). *Educating the whole child: Improving school climate to support student success.* Learning Policy Institute.

DeSmet, A., Van Ryckeghem, D., Compernolle, S., Baranowski, T., Thompson, D., Crombez, G., Poels, K., Van Lippevelde, W., Bastiaensens, S., & Van Cleemput, K. (2014). A meta-analysis of serious digital games for healthy lifestyle promotion. *Preventive Medicine, 69*, 95–107.

Djaouti, D., Alvarez, J., Jessel, J.-P., & Rampnoux, O. (2011). Origins of serious games. In *Serious games and edutainment applications* (pp. 25–43). Springer.

Duncan, L. R., Hieftje, K. D., Culyba, S., & Fiellin, L. E. (2014). Game playbooks: Tools to guide multidisciplinary teams in developing videogame-based behavior change interventions. *Translational Behavioral Medicine, 4*(1), 108–116. https://doi.org/10.1007/s13142-013-0246-8

Duncan, L. R., Hieftje, K. D., Pendergrass, T. M., Sawyer, B. G., & Fiellin, L. E. (2018). Preliminary investigation of a videogame prototype for cigarette and marijuana prevention in adolescents. *Substance Abuse*, 1–5. https://doi.org/10.1080/08897077.2018.1437862

Durlak, J. A., & DuPre, E. P. (2008). Implementation matters: A review of research on the influence of implementation on program outcomes and the factors affecting implementation. *American Journal of Community Psychology, 41*(3–4), 327–350.

Durlak, J. A., Weissberg, R. P., Dymnicki, A. B., Taylor, R. D., & Schellinger, K. B. (2011). The impact of enhancing students' social and emotional learning: A meta-analysis of school-based universal interventions. *Child development, 82*(1), 405–432.

Farber, M., & Rivers, S. E. (2020). Leveraging technology for SELF programmes. In *Rethinking learning: A review of social and emotional learning frameworks for education systems*. UNESCO MGIEP.

Fernandes, C. F., Taylor, C. K., Tran, A., Pendergrass, T., Hieftje, K., & Fiellin, L. E. (2020). A pilot randomized controlled trial to evaluate a cognitive-behavioral intervention: empowerED: Think it through digital stories. *Unpublished manuscript*.

Fiellin, L. E., Hieftje, K. D., & Duncan, L. R. (2014). Videogames, here for good. *Pediatrics, 134*(5), 849–851.

Fiellin, L. E., Hieftje, K. D., Pendergrass, T. M., Kyriakides, T. C., Duncan, L. R., Dziura, J. D., . . . & Fiellin, D. A. (2017). Video game intervention for sexual risk reduction in minority adolescents: Randomized controlled trial. *Journal of Medical Internet Research, 19*(9), e314. https://doi.org/10.2196/jmir.8148

Fiellin, L. E., Hieftje, K. D., Rosenthal, M. S., Camenga, D. R., & Edelman, J. E. (2012). *A qualitative study to inform the development of a videogame for minority adolescent HIV risk reduction and prevention*. 19th International AIDS Conference, Washington, DC.

Fiellin, L. E., Kyriakides, T. C., Hieftje, K. D., Pendergrass, T. M., Duncan, L. R., Dziura, J. D., Sawyer, B. G., & Fiellin, D. A. (2016). The design and implementation of a randomized controlled trial of a risk reduction and human immunodeficiency virus prevention videogame intervention in minority adolescents: PlayForward: Elm City Stories. *Clinical Trials, 13*(4), 400–408. https://doi.org/10.1177/1740774516637871

Hieftje, K. D., Duncan, L. R., & Fiellin, L. E. (2014). Novel methods to collect meaningful data from adolescents for the development of health interventions. *Health Promotion Practice, 15*(5), 714–722. https://doi.org/10.1177/1524839914521211

Hieftje, K. D., Duncan, L. R., Florsheim, O., Sawyer, B. G., & Fiellin, L. E. (2019). One night stan: Feasibility study of an HIV prevention and sexual risk reduction social card game for young Black women. *Games for Health Journal, 8*(2), 112–120.

Hieftje, K. D., Duncan, L. R., Pendergrass, T. M., Sawyer, B. G., & Fiellin, L. E. (2016). Development of an HIV prevention videogame intervention: Lessons learned. *International Journal of Serious Games, 3*(2), 83–90. https://doi.org/10.17083/ijsg.v1i4.47

Hieftje, K. D., Edelman, E. J., Camenga, D. R., & Fiellin, L. E. (2013). Electronic media—based health interventions promoting behavior change in youth: A systematic review. *JAMA Pediatr, 167*(6), 574–580.

Hieftje, K. D., Fernandes, C. F., Lin, I.-H., & Fiellin, L. E. (2019). Effectiveness of a web-based tobacco product use prevention videogame intervention on young adolescents' beliefs and knowledge. *Substance Abuse*, 1–7.

Hieftje, K. D., Pendergrass, T., Montanaro, E., Kyriakides, T., Florsheim, O., & Fiellin, L. E. (2018). *"But do they like it?" Participant satisfaction and gameplay experience of a public health videogame intervention in adolescents*. 2018 IEEE 6th International Conference on Serious Games and Applications for Health (SeGAH).

Hieftje, K. D., Rosenthal, M. S., Camenga, D. R., Edelman, E. J., & Fiellin, L. E. (2012a). A qualitative study to inform the development of a video game for adolescent HIV prevention. *Games for Health Journal, 1*(4), 294–298. https://doi.org/10.1089/g4h.2012.0025

Hieftje, K. D., Rosenthal, M. S., Camenga, D. R., Edelman, E. J., & Fiellin, L. E. (2012b). A qualitative study to inform the development of a videogame for adolescent human immunodeficiency virus prevention. *Games for Health Journal: Research, Development, and Clinical Applications, 1*(4), 1–5.

Janis, I. L., & Gilmore, J. B. (1965). The influence of incentive conditions on the success of role playing in modifying attitudes. *Journal of Personality and Social Psychology, 1*, 17–27.

Kato, P. M., Cole, S. W., Bradlyn, A. S., & Pollock, B. H. (2008). A video game improves behavioral outcomes in adolescents and young adults with cancer: A randomized trial. *Pediatrics, 122*(2), e305–317. https://doi.org/10.1542/peds.2007-3134

Kilgus, S. P., Reinke, W. M., & Jimerson, S. R. (2015). Understanding mental health intervention and assessment within a multi-tiered framework: Contemporary science, practice, and policy. *School Psychology Quarterly*, *30*(2), 159.

Kohler, H. P., Behrman, J. R., & Watkins, S. C. (2007). Social networks and HIV/AIDs risk perceptions. *Demography*, *44*(1), 1–33.

Lankenau, S. E., Teti, M., Silva, K., Bloom, J. J., Harocopos, A., & Treese, M. (2012). Initiation into prescription opioid misuse amongst young injection drug users. *International Journal of Drug Policy*, *23*(1), 37–44.

Lave, J., & Wenger, E. (1991). *Situated learning: Legitimate peripheral participation*. Cambridge University Press.

Lee, J. (2020). Mental health effects of school closures during COVID-19. *The Lancet Child & Adolescent Health*, *4*(6), 421.

Lenhart, A., Kahne, J., Middaugh, E., Macgill, A., & Vitak, J. (2008). Teens' gaming experiences are diverse and include significant social interaction and civic engagement. *Teens, Video Games, and Civics*.

Lewallen, T. C., Hunt, H., Potts-Datema, W., Zaza, S., & Giles, W. (2015). The whole school, whole community, whole child model: A new approach for improving educational attainment and healthy development for students. *Journal of School Health*, *85*(11), 729–739.

Liang, L., Ren, H., Cao, R., Hu, Y., Qin, Z., Li, C., & Mei, S. (2020). The effect of COVID-19 on youth mental health. *Psychiatric Quarterly*, 1–12.

Lieberman, D. (1997). Interactive video games for health promotion: Effects on knowledge, self-efficacy, social support, and health. In *Health promotion and interactive technology: Theoretical applications and future directions* (pp. 103–120). Lawrence Erlbaum Associates Publishers.

Liew, J., McTigue, E. M., & Kattingon, L. (2010). Educating the whole child: The role of social and emotional development in achievement and school success. In *Handbook of curriculum development* (pp. 465–478).

Montanaro, E., Fiellin, L. E., Fakhouri, T., Kyriakides, T. C., & Duncan, L. R. (2015). Using videogame apps to assess gains in adolescents' substance use knowledge: New opportunities for evaluating intervention exposure and content mastery. *Journal of Medical Internet Research*, *17*(10), e245. https://doi.org/10.2196/jmir.4377

Morris, Z. S., Wooding, S., & Grant, J. (2011). The answer is 17 years, what is the question: Understanding time lags in translational research. *Journal of the Royal Society of Medicine*, *104*(12), 510–520.

National Alliance on Mental Illness. (September 2019). *Mental Health By the Numbers*. Retrieved September 9, from www.nami.org/mhstats

Odgers, C., & Robb, M. B. (2020). *Tweens, teens, tech, and mental health: Coming of age in an increasingly digital, uncertain, and unequal world*. www.commonsensemedia.org/sites/default/files/uploads/pdfs/tweens-teens-tech-and-mental-health-full-report-final-for-web1.pdf

Payton, J. W., Wardlaw, D. M., Graczyk, P. A., Bloodworth, M. R., Tompsett, C. J., & Weissberg, R. P. (2000). Social and emotional learning: A framework for promoting mental health and reducing risk behavior in children and youth. *Journal of School Health*, *70*(5), 179–185.

Peng, W., Klein, J., & Lee, K. (2006). *Will role playing video game influence how you judge? Favoritism towards similar roles and social judgments towards criminality*. Annual meeting of the International Communication Association, Dresden International Congress Centre, Dresden, Germany. www.allacademic. Com/meta/p90645_index. Html.

Pentz, M. A., Hieftje, K. D., Pendergrass, T. M., Brito, S. A., Liu, M., Arora, T., Tindle, H. A., Krishnan-Sarin, S., & Fiellin, L. E. (2019). A videogame intervention for tobacco product use prevention in adolescents. *Addictive Behaviors*, *91*, 188–192.

Shaffer, D., Squire, K., Halverson, R., & Gee, J. (2005). Video games and the future of learning. *Phi Delta Kappan*, *87*(2), 105–111.

Shepley, C., & Grisham-Brown, J. (2019). Multi-tiered systems of support for preschool-aged children: A review and meta-analysis. *Early Childhood Research Quarterly*, *47*, 296–308.

Stokes, B. (2005). Videogames have changed: Time to considerserious games'? *Development Education Journal*, *11*(3), 12.

Street, R., Jr, & Rimal, R. (1997). Health promotion and interactive technology: A conceptual foundation. In *Health promotion and interactive technology: Theoretical applications and future directions* (pp. 1–18). Mahwah, NJ: Lawrence Erlbaum Associates Publishers.

Weissberg, R. P., Durlak, J. A., Domitrovich, C. E., & Gullotta, T. P. (Eds.). (2015). Social and emotional learning: Past, present, and future. In J. A. Durlak, C. E. Domitrovich, R. P. Weissberg, & T. P. Gullotta (Eds.), *Handbook of social and emotional learning: Research and practice* (pp. 3–19). The Guilford Press.

Weisz, J. R., Sandler, I. N., Durlak, J. A., & Anton, B. S. (2005). Promoting and protecting youth mental health through evidence-based prevention and treatment. *American Psychologist*, *60*(6), 628.

Wouters, P., Van Nimwegen, C., Van Oostendorp, H., & Van Der Spek, E. D. (2013). A meta-analysis of the cognitive and motivational effects of serious games. *Journal of Educational Psychology*, *105*(2), 249.

13

Using Games for Empathy, Compassion, and Care

Karen (Kat) Schrier

A compelling experience can change the way we view the world, and the way we view each other. A powerful song, a theater show, or a television series can share stories and perspectives. Games can also do this: they can enhance connectedness, help strangers become friends, and let people feel more like a community.

We may hear about commercial, popular games—*Fortnite, Fall Guys, Grand Theft Auto, Overwatch, NBA 2K*, or *Call of Duty*—and we may not readily imagine how these games could be used for prosocial purposes. We watch our kids scream and shout and compete, and we cannot see how they may enhance care or compassion. We also may hear about the fantastical content of many games—elves, dragons, aliens, and faraway worlds—and not understand how this may connect to our own lives, values, or systems. But many games (even the ones I have mentioned) can directly and indirectly connect us to each other and can enhance our empathy and compassion for others (Schrier, 2019c).

In this chapter, I will explore why and how games may support the learning and practice of social and emotional skills such as empathy, compassion, and care—as well as the limitations. Next, I will provide practical and logistical guidelines for using games in the high school classroom to support such as empathy and compassion. What are the best practices for choosing games and for using them for in-person and remote learning experiences?

What Is Empathy and Compassion—and Why Does It Matter?

Schools and policymakers tend to focus on teaching writing, reading, and arithmetic, as well as STEM subjects, and social studies. But social and emotional learning (SEL) and skills are also essential—and may even support greater practice and knowledge of other subject areas. It is part of—and perhaps even necessary to—full participation in our society (Levine & Kawashima-Ginsberg, 2017). It helps to enhance our practice of all different skills, helps us to believe in ourselves and our abilities, and helps us to participate in our broader communities (Durlack et al., 2011; Taylor et al., 2017). We need to be able to fully express who we are to fully connect with ourselves, with others, and with the world around us.

Social and emotional skills refer to the practices and behaviors around how we express and identify emotions, care and connect with others, and make ethical and sound decisions. CASEL is one framework that relays the types of skills associated with social and emotional learning, such as responsible decision-making, relationship skills, self-awareness, and social awareness (CASEL, 2020).

Empathy and compassion are widely cited as being integral to social and emotional learning. Empathy is defined as taking on someone else's perspectives or feelings. It has been seen as having cognitive, affective, and motivational components (Bailenson, 2018; Farber & Schrier, 2017; Schrier & Farber, 2019). It is different from compassion in that compassion requires action—we don't just understand someone else, but we act on it.

Perspective taking also has inconsistent results (Vescio et al., 2003; Castillo et al, 2011; Galinsky et al., 2005; Wang et al., 2014; Goldstein et al., 2014). On the other hand, empathy is a flickering experience and may not always be beneficial or useful. Bloom argues that empathy is problematic and does not always lead to prosocial outcomes (Bloom, 2016).

Perspective-taking, however, has inconsistent results in games and VR (Schrier, 2019b; van Loon et al., 2018). Some studies suggest that players use more stereotypes when playing as a Black avatar than a white one, and other studies suggest it reduces stereotypes (Groom et al., 2009; Banakou et al., 2016; Hasler et al., 2017). Olson and Harrell's research suggests that players' preconceived notions about race factor into how they are able to identify racism in a game (Olson & Harrell, 2020).

Why Might Games Support Empathy and Compassion?

Games have been used in all areas of education and learning. They are rich communities and interactive playgrounds that can enable authentic problem solving and connectedness (Kafai & Fields, 2019). The following are a few ways that games may specifically enable the practice of empathy and compassion. I also share limitations.

Games Can Enable Players to Explore Storyworlds

Some games may immerse players in storyworlds, or a shared universe with overlapping characters, storylines, objects, settings, and events (Schrier & Shaenfield, 2021; Deterding & Zagal, 2018). These worlds can enable players to experience perspectives in a dynamic, evolving virtual space, where mindsets and views may change over time depending on one's actions and interactions in a game.

Players may use a "willing suspension of disbelief for the moment," and engage with events and figures in fictional game worlds, in ways they may not (even do) in real life (Coleridge, 1817). Story helps to transport an audience to another realm, where people feel immersed, empowered, and that the stakes are higher because they are "really there experiencing the events" (Murphy et al., 2011). When people are engrossed in a narrative or story world, they may also be more open to new ideas, places, and peoples, as well as also more open to changing behaviors, attitudes, and perspectives. This is like other media, like film, opera, and television, except that with games, stories and perspectives can emerge from our active interactions with this world. It makes the story more personally relatable because we are able to directly explore perspectives and people's lives (Farber & Schrier, 2017).

For example, the game *Tell Me Why* (Dontnod, 2020) enables players to uncover a storyworld set in an Alaskan small town. Players play as identical twins Alyson and Tyler Ronan (one a cis woman and the other a trans man) and can explore the world while also exploring the differing perspectives and memories of the two main characters (Quian, 2020). Likewise, *SweetXHeart* (Small, 2019) enables us to play as the character Kara, a Black woman. Players need to spend five days interacting with others and making choices such as how to respond to catcalls or microaggressions in school and the workplace. These interactions affect Kara's stress level, which wavers throughout the play experience.

While stories can be compelling, there are also limits. Not all stories or storyworlds are equally transformative. Some people are motivated and engaged by types of stories and narrative interactions, while others may be turned off. "Some games can engage our hearts and minds, and some may not. The same game may be immersive for one person and not for another" (Farber & Schrier, 2017). Games, and their stories, are also limited by those who create them—their authenticity and richness relies on the experiences and resources of their creators. Moreover, stories can and should show all the nuances of humanity, and not just the triumphs, but the tribulations, too. "Like our own world, many of these new virtual worlds are problematic, and show different parts of humanity, including cruelty and violence, as well as love and compassion" (Schrier, 2019a). How can we enhance empathy while furthering our full understanding of the flaws and foibles of humanity?

Games Can Enable Us to Experience Multiple Perspectives

Games can also help players to reason through and reflect on their own perspectives and those of others, which can help them become more empathetic and culturally aware (Schrier, 2019a). Actively interacting with authentic perspectives can help players to better understand another's obstacles, emotions, and mindsets (Vescio et al., 2003; Castillo et al., 2011; Galinsky et al., 2005; Wang et al., 2014; Goldstein et al., 2014). Story can also help players experience and challenge their own biases and that of others, such that they could possibly change or expand their perspectives. Cragg explains that "to weaken the grip of prejudice in a society, people, particularly children have to be brought into contact with images, stories, experiences that challenge stereotypes and change perceptions" (Cragg, 1997). The more we interact with others' stories, the more familiar they become, and the less distant they seem from ourselves. This can support perspective-taking and can reduce the "othering" that leads to biased attitudes and behaviors.

For instance, *Mind Field* is an interactive video experience that helps people become more aware of different forms of racism, such as microaggressions (Carnegie Mellon/ETC, 2017). The game lets the player make dialogue choices while exploring fictionalized versions of real-life stories. In one vignette, players can interact with a study group, where the students are dividing up responsibilities on the project. After the vignette, we also hear a perspective, voiced by the real person behind the character who felt her role was diminished. The authenticity of this perspective further contributes to our ability to better understand her experience. Because we are making choices for a character in the game, we feel more responsible to the other characters, which may affect how we listen to and respond to those characters. Likewise, the interactive VR experience *I am a Man* (Ham, 2018) shows scenes from the Black civil rights movement in the U.S. and shares first-hand perspectives from participants in the movement.

However, perspective-taking can sometimes backfire. Performing empathy through a game may be problematic because it may make us think we can fully understand someone else's lives—but we cannot. This can possibly enhance misunderstandings, stigma, and more disconnection among disparate groups (Gloor & Puhl, 2016; Nario-Redmond et al., 2017).

Instead of reducing biases, perspective-taking through games can perpetuate biases, too (Schrier, 2019a, 2019b). Nario-Redmond, et al. found that it can lead to stereotypical understandings of others (Nario-Redmond et al., 2017. It can also make people feel so emotionally overwhelmed that they cannot connect further with people who are different from them (Sassenrath et al., 2016). It can even be a form of violence to "try on" and "take off" someone else's identity, such as being a type of digital Blackface (Nakamura, 2002; Roxworthy, 2014; Mortley, 2020).

Games Can Help Us to Explore Our Own and Others' Identities

Games can also motivate players to share and express their own identities, and to learn about others' identities, which helps to support perspective-taking and the practice of empathy (Schrier, 2019a, 2021).

First, games can help to encourage players to customize avatars or play as particular roles that express aspects of their identities or help them to learn about others. Darvasi, a teacher at an all-boys private school in Toronto, Canada, uses Twine to help students further explore their identities in a unit that centers on the game *What Remains of Edith Finch*. In the game, players need to interact with artifacts left behind by members of the Finch family, such as music boxes or photographs, which express the stories and identity of that person. The students crafted stories about themselves, as inspired by the story in the game that they played, which included their own meaningful items (Darvasi et al., 2019).

Games can also enable players to construct their own personal narratives, art assets, or paths through the game (Bagdasarov et al., 2012). For instance, in *Her Story* (Barlow, 2015), the players can search through a database of mini-video clips of character testimonies, each with their own piece of a story of what happened in a murder mystery. How the player decides to navigate that database (such as which search terms they use) ends up constructing a unique narrative, which eventually may reveal what really happened in the murder. Because of how many video clips are available in the database, the actual string of videos watched becomes one of hundreds of permutations of video sequences. By choosing the order of the videos, the player directly co-constructs the narrative of the game. Moreover, how the player then interprets the story of what happened is also a form of co-construction.

Likewise, educators can encourage students to create their own stories about the game, such as "fan fiction" type expansions on characters, or even machinima-like videos about the gameplay (Kafai & Burke, 2016). These types of creations within a creation could even happen in a game. In *Civics! An American Musical* (Fablevision, 2020) students can develop their own narrative and musical creations with the art assets in the game.

However, the ability to explore one's identity through games is limited. Some games may limit how or who can express their identity through a game, for instance, by limiting which hair textures or gender pronouns options can be accessed. Moreover, trying on someone else's identity through a game may be problematic. It can be appropriate to put on (and take off) a "costume" of an identity, without meaningfully understanding or accessing it. This can perpetuate biases and harm to those who express that identity (Schrier, 2019a, 2021; Nakamura, 2002). Finally, just as in all communities, certain identities may be systemically marginalized or excluded, and biases may be perpetuated or even propagated (Gray, 2020; Benjamin, 2019; Kafai et al., 2008; Kafai, Richard, & Tynes, 2016; Chess, 2017; Richard & Gray, 2018).

Games Can Encourage Practice of Decision-Making and Reflection

Games can provide the context through which players can make their own decisions. This includes games that relay interactive, non-linear stories, where participants are presented with several options to choose from, and are asked to decide on next steps. Some of these games may adapt and change based on student decisions, while in others, the results are functionally and narratively the same (Schrier, 2014, 2015).

For instance, in *Life is Strange*, players play as Max Caulfield, a high school student who is trying to help her best friend, Chloe Price. Throughout the game, the player (as Max) needs to make ethical choices that affect the story, such as which conversation responses to share with Kate, a girl who is thinking about committing suicide. The choices you make will impact whether you are able to help save her and keep her from committing suicide; it also impacts the rest of the game, such as how other people treat and view Max, and how Max feels about herself.

Games may also enable decisions that show both short-term and longer-term consequences, and the dynamism of a living social system (Schrier, 2021). This also can help players start to realize that their decisions can have uncertain and rippling impacts, much as they may in real life. In *Life is Strange*, for instance, players will experience both short-term and longer-term outcomes, such as a suspension from school or bullying from other characters. Sometimes the player can also rewind and redo choices to see differential outcomes (Schrier & Shaenfield, 2021).

Reflection on these decisions and choices is not only useful, but may be essential to learning (Villareale, Biemer, El-Nasr, & Zhu, 2020). *Life is Strange* (Square Enix, 2015) invites reflection when it enables players to rewind choices and see different outcomes, but it also has other reflective moments, such as when a player can sit on a bench in *Life is Strange: Before the Storm* (Dontnod, 2017) and recount events that have already happened, or in *Life is Strange 2* (Square Enix, 2018), where the player as Sean Diaz draws in their notebook and reflects on what they see.

One major limitation is how much a game world and story can change based on a player's decisions (see, e.g., Telltale's *Walking Dead* episode one). On the other hand, having limited endings, is that it is rather resource-heavy to have a world dynamically respond to a player. Having limited endings could also suggest to the player that while their ethical decisions matter, they may not have ultimate control over the final consequences of their actions. Systemic pressures and constraints may keep us from fully controlling our future. These games suggest that the outcomes were inevitable no matter what paths we chose, even if we, as the player of our lives, were changed along that path.

Moreover, reflection in games often comes outside of the game or beyond it. Teachers need to ensure that their students are not only making choices but reflecting on them. How can reflection be integrated more carefully into the game (or by the teacher) to enable reflection while the action is happening?

Games Can Encourage Friendship and Community

Games are communities. As such, players can connect and build relationships with other (real) players or NPCs (non-player characters). The character does not need to be humanoid—it can even be a digital object (such as the companion cube in the *Portal* series). Taking care of someone, such as a digital creature or character, may help to give the player a sense of responsibility, urgency, and desire to meet the goals of the game so they can help this other character (Schrier, 2021; Schrier & Shaenfield, 2015). In a game, we may need to make choices for and help other characters, or we may play alongside someone else (whether real or virtual) and rely on them to meet goals, furthering our connection to them. In the game *Way* (CoCo & Co., 2011), for instance, two (real) strangers play the game, simultaneously, with a split screen. The catch is that the two players cannot speak or write to each other, but they need to gesture to each other to be able to collaboratively play and complete the game together. One player, for instance, needs to show the other player where to jump, because the platforms are invisible to the jumping player. After relying on each other for the entirety of the game, players often comment that they feel like they are "friends." In my research on *Way*, I have found that players feel trust toward their partner and feel that they are someone they can rely on, because of how they played together (Schrier & Shaenfield, 2015).

Players who are already friends or acquainted outside of a game may also connect around and through games. For instance, players playing *Among Us* (InnerSloth, 2018) need to communicate and interact with each other to figure out, collectively, who the imposter is. In this online party game, which features up to ten players, one player is randomly assigned to be the "imposter," who secretly murders the other players. Players need to complete tasks and then vote together on whom they think the imposter is. By working and talking together, players bond over a collective, shared experience. Likewise, players may also connect by talking about games in other forums, such as in-person or through social media. Players may connect by talking about playing *Fall Guys*, an online Battle Royale, where players need to overcome silly obstacles to be the last one standing after a series of rounds. Or, they may connect by playing games together, either collaboratively, such as through the board game *Pandemic*, or competitively, through a *Super Smash Brothers* game.

However, while games may forge friendships, they may also fragment them. Players may take trash talking too far, or may use hate speech or bully others, just as they may in other types of communities. Players may take negative emotions and actions beyond a game and decide to stop playing, or halt friendships. And players may be harassed and even assaulted through games in ways that make them feel unwelcome, excluded, marginalized, or even violated (ADL, 2019). Teachers and designers need to be mindful of these possibilities—and reduce rather than propagate hate.

How to Use Games to Support Empathy and Compassion Practice

A key element of any educational experience is that it simply teaches what it needs to teach—that it is relevant to the unit, current event, skill, or topic that a teacher wants to teach (Schrier, 2018). The most useful and effective games fluidly match the pedagogical goals and curricular standards. In this section, I provide questions, guidelines, and principles to use to find and use games for empathy and compassion.

A Process for Choosing and Using Games for Empathy and Compassion

The following is a process for finding games to use in empathy and compassion practice, and social and emotional learning more generally. It is based on previous work (Becker, 2018; Schrier, 2015, 2018).

1. *Who is the audience?* Educators need to first think about the age of the students, what previous work they have done, their reading level or current skills, and their interest in the topic. They may need different games, different levels within the games, or even different types of support while playing the game.

2. *What are the learning goals and curricular needs?* Educators need to think about how a game might meet standards and particular curricular needs. For instance, perhaps an educator has a unit on identity, and wants to teach their students to develop their identity exploration and expression skills. They may then want to choose games that help develop these skills, or perhaps a suite of games that approach different skills. There are several ways to match the game to these goals. Educators can match their educational goals to the game's content, or they can match the skills and approaches that it teaches to the game's play.

3. *What is the context and ecosystem of use?* Educators also need to think about the context for the game. Where and how will the game be played? A game is not a standalone product, but part of a larger ecosystem, which includes the school, home, digital platforms, community of learners, the local civic community, the educators or mentors and their expertise, and the broader culture (Dishon & Kafai, 2019; Kafai & Burke, 2016). Are games being played in a library or after-school setting, in-person in a classroom, or in a remote learning environment?

4. *What are the technological limitations?* Educators need to understand how the game can be played given the technical resources available (such as the technological constraints of their physical or virtual classroom). How is the technology configured, who has access to these technological platforms, and what are the ways these connections may break down? Educators using digital games have to ensure that they have the right equipment, such as enough computers, VR headsets, or mobile devices. Just because the game works at home or in one setting, it may not work in another setting, such as online, in a classroom, or at a museum.

5. *What are the logistical limitations?* What are the logistical and practical limitations beyond the technology? Teachers need to make sure they have enough game copies or licenses to use so it can be deployed to multiple computers or accessed from students' homes. The time allotted to the game also matters, as the game may need to fit into a module, unit, class session, or Zoom meetup. Some games may work better outdoors or in a larger open space, such as *Werewolf* or *Mafia*.

Some games work better in person, while others do not need players to be co-located. Educators may need to also think about a game's particular limitations. Students may need to share one headset or iPad, and teachers may have to have sign-up sheets for a large class, which could be disruptive. A VR game might be dizzying and even nausea-inducing for some students, so limiting time on the headset may be beneficial, and teachers may want to include a school nurse or health official in on conversations on how to minimize harm.

6. *What is the play of the game?* Educators need to carefully evaluate and even critique the games they are thinking about using. There are a number of components of gameplay that should be considered, such as the mechanics (the actions that a player takes), the game goals, the characters, the storyline, and the themes. The elements of the gameplay should work together appropriately to match the learning goals (see Becker, 2018). Educators should also consider the game as both a text to be interpreted, a community that shares values, as well as a designed experience. Educators need to consider how they are designed and played, to "lift up the hood of the game" and see how it works, the values that are embedded, the biases it may express, or even how a game player may hack, cheat or transgress in a game (Flanagan et al., 2007; Flanagan & Nissenbaum, 2016).

7. *What are the activities around and within the game?* Educators also need to think about how to match the games they choose with either other games, or other types of activities, exercises, worksheets, or assessments.

8. *What are the training gaps?* A game is more effective in partnership with an educator who can help the students get the most out of the game. This requires the teacher to have knowledge about the game and how to use it in an educational setting. It requires some expertise in knowing how to adjust both the game and the students' expectations and abilities, to match each other. A teacher or mentor will be able to pause the game at particular moments, connect the game to the students' lives and educational needs in meaningful ways, or they may point out inaccuracies or problems with the game. They will know how to adapt the game to fit into their classroom's or informal learning environment's needs. However, experience and expertise in using games, VR, and AR takes time. Teacher training on how to use games should be part of other types of pedagogical training, whether through formal education or informal workshops. Some districts provide training in game-based learning, and some teacher education programs are starting to incorporate this topic into technology classes.

9. *What are the accessibility needs?* In addition to choosing the right game, thinking about the audience, and considering other challenges, educators need to think about the accessibility of their game. For instance, some games follow universal design best practices, or are required to

add in features, such as reading text aloud, or enlarging it. The Ablegamers Charity Ablegamers APX Cards and Toolkit can help people think through different accessibility needs and opportunities (Ablegamers Charity, 2020).

10. *How equitable is participation?* Another type of accessibility is to what extent players can participate in the game and game communities. Educators should consider how players' intersectional identities interact with the communities that emerge within and around the game. They should consider who belongs in the game and who is empowered, and how different people are allowed or not allowed to express themselves and their identities (Noble & Tynes, 2016; Gray, 2020; Benjamin, 2019; Gray & Leonard, 2018). The ADL Designing Inclusive Games toolkit can help educators and designers think through the relevant questions in relation to equity and inclusion (Schrier & ADL, 2021).

11. *How does the game connect to the "real world"?* Another big consideration is the extent to which the game connects to real-world social and emotional issues, topics, and communities. How is the game making the students more connected to the world beyond the classroom? How is the student being asked to express and share their own real-world identities and interests? When appropriate, games can be used to help make the real-world topics and needs more meaningful and relevant to students (Schrier, 2021).

12. *What are the ethical challenges?* Teachers need to think about the ethical implications of the game—such as who can access and participate in the game, how values and biases are embedded in the game—but also how privacy, transparency, culture, and power are negotiated through the game and its communities. Sometimes a game may interact with the students and their communities in surprising or even problematic ways. Are students being pressured to reveal too much or become too vulnerable? Are they being too emotionally overwhelmed or uncomfortable? Are they confronting their biases or furthering their misconceptions (Schrier, 2021)? The Values at Play framework can help the educator, along with the students, begin to sift through a game's values and the ethical challenges it may bring up (Flanagan et al., 2007).

13. *What are the assessment needs?* Educators need to think about how they will assess learning through and beyond the game. How do we know that the game we use is effective? How can games themselves serve as assessments for learning, or how can making games also serve as a way to understand behavioral, attitudinal, and conceptual change (Gibson & Webb, 2013; Simkins, 2014)?

Designers and educators can use these 13 questions as a starting point for designing games and playful activities that encourage empathy and compassion. While these questions may help in designing an effective educational experience, we particularly need to remain flexible to the evolving circumstances and needs of our learners. Given recent shifts to using more hybrid and remote learning, as well as rapidly changing socioeconomic situations, there may be an increasing need for social and emotional learning practice that is done virtually but still playfully. Amid fewer opportunities for connectedness, many yearn more and more for virtual communities that model and encourage empathy and compassion. How can designers create games that are supportive *and* adaptable? How can we create and share experiences that care about players as their needs and conditions change?

Resources

Games

Among Us (InnerSloth, 2018).
An online game for between four and ten players that can be played by class members over a local network or with others on the internet. You play as a crew mate on a spaceship with the objective of completing tasks while identifying imposters who want to sabotage the mission. Emphasis is on team communication and cooperation.

Civics! An American Musical (Fablevision, 2020).
Players take on the role of a theater producer and create a musical by adapting a historical event and using primary sources to create songs, sets, scripts, and costumes.

Her Story (Barlow, 2015).
An interactive narrative or video game film (FMV) where the player searches a database of police interviews to help identify the criminal and locate a missing person.

I am a Man (Ham, 2018).
A Virtual Reality (VR) experience that explores a series of 1968 Civil Rights movement events, such as the Memphis, Tennessee, sanitation strike, and gives players a firsthand experience of the struggles of people fighting for freedom and equity.

Life is Strange (Square Enix, 2015), *Life is Strange: Before the Storm* (Dontnod, 2017), *Life is Strange 2* (Square Enix, 2018).
A series of episodic games that feature choices and unique game mechanics. For instance, *Life is Strange* has a rewind game mechanic that allows the player as protagonist to rewind time and make an alternative decision and follow out its consequences.

Mind Field (Carnegie Mellon/ETC, 2017).
An interactive film that uses vignettes to explore micro-aggressions on a college campus from different perspectives.

SweetXHeart (Catt Small, 2019).
In this digital game, you play as Kara, a Black college student from the Bronx, New York City, as she navigates a typical week in her life. Players make choices on how to handle sexual harassment and the biases faced by Black women.

Tell Me Why (Dontnod, 2020).
Set in an Alaskan town, you play as twins Tyler and Alyson Ronan, making decisions based on the veracity of their contrasting narratives about the past. Players also explore Tlingit culture, an indigenous people of the far Northwest of the U.S. and Canada.

Way (CoCo & Co., 2011).
An online digital game that requires cooperation with another player to solve puzzles without the use of verbal language.

What Remains of Edith Finch (Giant Sparrow, 2017).
You explore the cursed ancestral home of the Finch family and learn about each member's strange death at the house as you move from room to room.

General Resources

Ablegamers Charity Accessible Player Experiences (APX), Ablegamers toolset https://accessible.games/accessible-player-experiences/ and cards at https://ablegamers.org/product/apx-cards/.
An organization that advocates for game players, such as people with disabilities, to better access and play games using assistive technology.

ADL (Anti-Defamation League): https://adl.org.
This organization was founded in 1913 to stop the defamation of Jewish people and secure justice and fair treatment to all, and it continues to fight all forms of hate and discrimination. The organization publishes many reports, including K. Schrier's paper on game design, identity, and empathy, *Designing Ourselves*, www.adl.org/designing-ourselves.

Schrier, K. (2021). *We the Gamers: How Games Teach Ethics & Civics*.
New York, NY: Oxford University Press.
This book explores how games are communities where civic deliberation and value sharing are already taking place. It also describes how games can be used in ethics, civics, and social studies education to inspire learning and civic change.

References

Ablegamers Charity. (2020). Accessible Player Experiences (APX) Ablegamers toolset https:// accessible.games/accessible-player-experiences/ and cards at https://ablegamers.org/ product/apx-cards/.

ADL. (2019). *Free to play?* www.adl.org/free-to-play

Bagdasarov, Z., Harkrider, L. N., Johnson, J. F., MacDougall, A. E., Devenport, L. D., Connelly, S., Mumford, M. D., Peacock, J., & Thiel, C. E. (2012). An investigation of case-based instructional strategies on learning, retention, and ethical decision-making. *Journal of Empirical Research and Human Research Ethics*, *7*, 79–86.

Bailenson, J. (2018). *Experience on demand: What virtual reality is.* New York: W.W. Norton & Company.

Banakou, D., Hamumanthu, P., & Slater, M. (2016). Virtual embodiment of White people in a Black virtual body leads to a sustained reduction in their implicit racial bias. *Frontiers in Human Neuroscience*, *10*, 601.

Becker, K. (2018). Choosing and using games in the classroom. In D. Gibson (Ed.), *International handbook of information technology in primary and secondary education.* Springer.

Benjamin, R. (2019). *Captivating technology.* Duke University Press.

Bloom, P. (2016) *Against empathy.* Ecco.

CASEL. (2020). *CASEL core competences.* Retrieved June 3, 2020, from https://casel.org/core-competencies/

Castillo, J.-L. Á., Cámara, C. P., & Eguizábal, A. J. (2011). Prejudice reduction in university programs for older adults. *Educational Gerontology*, *37*(2), 164–190.

Chess, S. (2017). *Ready player two.* University of Minnesota Press.

Coleridge, S. T. (1817). *Biographia Literaia.*

Cragg, W. (1997). Teaching business ethics: The role of ethics in business and in business education. *Journal of Business Ethics*, *16*, 231–245.

Darvasi, P., Farber, M., & iThrive. (2019). *Museum of me.* https://ithrivegames.org/ithrive-curriculum/ museum-of-me/

Deterding, S., & Zagal, J. (2018). *Role-playing game studies.* Routledge.

Dishon, G., & Kafai, Y. B. (2019). Connected civic gaming: rethinking the role of video games in civic education, *Interactive Learning Environments.* https://doi.org/10.1080/10494820.201 9.1704791.

Durlack, J., Weissberg, R. P., Dymnicki, A. B., Taylor, R. D., & Schellinger, K. B. (2011, January–February). The impact of enhancing students' social and emotional learning: A meta-analysis of school-based universal interventions. *Child Development*, *82*(1), 405–432. https://doi. org/10.1111/j.1467-8624.2010.01564.x

Farber, M., & Schrier, K. (2017). Strengths and limitations of games as "empathy machines". *UNESCO Whitepaper.* https://unesdoc.unesco.org/ark:/48223/pf0000261993_eng; http://ithrivegames. org/wp-content/uploads/2019/03/Empathy_ DesignKit_3.12.18.pdf

Flanagan, M., & Nissenbaum, H. (2016). *Values at play in digital games.* MIT Press.

Flanagan, M., Nissenbaum, H., Belman, J., & Diamond, J. (2007). *A method for discovering values in digital games.* DIGRA 2007 Conference Proceedings, Tokyo, Japan.

Galinsky, A. D., & Ku, G. (2004). The effects of perspective-taking on prejudice: The moderating role of self-evaluation. *Personality & Social Psychology Bulletin*, *30*(5), 594–604.

Galinsky, A. D., Ku, G., & Wang, C. S. (2005). Perspective-taking and self-other overlap: Fostering social bonds and facilitating social coordination. *Group Processes and Intergroup Relations*, *8*(2), 109–124.

Gibson, D., & Webb, M. (2013). Assessment as, for and of 21st century learning. In *International summit on ICT in education* (p. 17). Torun: EDUsummIT.

Gloor, J. L., & Puhl, R. M. (2016). Empathy and perspective-taking: Examination and comparison of strategies to reduce weight stigma. *Stigma and Health, 1*(4), 269–279. https://doi.org/10.1037/sah0000030

Goldstein, N. J., Vezich, S., & Shapiro, J. R. (2014). Perceived perspective-taking: When others walk in our shoes. *Journal of Personality and Social Psychology, 106*(6), 941–960.

Gray, K. (2020). *Intersectional tech: Black users in digital gaming.* LSU Press.

Gray, K., & Leonard, D. J. (2018). *Woke gaming.* University of Washington Press.

Groom, V., Bailenson, J. N., & Nass, C. (2009). The influence of racial embodiment on racial bias in immersive virtual environments. *Social Influence, 4*(1), 1–18.

Hasler, B., Spanlang, B., & Slater, M. (2017). Virtual race transformation reverses racial in-group bias. *PloS One, 12*(4), 2017. https://doi.org/10.1371/journal.pone.0174965.

Kafai, Y. B., & Burke, Q. (2016). *Connected gaming: What making video games can teach us about learning and literacy.* MIT Press.

Kafai, Y., & Fields, D. (2019). The ethics of play and participation in a tween virtual world: Continuity and change in cheating practices and perspectives in the Whyville community. *Cognitive Development, 49*, 33–42.

Kafai, Y., Heeter, C., Denner, J., & Sun, J. Y. (2008). *Beyond Barbie and Mortal Combat.* MIT Press.

Kafai, Y., Richard, G., & Tynes, B. (2016). *Diversifying Barbie and Mortal Combat.* ETC Press.

Levine, P., & Kawashima-Ginsberg, K. (2017). The Republic is still at risk. *Whitepaper.* www.civxnow.org/sites/default/files/resources/SummitWhitePaper.pdf.

Mortley, G. in T. Parker-Pope. (2020) How to Raise an Anti-Racist Kid. *New York Times,* www.nytimes.com/2020/06/24/well/family/how-to-raise-an-anti-racist-kid.html

Murphy, S. T., Frank, L. B., Moran, M. B., & Patnoe-Woodley, P. (2011). Involved, transported, or emotional? Exploring the determinants of change in knowledge, attitudes, and behavior in entertainment-education. *Journal of Communication, 61*, 407–431. https://doi.org/10.1111/j.1460-2466.2011.01554.x

Nakamura, L. (2002). *Cybertypes: Race, identity, and ethnicity on the internet.* Routledge.

Nario-Redmond, M. R., Gospodinov, D., & Cobb, A. (2017). The unintended negative consequences of disability simulations. *Rehabilitation Psychology, 62*(3), 324–333.

Noble, S., & Tynes, B. (Eds.). (2016). *The intersectional internet: Race, sex, class, and culture online.* Peter Lang.

Olson, D., & Harrell, F. (2020). *"I don't see color": Characterizing players' racial attitudes and experiences via an anti-bias simulation videogame.* FDG Conference.

Quian, J. (2020). Tell Me Why game review: A poetic exploration of memory against a stunning Alaskan landscape. *The Guardian.* www.theguardian.com/games/2020/sep/14/tell-me-why-game-review-a-poetic-exploration-of-memory-against-a-stunning-alaskan-landscape.

Richard, G., & Gray, K. L. (2018). Gendered play, racialized reality: Black cyberfeminism, inclusive communities of practice, and the intersections of learning, socialization, and resilience in online gaming. *Frontiers: A Journal of Women Studies, 39*(1), 112–148.

Roxworthy, E. (2014). Revitalizing Japanese American internment: Critical empathy and role-play in the musical "allegiance" and the video game "drama in the delta". *Theatre Journal, 66*(1), 93–115.

Sassenrath, C., Hodges, S. D., & Pfattheicher, S. (2016). It's all about the self: When perspective taking backfires. *Current Directions in Psychological Science, 25*(6), 405–410.

Schrier, K. (2014). Designing and using games to teach ethics and ethical thinking. In K. Schrier, (Ed.), *Learning, education and games, vol. 1: Curricular and design considerations.* ETC Press.

Schrier, K. (2015). EPIC: A framework for using video games for ethics education. *Journal of Moral Education, 44*(4), 393–424.

Schrier, K. (2018). Guiding questions for game-based learning. In D. Gibson (Ed.), *International handbook of information technology in primary and secondary education.* Springer.

Schrier, K. (2019a). Designing ourselves. *ADL Whitepaper*. www.adl.org/designing-ourselves

Schrier, K. (2019b, April). Reducing bias through gaming. *G/A/M/E Journal*. www.gamejournal.it/reducing-bias-through-gaming/

Schrier, K. (2021). *We the gamers: How games teach ethics & civics*. Oxford University Press.

Schrier, K. (Ed.). (2019c). *Learning, education & games vol. 3: 100 games to use in the classroom and beyond*. ETC Press (Carnegie Mellon).

Schrier, K., & ADL. (2021). *Designing inclusive games*. www.adl.org/designinginclusivegames

Schrier, K., & Farber, M. (2019). *Open questions for empathy and games*. Proceedings of Connected Learning Conference '18, ETC Press, Boston, MA.

Schrier, K., & Shaenfield, D. (2015). Collaboration and emotion in *way*. In S. Tettegah & W. Huang (Eds.), *Emotion, technology, and games*. Elvesier.

Schrier, K., & Shaenfield, D. (2021). *Life is strange* (S. Bacon). *Transmedia Companion*.

Simkins, D. (2014). Assessing video games for learning. In K. Schrier (Ed.), *Learning, education & games: Curricular and design considerations* (Vol. 1). Carnegie Mellon.

Taylor, R., Durlack, J., Oberle, E., & Weissberg, R. (2017). Promoting positive youth development through school-based social and emotional learning interventions: a meta-analysis of follow-up effects. *Child Development*, *88*(4), 1156–1171.

Van Loon, A., Bailenson, J., Zaki, J., Bostick, J., & Willer, R. (2018). Virtual reality perspective-taking increases cognitive empathy for specific others. *PloS ONE*, *13*(8), pe0202442.

Villareale, J., Biemer, C., El-Nasr, M. S., & Zhu, J. (2020). Reflection in game-based learning: A survey of programming games (Virtual: Foundations of Digital Games (FDG) Conference, 2020).

Vescio, T., Sechrist, G. B., & Paolucci, M. P. (2003). Perspective taking and prejudice reduction: The mediational role of empathy arousal and situational attributions. *European Journal of Social Psychology*, *33*(4), 455–472.

Wang, C. S., Tai, K., Ku, G., & Galinsky, A. D. (2014). Perspective-taking increases willingness to engage in intergroup contact. *PloS ONE*, *9*(1).

14

What We Learned
From Games to Make Assessment Playful

Yoon Jeon (YJ) Kim and Kevin Miklasz

Introduction

Assessment in the education system is, simply put, complicated. There is a deep divide between standardized testing, often believed to be a more objective measure of student learning, and classroom assessment, which is often criticized as being a "hodgepodge of factors" that often violate principles of measurement (Cross & Frary, 1999). The use of standardized assessment for the purposes beyond what was intended and that involves significantly shaping how the curriculum is designed has been heavily criticized. There is increasing interest in using big data and making school-level decisions based on the data. Assessment, often equated with testing, is considered playing a key role in generating the data needed for these decisions.

Assessment in the education system is wrongfully viewed and used as an accountability measure for teachers as well as to "summatively" measure students' relative performance, which in turn is then used to make high-stakes decisions (e.g., closing down a school, determining college entrance). Due to this, most assessment practices in schools center around standards-based and standardized tests. This led to overuse of massively outdated assessment methods that have serious threats to validity in schools—mainly relying on multiple-choice tests. While educational reform and improvement effort has never stopped, how students are assessed in schools has barely progressed. To better prepare learners for the future, we should first pay attention to how assessment is done in schools. Without having readily available assessment tools and practices to measure what students are really learning from more open-ended and student-centered pedagogical approaches, assessment will remain a barrier to innovating how students learn in formal educational settings. Furthermore, assessment in schools has been wrongfully used to further alienate and disadvantage the most vulnerable student populations instead of used to support them.

Given a long history of inadequate and often problematic assessment practices in our education system, we need a fundamentally different framework to challenge existing assumptions about assessment and focus on rigorous and valid assessment that can improve teaching and learning, particularly for educators who wish to experiment with student-centered creative ways of learning and might find that existing assessment methods are at odds with what they value. Therefore, the assessment needs of the formal structures of the education system often work as a barrier to implement the modern understanding of how people learn (National Research Council, 2001). Additionally, the most exciting assessment practices that are increasingly implemented in formal learning contexts embody constructivist principles of learning, such as being student-centered, creative, and playful, and serve to empower learners' choices, interest, and passion (Resnick, 2014). Many believe that these models can better prepare learners for future work environments where they need to be innovative and collaborative (e.g., Bergen, 2009; Fisher et al., 2011). It is apparent that the educational assessment community needs to provide alternative approaches to design and develop assessments that can measure and support various aspects of learners that go beyond skills and knowledge. Due to the lack of such frameworks, assessment is often disregarded entirely or conducted as an afterthought that is neither engaging nor rigorous. Additionally, teachers often find it challenging to create new ways of assessing the "soft-skills" that go beyond academic knowledge, which are closely aligned with the needs for the future generation's well-being and productivity in the 21st century economy.

So, what are the practical needs of educators that a new assessment framework needs to address? How can we provide teachers with student-centered assessments, without compromising rigor and flexibility?

In this chapter, we introduce the idea of ludic assessments: playful, or ludic, activities that are intentionally designed to provide performance-based evidence for both what and how students learn. Specifically, we discuss our vision for what assessment in schools should look like and why we believe the application of a playfulness lens to reimagine assessment could be beneficial. We will then discuss how educators can adopt the design principles of this playful approach in their own practices followed by a few examples from the MIT Playful Journey Lab.

Ludic Assessment

The idea of ludic assessment originally arose from game-based assessments. Games were meant to engage learners through play while offering a basic formative assessment of student knowledge on a topic. The idea behind the term could apply to a lot more than just games, though it begged the questions: What do games tell us about good assessment? What do we mean by good assessment?

To answer these questions, let us talk about the different characteristics of a ludic assessment: performance-based, authentic, multi-dimensional, ongoing, embedded, flexible, and playful.

Performance-based: To be able to measure complex learning in more open-ended and student-centered learning environments, assessment needs to be performance-based (Linn et al., 1991). The assessment needs to provide an authentic context or task where learners demonstrate what they can do, rather than simply showing what they know. Therefore, performance-based assessment engages learners to solve interesting and complex problems, show their work processes, and generate multiple types of data (e.g., artifacts, choices they made).

Authentic: The assessment should mimic real world practice with concrete, contextualized activities that require learners to use the concept or skill needed in the real world. Multiple choice tests often measure knowledge that is not practiced in the real world in a multiple test format. The way in which the knowledge, skill, or concept is used in the real world should be mimicked in the assessment format itself. This means any individual assessment task will be more specific and contextualized than the typical multiple choice test, or that the knowledge being tested might not be generalized or transferable to different contexts, such that generalizability must come from having multiple, ongoing ludic assessment tasks completed in a variety of contexts.

Multidimensional: Unlike many of the conventional assessments that measure discrete knowledge, authentic, performance-based assessment inherently draws upon multiple competencies. Solving an authentic problem that college graduates will face in the real world often requires the application of multiple competencies in an integrated manner. Therefore, educators need to carefully consider what underlying skills, knowledge, and disposition are required, and how they are related to a problem of practice. Also, data generated from such tasks can be used to make more comprehensive inferences about learners than other types of assessment.

Ongoing: The new generation of performance-based assessment should not be based on a single observation at a single point in time. Rather, evidence should be gathered over time and across contexts. Estimates of students' knowledge, skills, and other attributes are continually updated based on multiple observations in diverse contexts rather than a single observation at one point in time. These observations can be provided immediately to a learner as a form of formative assessment, or their full trajectory can be mapped over time to show progress and growth, summed into a summative assessment. In this way, ongoing assessments break down the traditional distinction between formative and summative assessment.

Embedded: Assessment should be seamlessly woven directly into the task or learning environment itself. Embeddedness is crucial to support ongoing data collection without interruption because in this model learners don't have to "stop and show" for external purposes, which allows the assessment to be ongoing and continuous throughout the learning process. Also, by making assessment embedded in the learning process itself, educators can blur the distinction between learning and assessment.

Flexible: Learners should be able to choose different paths, actions, and ways of solving problems within the assessment to demonstrate their competencies. This also means that the assessment designer needs to thoughtfully consider possible solutions and accommodate differences (e.g., universal design principles). This can mean either having assessments with more than one right answer, or it can mean allowing choice between multiple forms of assessment to acknowledge the same competency. The converse side of allowing flexibility of assessment to the learner is that every learner's demonstration of mastery will look different and unique to the teacher.

In addition to these features just described, we argue that the educational assessment community should consider another principle, *playfulness*, as a way to radically change how we approach assessment in education. The addition of playfulness would therefore lead to better assessment processes that engage learners and educators in empowered, transparent, and collaborative ways. Although this principle, unlike the earlier ones, is not directly related to the rigor of the assessment as a good assessment tool, we believe it should be considered a vital component of all 21st-century learning experiences.

Playful: The benefits of ludic activities and engagement for learning have been widely documented in early childhood education, K-12 education, and all the way to higher and adult education (Lillard, 2013), yet not much has been changed when it comes to assessment.

Defining fun, play, or what conditions lead to playful experiences is difficult (Juul, 2005), and not surprisingly, there is no consensus around the theory or terminology of playfulness (Deterding et al., 2011). The goal of our work is not to define what playfulness is or to establish the terminology of ludic assessment, but to apply the literature and processes of game design and playful user experience design (Deterding et al., 2011) for the purpose of transforming how assessment is conducted in education. When we say playful, we are describing a pleasurable and fun experience, yet stress that fun does not need to be easy. In fact, a challenging work can be as fun or more than an easier one. When people play a fun game, they often feel "pleasantly frustrated", yet they persist through challenging problems (Gee, 2003). We believe playfulness in assessment can mean that assessment can provide an opportunity for learners to explore and experiment within the assessment activity (Resnick, 2014), both individually and socially. Ludic assessment means that assessment activities are thoughtfully designed, so they are "flexible enough for players to inhabit and explore through meaningful play" (Salen & Zimmerman, 2004, p. 165). In practice, this means that ludic assessment needs to incorporate multiple pathways to solution(s) where learners can make meaningful choices and demonstrate multiple ways of solving problems by trying new things.

While playfulness is intricately connected with learning, attempts to connect assessment with playfulness have been limited thus far. Work in the context of game-based assessment (Kim & Ifenthaler, 2019) has investigated how games can be used as a vehicle for assessment, yet more work needs to be done to show how playfulness can broaden assessment practices in general. One challenge that we anticipate with this work is the fundamental tension that underlies the assessment development process. Because allowing learners to experiment, explore, and socially engage with learning experiences on the surface seems to conflict with the common beliefs or practices of assessment, where the assessor (i.e., teachers, assessment developers) predetermines what is or is not acceptable work.

Play itself can be an enigma to design for in practice. Play often feels like one of those items that we recognize when we see it, but have trouble explicitly describing what is and is not play. The purpose of play is to create engagement, and engagement in part comes from having a sense of agency. The Four Freedoms of Play (Osterweil, 2014) is one framework that can be used to describe when an experience has the right level of agency, or freedom, to be playfully engaging. We can build on this framework to develop the following that can be used to evaluate the playfulness of an assessment activity (adapted from Miklasz, 2020). In taking on the perspective of the learner being assessed, the more of these questions that one can answer "yes" to, the more playful the activity. Not every activity needs to have a "yes" answer to every question or freedom, but the more "yeses" one can answer, and the more strongly one can say "yes", the more playfulness is in your assessment.

- *Freedom to Experiment*
  - Can you decide how you will be assessed?
  - Is there more than one way to answer the assessment correctly?
  - Is there more than one correct answer to the assessment?
  - Can you easily go down worthless or suboptimal answer paths?

- *Freedom to Fail*
  - Most basically, can you fail?
  - Is it psychologically safe to fail?
  - Can you set the difficulty of your assessment?

- *Freedom to Try on Identities*
  - Can you take the assessment from different perspectives?
  - Can you decide what you are assessed on, and therefore what you can be declared competent at?
  - Can you choose which assessment results do and do not get publicly acknowledged and shared?

- *Freedom of Effort*
  - Can you decide not to be assessed?
  - Can you decide how much you will engage or hold back from the assessment?
  - Can you decide when to be assessed?

What makes an experience playful, as described using the preceding rubric, might feel at odds with assumptions that we make for traditional educational assessments in today's schools. Therefore, to apply these playful learning principles, we first need to critically examine existing assumptions about assessment. For example, most forms of assessment that we are familiar with constrain choices that one can make within the assessment task, and often there is only one right way of solving the problem or one right solution (i.e., correct vs. incorrect answer). This is usually true when the assessment intends to measure discrete knowledge or low-level skills. However, assessment can be more open-ended and allow exploration as demonstrated in disciplines like Art and Engineering Education. In challenging these assumptions, ludic assessments enter a realm of trade-offs. Ludic assessments exist at the intersection of three disciplines: learning science, assessment science, and game design. Or put another way, ludic assessments must simultaneously teach, assess, and engage at the same time. This puts them at the center of a three-part Venn diagram in Figure 14.1. This also means ludic assessments operate in a space of compromise. That is, a ludic assessment will never feel as efficient as a direct lecture, or never feel as precise as a fully validated test, or it will never be as fun as a well-designed casual game. But one structural issue with education is that these activities are often put in separate buckets, covered by separate products that each use separate class time. By achieving multiple classroom goals at once, ludic assessment adds a kind of cross-functional

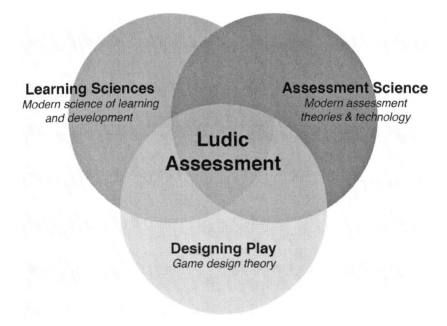

FIGURE 14.1 Three Domains of Playful Assessment

Source: Courtesy of Yoon Jeon (YJ) Kim and Kevin Miklasz©

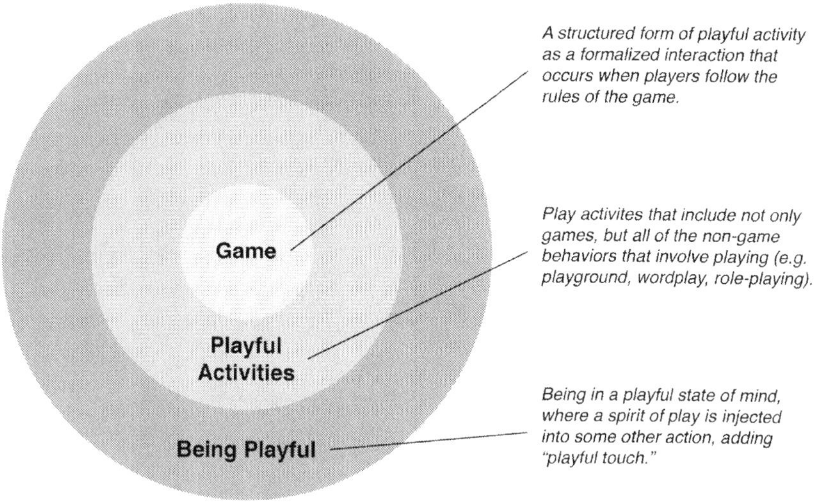

FIGURE 14.2 Levels of Playfulness (adapted from Salen & Zimmerman, 2004)

Source: Courtesy of Yoon Jeon (YJ) Kim and Kevin Miklasz©

efficiency to the job of education, taking more time to do any one of these three things, but less time to do all three at once.

Therefore, putting ludic assessment in practice requires educators to be aware of the emerging scientific understanding of how people learn (i.e., learning sciences) and how to measure what people know (i.e., assessment science) in addition to principles of designing play (what makes an activity playful, engaging, and enjoyable).

To what extent the assessment needs to be playful can also depend on the needs and purposes of the assessment. Assessment can be playful at different levels, and design choices that one make regarding the level of playfulness may lead to different trade-offs. Figure 14.2 (adapted from Salen et al. (2004)) illustrates different ways to think about play, from a game as the most structured form of playful activities, to playful activity—activity that is not a game, but involves non-gameplay behaviors (e.g., role playing, playing with words), and having a playful spirit (e.g., being silly and fun).

Practical Examples From the MIT Playful Journey Lab

Next, we will go into a few examples of ludic assessments from the MIT Playful Journey Lab.

For context, the MIT Playful Journey Lab (https://playful.mit.edu/) is a K-12 research lab that explores new frontiers in assessment learning by creating new forms of assessment that are playful, student-centered, and embedded in the process of learning. Most of the Playful Journey Lab's work is informed by innovative educators' pain-points. That is, when they try to bring a new pedagogy into their classrooms (e.g., games and makerspaces), they often encounter difficulties as the familiar assessment methods are not compatible.

We'll go through two examples—the first example fits more into the "game" category in Figure 14.2, while the second example fits more into the outer circles.

Practical Example 1: *Shadowspect*

Shadowspect (https://shadowspect.org) is a 3D digital puzzle game where the game has clearly defined goals, rules, and obstacles for the players to overcome. Each puzzle in the *Shadowspect* presents several silhouette views of a 3D figure where each figure is built by using a series of 3D geometric primitives such as cubes, cylinders, spheres, cones, or pyramids. The player then selects a set of geometric primitives to recreate a 3D figure by using the 3D game environment. *Shadowspect* was developed with the goal of creating a game that can be used by teachers to monitor students' progress with Common Core geometry standards while recognizing and celebrating other positive skills such as persistence and creative exploration. The teachers can also use this game as an enrichment activity or assignment where students play the game at home as much as they wish to or until they complete specific puzzles.

Shadowspect as a game is the most structured form of play, and it also illustrates multiple strengths of a ludic assessment. First, because of its pleasantly frustrating nature of the gameplay, students feel emotionally invested with the game and can sustain efforts longer compared to traditional math tasks. Second, because learner's actions and choices in the game can be used to understand more than one learning outcome, the educator can gain more holistic insights about what the student is learning and how the student is productively or unproductively engaging with the game. Third, *Shadowspect* presents authentic problems that mimic the use of geometric skills in real worlds, yet are abstract and playful enough to "hook" students to the puzzles.

Applying the Freedom of Play rubrics, *Shadowspect* is more constrained in the Freedom to Experiment as the game was designed and developed with specific behavioral indicators in mind that caused the puzzles to have a limited set of possible solutions. Therefore, the learner does not have much say in how she will be assessed. However, it does allow multiple solutions and allows the player to go down suboptimal answer paths (although assessed as unproductive persistence if it does not pan out at the end). *Shadowspect* offers a lot of room in terms of Freedom to Fail. Failing early on or with more difficult puzzles is expected. In fact, not getting a puzzle attempt right should not discourage the learners from trying again. Additionally, failing is part of the persistence metric, and how you fail and what you do when you first "fail" is a part of how persistence is being measured. Additionally, because the game allows the player to choose easy to hard, easy only, or hard puzzles, the learner has control of how difficult the whole assessment experience is.

In terms of Freedom of Effort, *Shadowspect* is a good example of allowing the player to choose how seriously or lightly she plays the game.

Practical Example 2: Beyond Rubrics

In 2019, MIT Playful Journey Lab, in collaboration with Maker Ed, developed Beyond Rubrics (BR)—an embedded assessment toolkit for hands-on learning that includes playful tools and activities enabling evidence collection and reflection in the process of making. The toolkit intends to engage three types of assessment activities—socially defining the learning outcome and success criteria, individually and collaboratively collecting evidence for learning, and meaning making with the collected evidence. The tools center around seven maker capacities including design process, trouble-shooting, and productive risk taking. Using Figure 14.2 to understand to what extent BR tools are playful, many of them have simple "playful touch" as they were inspired by playful objects and moments that you could find in classrooms or daily life that bring out joy or smiles for teachers and learners. For example, Sparkle Sleuth—an evidence collection tool where students document the aha or oh no moments when the teacher notices the delightful or ouch moments during the making process—was inspired by how young children get excited about getting sparkly stickers after the dentist office visit and celebrate those sparkly moments of learning that learners might not perceive as sparkly. Another tool—Maker Moment—demonstrates a playful activity that has a game-like mechanic to how learners collect evidence for learning. Maker Moment is inspired by the mechanic of Bingo in which students collaboratively document on the Maker Moment with different color pens to reflect later on how frequently they demonstrated different maker capacities.

BR demonstrates several strengths of ludic assessment. First, it is flexible in terms of how the learner chooses to demonstrate her skills. Second, it is ongoing because the learner can document the learning in the process instead of waiting until when learning is done. This strength is particularly of importance in the making context as messing up and getting stuck in the process is not only expected, but also an essential part of the learning process. Third, teachers and learners can have a better understanding of how multiple skills can be applied, and assessment can be more specific in the context.

Applying the Freedom of Play rubrics, BR tools aim to preserve learner's *Freedom to Experiment*, which is also a crucial element for productive making. That is, learners can choose what they think is a piece of evidence based on the common understanding of how the successful demonstration of maker capacities should look like that have been negotiated with the teacher and peers. They can also choose in what forms (e.g., written statement, a Polaroid picture, a short video) they demonstrate their skills. BR tools are also flexible enough for the teachers to design social norms around how and when to use the collected evidence, in relation to the *Freedom of Effort*. For example, a teacher can suggest that students request help only after they tried a different solution and strategy using Unstuck Station, instead of asking for help immediately. Or students can review the series of moments that were captured and choose one incident that they feel captures their experience best.

Conclusion

In this chapter, we discuss what ludic assessment is and how ludic assessment can challenge many of the existing assumptions about what counts as assessment in classrooms. Ludic assessment leverages the modern understanding of how people learn and how we should measure that learning. We also suggest that playfulness in assessment can be achieved by exploring how well the assessment allows for the Four Freedoms of Play. We also discussed how ludic assessment can lead to different trade-offs because it sits on the intersection of play, learning, and assessment. Although a teacher might feel uncomfortable trying out ludic assessment, especially given the assessment culture of prioritizing certain types of rigor (e.g., reliability and objectiveness), there can be long-term payoff as it can lead to a classroom culture of learning, where students are empowered and given agency to decide how and when they are being assessed.

The pandemic we are currently in, and the sudden shift to remote learning, has certainly changed not only the nature of learning but of assessment too. There has been a sudden shift to digital solutions, and in particular asynchronous learning, and a cancellation of normal standardized testing. This creates a potential opportunity to transform how learning and assessment happens in this new normal. For the education industry, it's worth thinking about how the solutions in this space reinforce our existing assessment paradigm or move towards a new solution. Where do we invest? What new habits do we create? What designs do we build? For instance, do we treat at-home assessment as a problem to be fixed with digital surveillance solutions, or an opportunity to reinvent flexible, performance-based assessments that students complete at their own pace about their own interests? Many of the ideas offered about ludic assessments are easier to implement in a digital environment, and the opportunity to shift to a new assessment paradigm is ripe.

A ludic assessment can be a powerful way to address disengagement and lack of play in the synchronous online learning models that are commonly found in today's schools during the pandemic. That is, school educators have the potential to be more flexible about what counts as assessment when the individual student's context widely varies. Therefore, to support all students, from the one who disappears from the online classroom to take care of her younger sister to the one who does not have a reliable interaction connection, it is more critical than ever to challenge some assumptions about what is a good, reliable assessment. Perhaps the ability to accommodate different students in different situations should be valued above a uniform distribution in a single format? Finally, this pandemic has been affecting many young people's social and emotional health and many of them are very "zoomed out". A pinch of playfulness embedded in their learning and assessment can be helpful to boost desperately needed engagement and enjoyment.

We hope the ideas offered here can provide a better path forward, not only during this pandemic's shift to remote learning but for education in general. Let's think about how to reinvent the future of both learning and assessment in a way that better helps students live up to their full potential.

References

Bergen, D. (2009). Play as the learning medium for future scientists, mathematicians, and engineers. *American Journal of Play*, *1*(4), 413–428.

Cross, L. H., & Frary, R. B. (1999). Hodgepodge grading: Endorsed by students and teachers alike. *Applied Measurement in Education*, *12*(1), 53–72.

Deterding, S., Dixon, D., Khaled, R., & Nacke, L. (2011). From game design elements to gamefulness: Defining "gamification". In *Proceedings of the 15th international academic MindTrek conference: Envisioning future media environments*. Association for Computing Machinery Digital Library (pp. 9–15).

Fisher, K., Hirsh-Pasek, K., Golinkoff, R. M., Singer, D. G., & Berk, L. (2011). Playing around in school: Implications for learning and educational policy. *The Oxford Handbook of the Development of Play*, 2010.

Gee, J. P. (2003). What video games have to teach us about learning and literacy. *Computers in Entertainment (CIE)*, *1*(1), 20–20.

Juul, J. (2005). *Half-real: Video games between real rules and fictional worlds*. MIT Press.

Kim, Y. J., & Ifenthaler, D. (2019). Game-based assessment: The past ten years and moving forward. In *Game-based assessment revisited* (pp. 3–11). Springer.

Lillard, A. S. (2013). Playful learning and Montessori education. *NAMTA Journal*, *38*(2), 137–174.

Linn, R. L., Baker, E. L., & Dunbar, S. B. (1991). Complex, performance-based assessment: Expectations and validation criteria. *Educational Researcher*, *20*(8), 15–21.

Miklasz, K. (2020). *Intrinsic rewards in games and learning*. ETC Press.

National Research Council. (2001). *Knowing what students know: The science and design of educational assessment*. National Academies Press.

Osterweil, S. (2014). *The four freedoms of play and learning* [Video]. YouTube. https://youtu.be/-66lm9T4bNk.

Resnick, M. (2014). *Give P's a chance: Projects, peers, passion, play*. Constructionism and Creativity: Proceedings of the Third International Constructionism Conference. Austrian Computer Society, Vienna, 13–20.

Salen, K., Tekinbaş, K. S., & Zimmerman, E. (2004). *Rules of play: Game design fundamentals*. MIT Press.

Conclusion
Once We Defeat the COVID-19 Boss Battle, What Then?

David Seelow

Five Ways Game-Based Learning Can Transform Students

Let me begin my end with a snippet describing a busy, jam packed metropolis suddenly turning into a ghost town of sorts, "it was a most surprising thing, to see those streets, which were usually so thronged, now grown desolate, and so few People to be seen in them" (Defoe, 1722). The quote adequately describes New York City's famous Fifth Avenue during March 2020 when the COVID-19 virus brought America's most populated and vibrant city to the breaking point. However, the description refers to another great city, London, the year 1665, and the cause: The Great Plague. That is over 350 years ago, but a new virus has proven just as daunting in the technology rich early 21st century as it did to a medically primitive society in the last third of the 17th century. The massive leaps in technology, medicine, and scientific research . . . advances Daniel Defoe could not have even imagined, over the last three and a half centuries are still humbled by nature's power.

Technology has not, and will not save us from natural disasters, or the educational limitations this book seeks to redress. We need to rethink education, and COVID-19 has allowed us the pause to reflect on what needs to be done. Writing in *The Atlantic*, Erika Christakis (2020) makes my point about secondary education regarding elementary education:

> Like a tsunami that pulls away from the coast, leaving an exposed stretch of land, the pandemic has revealed long-standing inattention to children's developmental needs—needs as basic as exercise, outdoor time, conversation, play, even sleep. All the challenges of educating young children [and not so young] that we have minimized for years have suddenly appeared like flotsam on a beach at low tide, reeking and impossible to ignore.

Bullseye. She is on target. Christakis's answer to the previous wasted opportunities for learning emphasizes "achievement that is not narrowly academic," which this book has also argued from various angles in every chapter. Let me conclude with five ways game-based learning can promote the kind of learning necessary in a post-pandemic world: 1) systems thinking, 2) co-operation/collaboration, 3) strategic thinking, 4) intelligent decision making, and 5) ethics.

They are five skills or ways of thinking teachers can encourage to transform student learning in fundamental ways. Specific games are concrete ways of realizing this innovative way of thinking and educating.

First, *systems thinking*. The global public health crisis engendered by COVID-19 also brought about simultaneous crises in education and economics/business, at a minimum. If schools close, parents must arrange for supervision, and that, in turn, interferes with their work schedule, if they are fortunate enough to still be working. Systems are dynamic; a change in one part of the system causes changes in all other parts of the system. Thinking about systems requires an ability to see the big picture and how all the different parts work together. Running a city or a public health department involves high level systems thinking. Where is this taught in school? Games, especially open world games, such as Massively Multiplayer Online Role Playing Games (e.g., *World of Warcraft*), as well as controversial games like the Grand Theft Auto series or the noncontroversial Sims series (see Gee, 2010) compel players to work with systems all the time.

Second, *teamwork and cooperation/collaboration*. You cannot successfully solve complex, multisystemic problems as an individual. Vaccines are discovered by teams of research scientists, and larger public health issues, as an example, require cooperation between local, state, and federal government agencies as well as public health officials, the public, medical professionals, and many more. Climate change requires the same level of cooperation and collaboration. Several casual, entertaining games teach teamwork very well. For instance, during the pandemic, the game *Among Us* (2018) suddenly became enormously popular among high school and college students. It is a simple game to play. You are part of a space crew completing tasks necessary to guide your spaceship safely toward its destination. However, there is an imposter among the crew. Players must root out the imposter before they sabotage the ship. Can students tell the real from the fake? Many Americans cannot discern accurate from inaccurate information anymore, so that is one worthwhile skill the game requires. Moreover, the game requires a majority vote for a possible imposter to be voted out. Working as a team makes a difference in this game. That is the entire point. Students can play with classmates over a wireless network (up to ten students) or online with strangers or distant friends.

Third, *strategic thinking*. A strategic thinker has a goal, flexibility, and an ability to forecast and imagine new possibilities based upon current situations. Such thinkers combine the Arts and Sciences in equal measure. A strategic thinker must use the precision of mathematics and the imagination of poetry. You cannot build a bridge unless you first imagine it. Chess can be considered the preeminent strategy game. It should be available and encouraged in every school.

During the pandemic, the Netflix limited series *The Queen's Gambit* (2020) emerged as a surprise hit. Audiences apparently found the show about chess as exciting as the action and horror shows that more often draw the largest ratings. No doubt, the Rocky Balboa mythos played a part, as 9-year-old underdog orphan Beth Harmon fights her way from high school matches to defeat the Russian World Chess Champion Vasily Borgov. That a girl—becoming a young woman—could beat all the men and achieve the pinnacle of success in a staunchly patriarchal game culture has special satisfaction. We can learn some important lessons about games and strategic thinking from this series and the ancient game of chess.

As Beth pursues her interest in chess, we learn what makes a Chess Master and, ultimately, a Grandmaster. These are the qualities that also make an expert strategic thinker. First, practice, practice, practice. Beth plays chess incessantly. She plays everyone who is willing to play while also imagining games in her head. Second, study hard. Beth reads and studies books about chess, and the skills and game play of other chess players from the past and present. No matter how much natural talent you might have that talent will not be fully realized without constant practice. Being good at something is hard work, whether that something is *Tetris*, *Fortnite* or Biology.

The third quality for being an expert strategic thinker is to challenge yourself. There will always be someone better (well for all but a select few). Beth plays the members of the all-male chess club at the local high school. She beats them all. In fact, Beth plays the entire team simultaneously and still beats them all. Watching these matches reminded me of the young Bobby Fisher. Beth goes on to state tournaments, regional, national, and international tournaments, i.e., bigger and bigger challenges. Do not let students take the easy way out. No easy "A's." That serves students poorly. You do not grow without challenge. What might seem easy in high school most likely will not be easy in college.

In terms of strategic thinking, students must therefore study, master the subject. Beth needs to know every possible move at any point in the game as well as how her opponents have played similar situations in other games. At the same time, these precisely calculated moves must also draw upon her imagination. Beth must see all the possible ways a situation might play out over the duration of the game. In the show, we see her envision a game in her head as she looks up at the ceiling and imagines multiple ways to move pieces many moves in advance. Games involve decisions and consequences for those decisions. In *Life is Strange*, for instance, you play the character Max who can rewind time, and revisit a decision. In chess you need to think multiple moves in advance before you make a move in the present. Strategic thinking really demands this ability to look at the future, and project from the present forward. You need to see possibilities to progress.

Fourth, *intelligent decision making*. There is a moment in the final episode of *The Queen's Gambit* during the championship match when Borgov offers Beth a draw. The game is in a late stage. Borgov has the advantage on the board, and his end game is virtually unbeatable. Beth must make a critical choice. These critical existential choices confront all of us, and, sometimes, our decision affects more than us. Beth turns down the offer, a risky decision, but one that pays off. We want students to make smart choices when it comes to school and life: turn down the offer of an unfamiliar pill at a party and so on. Dr. Ferrnandes and her Yale colleagues discussed these kinds of situations in

Chapter 12. COVID-19 is a case in point. Every student, like every citizen, had to make a personal choice of whether to wear a mask. Not choosing to wear a mask not only put oneself at risk for contracting the virus but put other people's health a risk. Sadly, many Americans chose to make the poor choice and not wear a mask. That decision resulted in unnecessary deaths. Those people who offered civil liberties as the reason for not wearing a mask showed neither understanding of the constitution nor understanding of civil rights. We cannot educate people to make these kinds of uninformed harmful decisions.

In his book on designing behavioral games, Aaron Dignan draws attention to the existential choices necessary for any important change to occur. "Today we face global issues that go beyond our personal development. Unlike problems that we can solve with policy alone, these issues almost certainly require that we change behavior at the individual and family level, because *we're* the problem" (2011, p. 165). Games are ideal both for helping us educate students in smart decision making and effecting positive behavioral change. Unlike a novel, in a game, the player reaches multiple points in the story where she has to make a key decision and that decision has an outcome, both short term and long term, on the game. These decision points are perfect teachable moments.

Games can also encourage and promote pro social behaviors that benefit one's well-being. Thought and action must work in concert. People generally know when taking a prescribed medication is a good idea, but they often do not adhere to the medication schedule and risk self-harm. Middle and high school students often make poor behavior choices, and games that target behavior like resisting peer pressure, not vaping, and attending a tutoring session can have a positive effect on behavior.

Fifth, *ethics*. In her chapter Karen (Kat) Schrier shows how games can contribute to empathy and compassion. For students to make positive behavior changes and smart decisions they need to know when a decision is right and when it is not. Ethics are not relative. Not wearing a mask is wrong. Period. Knowing that decision is wrong requires compassion—you need to realize your action impacts another person, as well as an underlying understanding of what makes a decision responsible and informed. Ethics should be taught in every school—elementary, middle, high school, college, and professional schools. Our education system has failed miserably on this account. Look at national politics, where leaders make partisan decisions that benefit their re-election a priority over their constituency and the national citizenry. The corporate world, even worse. The opioid epidemic results in no small measure from Big Pharma pushing a highly addictive drug that has ruined lives and communities under the absurd pretense that the drugs are helping the very people whose lives are being ruined. Species are going extinct because of how we pollute the ocean and decimate the rest of the world's species in relentless short sighted, selfish development. Climate change continues to a point of no return and collectively the world watches, but there are no innocent bystanders.

There is hope. In fact, students have become the real leaders today. Greta Thunberg, Malala Yousafzai, Emma Gonzalez, Alex Wind, Cameron Kasky, and Jaclyn Corin are all leaders and activists as high school students making world changing impact through responsible ethical action. Games can help encourage an understanding of and engagement with ethics, even games you might frown upon as frivolous or escapist.

The transmedia phenomena *The Walking Dead* created by Robert Kirkman combines a first-class narrative with major decision points for the player. You play as Lee Everett, a convicted murderer, who also happens to be a history professor at Georgetown. Lee happens upon a zombie invasion—a metaphor for any mass attack of the "other," and he must, as circumstances evolve, protect a 9-year-old girl named Clementine from these walking dead. Zombies may seem strange, but on one level *Hamlet* is also a ghost story— and a very gory one at that. *Walking Dead* is also a survival story (*Hamlet* had no such fortune). Surviving means protecting the innocent girl, while making life or death decisions. These are moral decisions, not simple choices like many point-and-click or choose-your-own-adventure narratives. Each key decision is saved and returns in later episodes/issues having made an impact on the story. Trying to teach Kant, even in graduate school, is a tall order, but using a horror story that high school students thrive on and will immerse themselves in allows you to bring ethical theories to bear on students' choices, and then you can debate them in class. This is game-based learning at its best: engaging, exciting, fun, thought provoking, authentic, and powerful.

Implementation Tips

Hopefully, this book has convinced you of the value game-based learning offers. How do you make it happen? Start small. Go back and re-read Kate Litman's chapter to see how Quest to Learn makes it happen. Begin with a single unit of one of your courses, assess the unit, revise it, and teach again after tweaking. Find other teachers in your department or school building with an interest in games and brainstorm together. Form a support/study group. Work on support from the department chair and then the building principal and then the curriculum director. Make professional development a priority. Join email lists, organizations (e.g., the local chapter of the Independent Game Developers Association), and LinkedIn groups (e.g., Games Learning & Society) that value game-based learning. Attend conferences, virtual or in person, (e.g., Games for Change, Serious Play), and network. My Revolutionary Learning blog at www.revolutionarylearning.net has discussions of numerous games that can be used in the classroom, both traditional and online. You can help design after-school clubs/programs that cross district lines and combine game play with literacy and other important life skills. The teacher's union can help as well. For change to happen on a state and national level, political action will be necessary. Finally, all the contributors to this book are enthusiastic supporters and practitioners of game-based learning. Reach out to us. Finally, consider this book an invitation to play and turn stale classrooms into dynamic learning experiences.

References

Christakis, E. (2020, December). School wasn't so great before COVID, either. *The Atlantic*. Retrieved January 12, 2020, from www.theatlantic.com/magazine/archive/2020/12/school-wsnt-so-great-before-covi-either/6116923

Defoe, D. (1990). *A journal of the plague year*. Oxford World Classics. Originally published in 1722.

Dignan. A. (2011). *Game frame: Using games for strategy and success*. Free Press.

Gee, J. P. (2010). *Women and gaming: The Sims and 21ˢᵗ century learning*. Palgrave Macmillan.

Queen's Gambit (2020). Director: Scott Frank. Netflix streaming series.

The Walking Dead (2012–). Telltale Games. Video game.

Afterword

Justin Reich

I hope that after reading the diverse chapters in this book, tackling math, history, science, social and emotional learning, executive function, and other topics, you are inspired to reconsider the role that games might play in teaching and learning in the future. For readers who are practicing educators, let me offer two frameworks for guiding reimagining your teaching and curriculum.

What is so important for students to learn that it's worth the time and effort to reimagine a lesson, unit, or course through the lens of game-based learning? In their recent study of U.S. high schools, *In Search of Deeper Learning*, Jal Mehta and Sarah Fine (2019) observed a wide range of schools adopting different pedagogical approaches. They toured project-based learning schools, International Baccalaureate schools, "no excuses" charter schools, and others. While they found many differences in pedagogical approaches in these different schools, they discovered a great deal of agreement about what constituted "deeper learning" that would prepare students well for the complex future ahead.

For many educators, deeper learning includes three dimensions: content mastery, creative expression, and identity development. When a student learns something deeply, she has a mastery of relevant facts and skills, she can use those facts and skills to make novel performances and products (a new robot, a new proof, a new play, a new argument), and she undergoes a shift in identity that integrates her newfound disciplinary skills into her sense of self—she goes from doing physics to being a physicist. Different pedagogical philosophies sequenced these dimensions differently—"no excuses" charter schools tend to start with content mastery before moving students on to creative expression and identity development, while project-based learning schools tend to start with creative expression before turning to the other two dimensions, but educators who disagree about the means of education often share a sense of the ends.

These three dimensions of the aims of deeper learning offer footholds for thinking about where gaming and game-based learning might fit into your teaching. In many domains, some fraction of content mastery is drudgery, and gameful approaches can provide motivation and structure for memorizing key facts or developing new skills. Games are powerful places for exploring new identities, where fictional worlds can inspire students to playfully inhabit new roles. A student who doesn't feel much like a real scientist in a high school lab class might have a better chance of adopting—at least for a little while—a scientist's persona while donning a VR headset to begin exploring the inside of a cell. Game worlds can also generate new contexts for problem solving and creative expression, such as the designers in *Minecraft* worlds applying ideas of style, proportion, and other architectural concepts to the creation of new kinds of buildings and spaces, or applying ideas about democracy, justice, and public policy to the rule set governing a new world. And when learners are given the opportunity to create text adventures or other kinds of games, they have a new format with which to apply their content knowledge and disciplinary skills. The deeper learning framework of mastery, creativity, and identity gives teachers three kinds of entry points for thinking about where games might fit into a new or revised curriculum.

A second useful tool for thinking about curriculum change is what education technologist Stone Wiske and colleagues (2005) called a "target of difficulty." Most teachers are unlikely to start incorporating game-based learning into their practice by throwing away an entire syllabus and starting over from scratch. Sensibly, most teachers want to start with a more modest change to a lesson or unit before diving into remodeling an entire course. But where to start? A target of difficulty is a place in a teacher's curriculum that is worth the effort to redesign, and it has three components. First, the content of the curriculum is something of importance to the learning course of the course. If a teacher is going to put new effort into curriculum redesign, it's best to put that work into something really important. A good target of difficulty is central, not peripheral, to the aims of a course. Second, the lesson or unit to target should be one that's hard to teach, or not working particularly well. If a teacher has a part of their course that's working really well, leave that alone. A better place to start is with a section or unit that regularly isn't clicking for some or many students. Finally, a target of difficulty is a place where innovation is likely to have some leverage—in this case, a place where gameful learning seems likely to have some purchase in tackling a curricular problem. A target of difficulty is something important to teach, hard to teach, or not working well under the current design, and in a topic where a game-based approach might align well with the teaching goals. For teachers wondering where to start trying a gameful approach to teaching and learning, the concept of a target of difficulty offers a useful place to start.

For a few educators reading this book, the stories and examples within might be enough to spark a passion for completely reimaging a class, a program, or an entire school. But most educators are not ready revolutionaries; most of us like to dip our toes into new ideas before diving in completely. Mehta and Fine's dimensions of deeper learning and Wiske's target of difficulty provide two ways of thinking about where the waters might be most inviting for that first dip. For educators who find some success in those first efforts at reinvention, early experiments can whet the appetite for greater and more substantive changes.

As the preceding chapters show, the rewards for this kind of experimentation can be substantial across the curriculum. More gameful learning can lead to classrooms where students find new entry points into topics and disciplines, have more opportunities for creative expression, and find greater motivation for the work and challenges of school.

References

Mehta, J., & Fine, S. (2019). *In search of deeper learning: The quest to remake the American high school.* Harvard University Press.

Wiske, M. S., Franz, K. R., & Breit, L. (2005). *Teaching for understanding with technology.* Jossey-Bass.

Acknowledgments

First and foremost, I want to thank the many contributors to this volume. Their comprehensive knowledge, expert skills, and enthusiastic dedication to game-based learning and the improvement of middle and high school education make this book the invaluable work I believe it to be. I thank Barry Fishman and Claudia-Santi F. Fernandes for their incredibly careful and helpful feedback on my Introduction and Conclusion. I am indebted to their collective voice and support of this effort. At Routledge, I thank Daniel Schwartz who first approached me with the idea for this book. He felt a book on game-based learning would be timely and valuable. His expert guidance and advice on the volume is much appreciated. Olivia Powers answered innumerable queries throughout the writing and editing of the book. She responded tirelessly with precision and support. Katherine Tsamparlis got the entire process rolling many months ago.

My embrace and promotion of game-based learning began in earnest around 2012. Many designers, educators, and visionaries have encouraged, supported, and improved my work over the last nine years. I owe no one more than John F. Ebersole, RIP, (1949–2016), the former president of Excelsior College. A Vietnam vet with a long dedication to the power of games and simulations for learning and training, John gave me an opportunity of a lifetime in founding the Center for Game and Simulation-Based Learning. John's full support never wavered, and no setback ever deterred his vision for learning. I will never forget him sending me an email of support from his hospital room in Boston just months before he passed saying how happy he was for my Revolutionary Learning 2016 Conference.

Several other professionals helped make my early symposia on games and learning a success, both in person and online. I thank Clark Aldrich, a pioneer of serious games and learning by doing, who graciously and expertly moderated the first two symposia. Other contributors I thank with applause are Jon Aleckson, CEO of Web Courseworks in Madison, WI; Andy Phelps, at the time chair of RIT's (Rochester Institute of Technology) game program, founder of the extraordinary MAGIC Center at that campus and now at American University; Joey Lee, Teacher's College, Columbia University; Ben DeVane, University of Iowa; standing applause for Tobi Saulnier, CEO and founder of the woman owned 1st Playable Productions in Troy, NY. Tobi's studio created the seriously fun writing game *Paper Capers* for the Online Writing

Lab I created. Jesse Schell, star game designer and CEO of Schell Games in Pittsburgh, served as keynote speaker at the Rayburn Building in Washington DC that inaugurated the Center for Game and Simulation-Based Learning. Super women Victoria Van Voorhis, CEO of Second Avenue Learning; Elena Bertozzi from Quinnipiac University; and Sharon Sloane, Founder and CEO of WILL Interactive, have all been enduring supporters. Randy Brown, Vice President of Applied Research Associates, Inc. and Division Manager of their Virtual Heroes division, a superb studio dedicated to designing serious games, Jennifer McNamara and Walter Cheek, Vice Presidents at the stellar BreakAway Games, were all ardent supporters. Gerol Petruzzella from Massachusetts College of Liberal Arts has been a wonderful collaborator over the years.

Holding a conference in New York City was a mammoth undertaking for a small online college and a nascent Center for Game and Simulation-Based Learning but many people made that a rousing success including Designing Events (Michele Issing and Erin Highlander-Williams did all the planning and logistics); stellar education journalist and writer Greg Toppo moderated a panel on games and assessment; Eric Zimmerman, noted game designer and NYU professor, emceed the pitch contest; and Rebecca Rufo-Tepper gave an inspiring closing keynote. Avery Rueb from Affordance Studios in Montreal has been an enthusiastic supporter. Across the Atlantic, Jacqueline Cawston and her colleagues from Coventry University in the U.K. have been fantastic supporters and advocates for game-based learning, and for sure, game industry pioneer, the legendary Ian Livingstone, who graciously served as the keynote speaker at my 2016 conference. I am also indebted to former New York State Senator Martin J. Golden (served from 2003–2018) from Brooklyn's 22nd Senate District who appeared at the conference's final day arcade show. At the time, Senator Golden served as chair of the Select Committee on Science, Technology, Incubation and Entrepreneurship. He has been a strong advocate for the games industry in New York State.

Speaking of assessment, Kristin DiCerbo, now Chief Learning Officer at Kahn Academy, has appeared with me a few times at conferences and suggested Dr. Yoon Jeon (YJ) Kim, the author of this book's final chapter, to me. William G. Harris, founder and CEO of the Association of Test Publishers, has been a fantastic longtime supporter of mine and a major advocate for the progressive use of games in assessment. His support is very appreciated. Don Dea, Cofounder of Fusion Productions and Board Member at Excelsior College, always supported me and offered expert technology advice. Scott Dalrymple, my former dean and former president of Columbia College in Missouri, supported my pitch for the Center for Game and Simulation-Based Learning to the Board of Trustees; Scott's vision and advocacy have meant much to me. John Prusch always provided an ear and good advice on instructional design when I initiated an online game-based learning pilot program. That program, in turn, owes its success to the wonderful trio at Muzzy Lane Software, north of Boston: Dave McCool, Conall Ryan, and Bert Snow. We proved even Red Sox and Yankees fans can find common ground on the larger field of learning.

An incredibly special thank you to my friend Lee Sheldon. Expert designer, master writer, professor of practice, and advocate for games in learning, Lee designed the online game *Secrets: A Cyberculture Mystery Game* that represents the gold standard for online education.

This is a book to help educators in grades 6–12, so I must give special thanks to those educators who encouraged me to explore public education. Kate Velsor at the State University of New York College at Old Westbury encouraged and convinced me to move from the Humanities Department to the School of Education in 1998. This launched another career of sorts and allowed me to oversee hundreds of student teachers across Long Island and parts of New York City. During this time, I also had the privilege of working closely with two terrific former teachers, Maxine Kline from the Long Beach City School District and the late Betty Friedman, RIP (1927–2006), from the Syosset Central School District. Finally, my own high school teaching practice owes most to Dr. Veronica McDermott, former superintendent of the Patchogue-Medford School District—Veronica remains a staunch supporter of education equity—and that district's former English chair, Gail Braverman.

I also give thanks to David Morrow and Brian Sweeney, former and current chairs of English at the College of Saint Rose, for giving me the opportunity and freedom to teach game-based courses. They are exemplary chairpersons, and the courses they have supported have always been extremely popular with students as evidenced by frequent requests for over enrollment.

Most of all, on a personal level I give a super abundance of thanks to Beth Ellen Tedford who always provides a listening ear, balanced feedback, and a sense of hope to my work. Her kind heart and gentle soul keep me going. Last, but in no way least, a little pug named Roderick. Any game with Roderick is a game I treasure forever.

Image Credits

About the Contributors

Sandra Schamroth Abrams, Ph.D., is Professor in the School of Education at St. John's University in New York. Abrams's investigations of digital literacies, videogaming, and technology integration explore layered meaning making and agentive learning. Abrams is author/editor of over 70 works, including eight books and six special issues. She has received various research awards, including the USDLA award for the article Gamification and Accessibility and an AECT award for her article Peer Review and Nuanced Power Structures. Abrams's recent publications are featured in *Teachers College Record, Journal of Adolescent & Adult Literacy*, and *Journal of Media Literacy Education*. Abrams serves on multiple editorial boards and is an Associate Editor for the *International Journal of Multiple Research Approaches* and a founding co-editor of the Gaming Ecologies and Pedagogies book series (Brill).

Chris Angelli has been teaching various biology courses at Somerville High School for 13 years. He has a bachelor's degree in biology from Assumption College, and master's degrees in cell and molecular biology and clinical lab science from The University of Rhode Island. He currently teaches AP biology and a course that he developed himself, biotechnology, at Somerville High School. Chris has a lifelong interest in digital games and simulations and is fascinated by creating a way to merge gaming and science education. In his spare time, Chris enjoys traveling, reading, and gaming.

Hap Aziz has been transforming learning through play as an educator, interactive experience designer, and learning technology visionary for the past three decades. He has worked extensively to create new and compelling experiences for learners in both physical and virtual learning spaces making use of serious play technologies. Hap has partnered with a number of colleges and universities to launch complete learning ecosystems, online academic programs, and professional development training that considers pedagogy through the lens of narrative, interactivity, and engagement, and he currently serves as the Director of Learning for AdventHealth. He holds a BA degree in computer science from Rollins College, an M.Ed. from Nova Southeastern University, and an EdD in curriculum and instruction from the University of Florida.

Joy Baker graduated with a degree in elementary education in 2000. Early in her career, she taught 2nd grade for three years. Following her adventure in elementary education, Joy obtained her state certification for Middle School Social Sciences in 2008, and she has been a middle school history teacher (7th and 8th grade) for the past 12 years, currently instructing students at International Community School in Winter Park, Florida. Convinced that learning happens in more than just the mind, she is passionate about teaching the whole child. In her teaching Joy strives to reach students with all learning styles so each child is able to engage with the material in a way that promotes success and lifetime learning.

Tyra M. Pendergrass Boomer brings a diverse educational background and unique work experiences to the play2PREVENT team. She received her Bachelor of Science in biology from Howard University and her Master of Environmental Management from Yale University. In her capacity of deputy director for the play2PREVENT Lab at the Yale Center for Health & Learning Games, Tyra is instrumental in building and maintaining community partnerships, overseeing the day to day operations of the lab, and presenting the lab's research in local, national, and international settings. Tyra was a 2013 Connecticut Health Foundation Health Leader Fellow. She was also 2018–2019 Advanced Health Science Research Fellow with the Yale School of Medicine.

Jonathan Cassie is the Director of Curriculum and Innovation at TVT Community Day School in Irvine, California. An educator with more than 20 years' experience teaching and leading in independent schools across the country, he has used his personal commitment to mission-alignment, strategic focus, and transformation to empower faculty and students to change their schools in response to the dynamic reality of the 21st century. He is also a game designer and writer with a special interest in tabletop roleplaying games, gamified instruction, and game-based learning. His book *Level Up Your Classroom*, was published in 2016, winning "best technical nonfiction book" from Association Media and Publishing in 2017. He is also one of the hosts of the education podcast "Many Windows."

Paul Darvasi, Ph.D., is an educator, game designer, speaker, and writer whose work looks at the intersection of games, culture, and learning. He teaches English and media studies, and is a founding member of the Play Lab at the University of Toronto. His research explores how commercial video games can be used as texts for critical analysis by adolescents. He has designed pervasive games that include *The Ward Game, Blind Protocol*, a cyber warfare simulation that instructs on online security, and a series of orientation games for McGill University. Darvasi has worked with various universities, the U.S. Department of Education, UNESCO, foundry10, Consumers International, iThrive, and Connected Camps and has participated in several international research projects. His work has been featured on PBS, NPR, CBC, the Huffington Post,

Polygon, Killscreen, Gamasutra, Sterne, Endgadget, Edsurge, Edutopia, and MindShift.

Andrew Evanko is a high school social studies teacher in Connecticut. He has worked as an educator for seven years and has long been interested in the pedagogical efficacy of utilizing games and simulations in the classroom. Andrew has attained a MA in history from Southern Connecticut State University. In his spare time, he spends too many hours perfecting his *Crazy Taxi* high score.

Claudia-Santi F. Fernandes, EdD, LPC, MCHES, NCC, is an adolescent mental health and wellness expert with experience in public schools, clinical settings, and research institutions. Dr. Fernandes taught in a public school and developed a compelling interest in school-based support services. This interest led her to become a bilingual school counselor where she supported student development through evidence-based counseling interventions and programs. She also played a leadership role in opening a Bard High School Early College in Newark, New Jersey. She was the Director of Student Activities and organized school-wide initiatives that concentrated on social and emotional learning and school climate as students worked toward a high school diploma and an AA degree from Bard College. Currently, Dr. Fernandes is a deputy director at the play2PREVENT Lab at the Yale Center for Health & Learning Games and an associate research scientist at the Yale University School of Medicine. As part the Lab, she conducts research involving the design, development, and evaluation of videogame interventions and she is committed to a focus of her work on mental health and well-being in youth and emerging adults. Currently, she is the Project Director of a National Institutes of Health (NIH)/National Institute of Drug Abuse (NIDA) initiative, Helping to End Addiction Long-term (HEAL) grant (Principal Investigator: Lynn E. Fiellin, MD) to prevent opioid misuse in older adolescents. She also practices as a licensed professional counselor and serves on the Board of Directors for the Connecticut Association of School-Based Health Centers.

Lynn E. Fiellin, MD, is a professor of medicine in the Section of General Internal Medicine at the Yale University School of Medicine, the Yale Child Study Center and the Yale School of Public Health (Social and Behavioral Sciences). She has received funding from the CVS Health Foundation, Robert Wood Johnson Foundation, the Health Resources and Services Administration, NIDA, NICHD, and NIAAA for her work. With the award of a five-year R01 in 2009 from the Eunice Kennedy Shriver National Institute of Child Health and Human Development, she changed her focus to developing and testing technology-based interventions for the purpose of improving outcomes in adolescents. In 2009, she founded the play2PREVENT Lab at Yale and subsequently founded and now directs the Lab and the Yale Center for Health & Learning Games. Her Lab/Center focuses on the development and evaluation of videogame interventions targeting a range of outcomes including HIV prevention, promotion of HIV/STI testing, and substance use prevention including opioids, tobacco, electronic cigarettes, vaping, and marijuana. Her team also forges successful collaborations and partnerships between scientists, educators, videogame designers/developers, community-based organizations, and others with the goal to develop innovative targeted interventions and educational materials for risk reduction and prevention in youth and young adults.

Sarah Fiess is the Assistant Principal and School Outreach Coordinator at Tech Valley High School. She holds a MA in Teaching of English from Columbia Teachers College, and an SBL/SDL Advanced Certificate from the College of St. Rose. In her community work, she supports educators throughout the Capital Region by offering professional learning experiences and coaching teachers in project-based learning.

Barry Fishman is Arthur F. Thurnau Professor of Learning Technologies at the University of Michigan School of Information and School of Education. His research focuses on the sustainable transformation of educational systems to build learner autonomy and engagement, including the development of gameful pedagogy, GradeCraft, and Design-Based Implementation Research methodology for partnership research. He earned his PhD in learning sciences from Northwestern University in 1996.

Randall Fujimoto is the Executive Director of GameTrain Learning, an educational nonprofit organization that promotes game-based learning in schools and organizations. Randall designs and develops various game-based educational and training programs, including educational immersive theater projects and educational escape game workshops. Previously, he was an executive producer in the video games industry and has master's degrees in education (instructional design) and business (MBA).

James Paul Gee retired in January 2020 to live on his small farm and take care of his animals. He was a professor at seven universities, tenured at eight, and held endowed chairs at three. His last job was as the Mary Lou Fulton Presidential Professor of Literacy Studies and Regents Professor at Arizona State University.

Hannah R. Gerber, Ph.D., is Professor at Sam Houston State University College of Education and an Honorary Professor at the University of South Africa, Department of Language Education, Arts, and Culture. Currently she is President of the International Council for Educational Media. Her research focuses on youth culture and digital practices, particularly adolescent videogaming practices and the literacy experiences that are developed within. Gerber's work has won multiple research awards and has been discussed in mainstream media venues, such as *Wired Magazine*. With over 80 published works to date, including seven books, her most recent articles can be found in the *Journal of Adolescent & Adult Literacy*, *Educational Media International*, *Tech Trends*, and the *International Journal for Multiple Research Approaches*.

Caitlin Hayward is Associate Director for Research & Development at the Center for Academic Innovation at the University of Michigan. Caitlin co-founded and led the development of the GradeCraft gameful learning management system. In parallel to developing GradeCraft, she completed her PhD in Information Science, with a focus on learning analytics, the theoretical foundations of gameful pedagogy, and novel educational technologies.

Kimberly Hieftje, Ph.D., is a research scientist at the Yale School of Medicine and the Deputy Director of the Yale Center for Health & Learning Games and play2PREVENT Lab, which focuses on the development and evaluation of videogame interventions for health prevention and promotion, behavior change, and education in adolescents and young adults. Dr. Hieftje is also the Director of the play4REAL XR Lab, which focuses on the use of XR (extended reality) in games. She is currently involved in the development and testing of several health behavior change videogames and has published frequently on developing, evaluating, and implementing serious games. She has worked on games that have focused on topics including JUUL/e-cigarette prevention, tobacco use prevention, risk reduction in adolescents, HIV/STI prevention, HIV/STI testing, empowering young women around sexual health, bystander intervention, LGBTQ bullying, school climate, and alcohol harm use prevention and reduction. Dr. Hieftje is currently the Editor-in-Chief of the *Games for Health Journal*.

Krithika Jagannath is a Ph.D., candidate in the Informatics Department at the University of California Irvine, where she works with Professor Katie Salen Tekinbaş in the *MadeWithPlay* and Connected Learning Labs. Her dissertation research is focused on governance in online "kid-friendly" gaming communities in *Minecraft*, and Discird. Krithika uses digital ethnographic and design-led research approaches to understand how technology might be designed to support positive youth development, particularly during early adolescence. She holds a bachelor's degree in Computer Science Engineering from Bangalore University and a Master's in Technology, Innovation, and Education from Harvard.

Douglas Kiang has taught for 30 years at all grade levels. His focus is on improving access for girls and minorities in STEM fields. He currently teaches computer science at Menlo School and consults with the College Board on the AP computer science principles course. He recently published a computer science curriculum focusing on maker education. Douglas has keynoted and presented day-long workshops at schools all over the world. He is an Apple Distinguished Educator and is a 2015 recipient of the NCWIT Educator Award, for support and encouragement of young women's interest in computing and information technology.

Yoon Jeon (YJ) Kim is the Executive Director of the MIT Playful Journey Lab. Her work has centered on the topic of innovative assessment and how technological advancement influences what we are measuring about student learning and how we are measuring it. For more than ten years, she has been involved in many game- and simulation-based assessment development and evaluation projects using evidence-centered design in combination with educational data mining techniques. At the Playful Journey Lab, she and her colleagues explore playful, authentic, yet rigorous assessment approaches in both digital and non-digital learning environments. The core of her work is close collaboration with practitioners—empowering teachers to innovate around classroom assessment and use playful assessment tools that can truly impact student learning.

Kate Litman began her career in New York City as a Teaching Fellow in 2005. Kate has taught Codeworlds at Quest to Learn for nine years and was the founding eighth grade math teacher. Kate holds a BA in English and American Literature from NYU and a master's degree in Mathematics Education from City College of New York. She is a Master Teacher with Math for America, a former facilitator for Institute of Play, and has achieved Peer Collaborative Teacher status with the New York City Department of Education. In this role, she acts as a curriculum developer, teaches a full schedule, and facilitates engaging PD for her colleagues. Whether teachers are building teamwork through a BreakoutEDU puzzle, brainstorming solutions to complex problems using LEGO Serious Play, or taking on the role of a secret agent at the Spyscape museum in Manhattan – they are sure to have an inspiring experience that embodies the principles of game-like learning. Kate has designed many games including *The Whole Enchilada, FracJack, Get to the Point* and *Lazy Triangles*.

Kevin Miklasz has worked in and around the fields of game design and education for the last ten years. As a trained scientist, he has a BA in physics from the University of Chicago and a PhD in biology from Stanford University, but has spent his time since gaining a smattering of diverse experiences in education: designing science curriculum, developing learning analytics for playful experiences, teaching after-school science programs, designing science games, developing learning experience prototypes in emerging technologies, managing an educational science and cooking blog, running game jams for kids, and running professional development for teachers and professional engineers. Kevin is the author of *Intrinsic Rewards in Games and Learning*, which explores how the game industry's innovations in reward structures can be used in educational settings, and is currently the Senior Director, Learning Analytics at Noggin.

Erin Milsom completed her Master of Science in secondary education at SUNY Albany, with a concentration in chemistry, and is now teaching earth science at Schalmont Middle School. She has worked as a researcher at the Wadsworth Center prior to entering education.

Rachel Niemer is the Director of Outreach and Access in the Center for Academic Innovation at the University of Michigan (U-M). Rachel helps instructors and administrators at U-M identify, design, and implement innovative solutions to meet the needs of pre-college, residential, and lifelong learners. She oversees the center's diversity, equity, and inclusivity initiatives as well as the Public Engagement team which works to prepare scholars across the university to use innovative techniques and new technologies to influence decision makers, share and disseminate knowledge, and learn from and co-create knowledge with the University of Michigan's publics.

Ashley Phillips teaches biology and environmental science at Tech Valley High School. Prior to earning her MAT from State University of New York Empire State College, Ashley worked as a museum educator and outreach coordinator at CMOST.

Lindsay Portnoy is Associate Teaching Professor within the Graduate School of Education at Northeastern University. Dr. Portnoy is a learning scientist leveraging training in cognitive psychology to develop immersive and impactful learning experiences that foster experiential learning and applied practice to set our youngest citizens on pathways to success. She is the author of *Designed to Learn: Using Design Thinking to Bring Purpose and Passion to the Classroom*, which features some of the work she did with Tech Valley High School. She is also the Co-founder of Killer Snails, which develops digital, VR, and tabletop games to teach science.

Justin Reich is an Associate Professor of digital media at MIT, the Director of the MIT Teaching Systems Lab, host of the TeachLab podcast, and the author of *Failure to Disrupt: Why Technology Alone Can't Transform Education.*

Dr. Karen (Kat) Schrier, associate professor, is the founding Director of the Games & Emerging Media program and Play Innovation Lab at Marist College. From 2018–2019, she served as a Belfer Fellow for the Anti-Defamation League's Center for Technology & Society, where she researched games, empathy, and identity. Dr. Schrier is also the founder and CEO of PlatyPlay, LLC, a company that specializes in designing and researching games for learning, empathy, civics, and inclusion. She has two decades of experience designing and producing websites, apps, and games, and has previously worked at organizations such as Scholastic, Nickelodeon, and BrainPOP. She is the Editor of the book series, Learning, Education & Games, published by ETC Press (Carnegie Mellon), and Co-editor of two books on games and ethics. She has written and/or edited over 100 scholarly publications and educational materials, including articles published in journals such as *Educational Technology Research & Development* and the *Journal of Moral Education*. Her book, *Knowledge Games: How Playing Games Can Help Solve Problems, Create Insight, and Make Change*, was published in 2016 by Johns Hopkins University Press and her book We the Gamers: How Games Teach Ethics and Civics was published in 2021 by Oxford University Press. She is currently working on a book on using games for civics and ethics education. Dr. Schrier holds a doctorate from Columbia University/Teachers College, master's degree from MIT, and a bachelor's degree from Amherst College.

Katie Salen Tekinbaş is a professor in the Department of Informatics at the University of California at Irvine, a member of the Connected Learning Lab, as well as Chief Designer and Co-founder of Connected Camps, an online learning platform powered by youth gaming experts. She is founding Executive Director of Institute of Play and led the design of Quest to Learn, an innovative New York City public school, which opened in 2009. Katie is co-author of *Affinity Online: How Connection and Shared Interest Fuel Learning* (NYU Press), *Rules of Play, The Game Design Reader, Quest to Learn: Growing a School for Digital Kids,* and Editor of *The Ecology of Games: Connecting Youth, Games, and Learning,* all from MIT Press. She has worked as a game designer for over 15 years and has been involved in the design of slow games, online games, mobile games, and big games in both the commercial and independent games sectors. Katie was an early advocate of the then-hidden world of machinima, and her current research focuses on the design of kid-friendly online communities, systems for peer mentorship, and conflict resolution in multiplayer games.

Meredith Thompson draws upon her background in science education and outreach as a research scientist at the Teaching Systems Lab, the Education Arcade, and as an instructor for the Scheller Teacher Education Program. Her research interests are in collaborative learning, STEM educational games, simulations as learning tools, STEM teacher preparation, and using virtual and simulated environments for learning STEM topics. In her research, she has explored using Virtual Reality and multiuser virtual environments in STEM education. She has partnered with K12 educators in developing and disseminating practical strategies for using VR in the classroom in the book Envisioning Virtual Reality: A toolkit for introducing virtual reality into the K12 classroom. She has also studied how online application-based, easily authorable "practice spaces" can be used to help better prepare novice teachers for the classroom. She uses those games and simulations when she teaches the STEP course: Understanding and Evaluating Education. In her spare time, Meredith writes and sings music with her twin sister Chris (HYPERLINK "http://www.cmthompson.com"www.cmthompson.com), writes poetry, and enjoys hiking in the woods with her two boys and her "found hound" Lindy.

Cigdem Uz-Bilgin holds a master's in Computer Education and Instructional Technology from Hacettepe University and a doctorate in Computer Education and Instructional Technology from Middle East Technical University. Her research focuses on using virtual environments and games for playful experiences for teachers and students. Cigdem is a research assistant at Yildiz Technical University, and she is currently working as a researcher for the Collaborative Learning Environments for Virtual Reality (CLEVR) project and the Reach Every Reader project in the Education Arcade/Scheller Teacher Education Program at MIT.

Rebecca Webster has been teaching math and science courses at Greater Lawrence Technical School for 22 years. She has a bachelor's degree in biochemistry and genetics from the University of New Hampshire and a master's degree in curriculum and development from the University of Phoenix. She currently teaches Honors biology and a course she designed called Modern Applications of Science. She also is the Kaleidoscope Club and Class of 2021 Advisor. Rebecca has been a coach in the Merrimack Valley for the past 20 years in the sports of swimming, diving, and tennis.

Diana "Dee" Weldon teaches engineering, technology, chemistry, and nanoscience. Diana earned a Bachelor of Science degree in chemical engineering from MIT and worked for GE for 17 years prior to entering the classroom.